State and Society in China

The Consequences of Reform

edited by
Arthur Lewis Rosenbaum
Claremont McKenna College

Westview Press
BOULDER • SAN FRANCISCO • OXFORD

Published in 1992 in the United States of America by Westview Press, Inc., 5500 Central Avenue, Boulder, Colorado 80301-2847, and in the United Kingdom by Westview Press, 36 Lonsdale Road, Summertown, Oxford OX2 7EW

Library of Congress Cataloging-in-Publication Data
State and society in China : the consequences of reform / edited by
Arthur Lewis Rosenbaum.
p. cm.
Includes bibliographical references and index.
ISBN 0-8133-1175-6. — ISBN 0-8133-1176-4 (pbk.)
1. China—Politics and government—1976– . 2. China—Social conditions—1976– . I. Rosenbaum, Arthur Lewis, 1939– .
DS779.26.S74 1992
951.05—dc20 91-39419
CIP

Printed and bound in the United States of America

The paper used in this publication meets the requirements of the American National Standard for Permanence of Paper for Printed Library Materials Z39.48-1984.

10 9 8 7 6 5 4 3 2 1

Contents

Acknowledgments

I would like to express my gratitude to the eight contributors to this volume. I also wish to express great appreciation to the Keck Center and to Larry David for their generous financial backing of this project. Chae-Jin Lee, director of the Keck Center, provided indispensable counsel and support throughout the entire endeavor. Mary Anderson graciously assumed administrative responsibility for keeping the project on track, especially when I was in China as a Fulbright lecturer.

I wish to thank many unnamed Chinese friends and colleagues for freely sharing their experiences and views. Diana and William Tillinghast deserve special recognition for their thoughtful comments on the various drafts of my essay. Norman Bock constantly challenged my arguments. Faye Rosenbaum was a critical reader of everything I wrote, always demanding that I maintain the standards I exact of her. My wife, Chiao-ling Rosenbaum, was a continual source of intellectual inspiration and a most perceptive observer of the Chinese scene.

Additional thanks go to the editorial staff of Westview Press: to acquisitions editor Susan McEachern and the anonymous readers of the manuscript for identifying major areas of weakness, and to Alice Colwell for her careful editing.

This book is dedicated to Frank Rosenbaum and Joyce Rosenbaum, whose insistence on intellectual rigor and clarity of thought inspired all their children.

Arthur Lewis Rosenbaum

1

Introduction

Arthur Lewis Rosenbaum

On the night of June 3–4, 1989, columns of tanks and armed soldiers rolled down Changan Boulevard in Beijing and applied merciless force to clear the streets of antigovernment demonstrators, shattering the evanescent hopes of millions who had believed that the "will of the people" would triumph. It has been more than two years since clanking tank treads sounded an end to short-lived Chinese feelings of hope, liberation, and solidarity. The physical scars of that night are now gone, concealed beneath the paint and refurbishment that accompanied the preparations for the 1990 Asian Games in Beijing. The psychological and political consequences, however, have not been dispelled. The massacre in Tiananmen Square changed everything in China, and yet it changed nothing.

The violent repression of the protesters, subsequent purge of leading reformers, and stilling of all forms of open dissent transformed the mood in Beijing without altering the underlying situation that created the crisis. An embittered population glumly observes the government's machinations, aware that public opinion does not influence decision-making. Even minor issues, which local leaders in a school or factory used to decide, are now deferred to higher levels. A bleakness of spirit immediately attracts the attention of visitors to Beijing.

Obsessed with "unity and stability," the party-state has blocked expression of popular opinion, subsidized failing state enterprises to prevent further unemployment, and limited growth to control inflation. Yet even as conservative-oriented planners talk of retrenchment and recentralizing parts of the economy, the South China coast experiences astounding rates of growth as it continues to privatize commerce. The National People's Congress, held in late March through early April

1991, displayed the same schizophrenic tendency, balancing talk of "open doors" and "reform" against rhetoric emphasizing the superiority of planning and stability.

U.S. distaste for the massacre of June 3–4 and for subsequent human rights violations is so great as to warp our perspective. By any objective standard, the massacre at Tiananmen and the current level of repression scarcely approach what many Chinese endured during the antirightist campaigns of the 1950s and the decade of the Cultural Revolution (1966–1976). The current economic compromises, which leave China awkwardly caught between a planned economy and a market economy, confound sound Western economic theory. But despite chronic government deficits, there is growth, and stores are filled with goods—some of which people actually wish to buy. If some aspects of Chinese polity and society are frozen or have regressed, others continue to evolve along pre-Tiananmen lines.

The conservative backlash cannot undo a decade of reform, nor can it completely change China's agenda. Every Chinese government since the 1880s has sought national wealth and power, both to enhance China's international position and to improve living conditions at home. Because in today's world such a quest requires access to foreign countries (capital, trade, and technology) and a domestic infrastructure that supports modernization, the search for wealth and power constrains conservative options. As long as Chinese conservatives acknowledge the importance of modernization, they cannot resolve the contradiction between party control and modern economic growth. Furthermore, the erosion of party authority undermines the political and social mechanisms used to enforce official policies. Authorities can restrain "deviant" behavior, but they can no longer compel people to believe or cooperate.

Even within the upper political echelons, the hard-liners' victory is incomplete. June 1989 effectively removed radical reformers from sensitive positions of influence at the top, but intra-elite divisions between "moderate" and "conservative" reformers continue. Disagreements between Deng Xiaoping and Chen Yun over economic reform caused a four-month delay in holding the Seventh Plenum in December 1990. They also forced a compromise on the Eighth Five-Year Plan, which offers no clear direction for the future.

China has entered a deathwatch similar to that of the last years under Mao Zedong. Since 1956 every individual groomed as the future leader of China—Liu Shaoqi, Lin Biao, Deng Xiaoping, Hua Guofeng, Hu Yaobang, and Zhao Ziyang—has been purged from office. Deng Xiaoping recovered his footing, but not before being twice purged. The impending deaths of the entire senior leadership of octogenarians will force the current "chosen successors," Li Peng and Jiang Zemin, to operate without their patrons. It will also bring to power a new generation of leaders whose political orientations are still unclear. The actors and political dynamics of a post-Deng era may be different, but the underlying problems and choices will remain.

State and Society in China attempts to identify the political dynamics, problems, and choices that have preoccupied—and will continue to preoccupy—China. The following introduction is intended to place the chapters into a broader perspective. It also provides a general overview of unifying themes and contributors' areas of disagreement. Four of the contributors—Thomas Bernstein, Dorothy Solinger, Stanley Rosen, and Hong Yung Lee—generalize from new research data; their chapters are appropriate for scholarly journals, but the introductions and conclusions give them greater breadth than the usual journal article. Essays by Martin Whyte, Andrew Walder, Merle Goldman, and Lowell Dittmer are close to "think pieces" in which the authors draw upon past research to speculate about the implications of the issues or suggest new approaches to the topic.

Some political realities of post-Tiananmen China, especially the overpowering influence of first-generation revolutionaries in the upper echelons, may not outlast Deng Xiaoping's generation, but others will continue. The years covered in this volume, 1978–1990, span at least four cycles of reform and retrenchment, thereby allowing the authors to distinguish cyclical from long-term change, momentary setbacks from irreversible regression.

The theme of this book might be summed up as the prospects for both systemic transformation of the party-state and the development of a "civil society." Systemic transformation and the development of civil society are interrelated but distinct. A fundamental change in the organization and operation of state power in China most likely will facilitate greater social autonomy but does not necessarily mean the acceptance and institutionalization of civil society. Conversely, the rise of civil society and of more autonomous social groups is often seen as a precondition for a transition from authoritarianism to democracy, but by itself it does not guarantee the dismantling of existing authoritarian political structures. Although Whyte and Solinger deal most explicitly with this issue, all chapters implicitly question whether long-term trends in China favor the emergence of a pluralistic civil society or retention of state-controlled society, either in its Marxist-Leninist guise or in a modernizing authoritarian reincarnation.

In early 1989 China was following a "predictable" pattern of incremental reforms and alternating cycles of ascendency by "radical" and "conservative" reformers. On the horizon were signs of rising popular discontent directed against economic mismanagement, corruption, and inflation, including the dramatic decision to postpone price and wage reform. But no one foresaw the historic upheavals of that spring. The euphoria experienced by many U.S. experts during the halcyon days of the democratic movement soon gave way to pessimism and despair over its failure. That autumn the stunning triumph of popular movements in Eastern Europe added to a feeling that much of China's reform program had been illusionary.

Although the shadow of Tiananmen has not disappeared, enough time has passed to permit U.S. scholars to move beyond the immediate images and emotions of Tiananmen. What emerges is a balanced, critical picture that identifies areas of paralyzing dysfunction and acute tension but does not neglect the achievements of reform and the potential for further change. Much of the writing on Chinese politics is quickly dated by sudden turns of events. *State and Society* is one of the first works to seriously reexamine Chinese reform after Tiananmen. More important, it focuses on long-term social and political trends rather than the short-term vagaries of factional struggle.

Theoretical Approaches

At least four differing paradigms dominate our scholarly approaches to understanding the root causes of the contemporary crisis in state-society relations in China: Leninist systems, the Confucian legacy, disequilibriating reforms, and stunted reform. These four approaches are not mutually exclusive, but each offers a perspective and calls to mind different images and historical parallels.

The Leninist Systems Approach

China's problems stem from generic defects of the Leninist party-state. Signs of systemic disintegration in China—the declining authority of a once all-powerful party, the collapse of faith in ideological orthodoxy, and a stagnating centrally planned economy—are typical of other contemporary Leninist states. When the deficiencies of centrally planned economies became more obvious and limited reforms failed to increase economic performance, the authority and legitimacy of the party-state was called into question. Corruption, nepotism, and depressed standards of living are intrinsic to contemporary Leninist patterns of governance. Under these circumstances, leadership based on the unchallenged organizational structure of an omnipotent Communist party and legitimized by a sacrosanct ideology could not be maintained. Rising demands for change made interelite unity difficult, further undermining the will of authorities to act decisively in defense of their privileged position.

The Confucian Legacy Approach

Many of China's current problems—and successes—can be attributed to a political culture influenced by imperial Confucianism. Bureaucratic domination, a single orthodoxy, and the belief in the supremacy of the group over the individual frustrated contemporary reformers. These phenomena may be Leninist in their absolutism, but they were already found in imperial Confucianism and traditional social attitudes. Yet heritage can also be a positive asset. The remarkable surge of economic growth since 1978 builds on a foundation of peasant responsiveness to market opportunities. South China's enthusiastic adaptation to privatized commercial opportunities, especially striking in comparison to the more conservative north, continues a pattern that is centuries old.

Certain difficulties derive from the vacuum left by the disintegration of the traditional order. Contemporary China's search for a political model that can reorder society and modernize the nation while preserving special Chinese characteristics dates back to the late nineteenth century. Western imperialism and internal rebellion sapped the vitality of the imperial Confucian state. Ineffective attempts to graft Western technology onto traditional Chinese values and institutions were followed by a series of more fundamental reforms of basic structures from 1901 to 1911. Creation of constitutional assemblies, promotion of industrialization, development of a Western-educated bureaucracy, and the abolition of the Confucian examination system eliminated those institutions that had held together the empire for two millennia—Confucianism, the scholar-official elite, and imperial authority. New institutions and values could not be established fast enough to replace what was being lost.

The late Qing reforms contributed to total political dissolution: the fall of the dynasty in 1911, four chaotic decades of warlordism, civil war, and regionalism. During this period, power was based on naked coercion or personal loyalty. The autonomy of local centers of power, the weakness of intra-elite cohesion, and the absence of legitimating ideologies and values impeded the reintegration of the political system. The Maoist system was the most successful of the twentieth-century efforts to reorder polity and end national disintegration, but its collapse after Mao's death in 1976 again set in motion experiments with alternative models of political organization. The origins of systemic political stability thus derive from the inherited political culture.

The Disequilibriating Reforms Approach

Reform creates disequilibrium by its successes in liberating social forces, discrediting old values, and generating rising expectations; unless political structures change fast enough to accommodate the developments, the disequilibrium can destroy the government. Thirteen years of reform initiated by Deng Xiaoping dramatically weakened the state and rejuvenated society but did not end the domination of the hegemonic party-state.

The death of Mao and the purge of the extreme Left brought to an end the years of messianic upheaval. In 1978 the Third Plenum of the Eleventh Party Congress defined the task of the revolution as socialist modernization and reform, not class-based struggle. Reform broke up a relatively monolithic elite tied to the Leninist party-state and altered the status of all social groupings. The party's partial withdrawal from micromanagement of all aspects of life and the new availability of goods and services through channels outside the control of the party-state gave a greater degree of independence to intellectuals, merchants, workers, and farmers.

Since 1978 the post-Mao leadership has pushed reforms it believes essential for a modernized, socialist China. It refashioned the bureaucracy to make it younger, more professional, and better educated. Economic reforms opened up China to foreign trade and investment, abolished collective agriculture, and introduced a mixed economy combining market mechanisms with state planning. Administrative decentralization and the weakening of social controls encouraged local leadership to respond to certain types of grassroots pressure. Entire provinces on the coast, most notably Guangdong, discovered that access to overseas capital and trade made it possible to circumvent many of Beijing's policy directives. A decline in wholesale, arbitrary party interference in cultural and educational affairs opened the door to new forms of expression, despite fierce official hostility to many of those ideas.

Finally, implementation of reforms left China vulnerable to new types of problems. Establishment of markets and the availability of consumer goods were accompanied by inflation and corruption. Access to outside ideas and privatization of values made life more humane but discredited official values and boosted unrealistic expectations.

The Stunted Reform Approach

Popular dissatisfaction arises from the failure of the reforms to attack the root problems of the old regime. Deng's strategy of partial reform deferred action on unpopular or controversial measures. Failure to deal decisively with structural weaknesses in the economy and politics eventually left the system unable to cope with the demands placed upon it. Even at its apogee (late 1986 or at the Thirteenth Party Congress of 1987) the reform program was illusionary because it left intact the Communist political system. Although the leadership was committed to economic modernization and liberalization, its desire to preserve the party-state's dominant role and "socialism with Chinese characteristics" set limits on reform. Each attempted reform intensified the inherent contradiction between modernization and Leninism. Hence the party-state's rearguard struggle to retain its dominant position is the primary cause of mass discontent and intra-elite disagreement.

Combining the Four Approaches

Because these approaches are not mutually exclusive, most authors feel free to adopt elements of each. The Confucian legacy approach is most strongly incorporated into the chapters of Goldman, Solinger, and Whyte, each of whom sees strong parallels between current and past problems. Elements of the Leninist systems approach are especially implicit in the contributions by Bernstein, Whyte, Walder, Lee, and Goldman. It is significant that all the contributors emphasize the unique aspects of Chinese communism that distinguish China from the Soviet Union: Maoist "deviations" from the Soviet model, the impact of the Cultural Revolution and Maoist excesses on elite consciousness, the consequences of having first-generation revolutionaries still in power, and economic prosperity during the first stages of reform. The disequilibriating reform model appears most emphatically in discussion of newly emergent social strata, privatization of values, and the decline of Communist control mechanisms. The stunted reform model dominates discussion of political institutionalization, the consequences of partial reform, and the failure to open up the political system. Dittmer adopts elements of the stunted reform approach, especially when he treats the failure to establish formal institutions of power to replace the informal style of leadership characteristic of the Deng era. Rosen, though extremely critical of the regime's failure to pursue political reform beyond certain narrow limits, argues that youth's dissatisfaction has been stimulated by rising expectations generated by the success of the youth reform.

Each approach provides a different perspective. The Leninist systems model sees China dealing with the same problems that have beset other Leninist states. A Confucian legacy model implies that contemporary China faces issues similar to those that confronted previous Chinese governments after 1860. The disequilibriating reforms approach compares China to other governments that attempt fundamental reform (e.g., France prior to the Revolution or the Meiji restoration in Japan). Finally, the stunted reform approach looks to examples of governments that are held back by a commitment to preserve key elements of the old order.

In his analysis of the conflict between formal institutional and informal personal power, Lowell Dittmer argues that the vaunted reforms of party and state structures really were designed to enhance Deng's personal power. Improved procedures, personnel changes, separation of state and government, retirement of senior people, and the establishment of a collective leadership provided the pretext for ousting opponents and allowed a deliberate fragmentation of formal power to prevent a challenge from below.

Although some formal institutions may become important in the future, a handful of first-generation revolutionaries still run China from behind the scenes. The supremacy of informal over formal institutional power prevented formal leaders, such as Hu Yaobang and Zhao Ziyang, from successfully asserting their constitutional authority over Deng Xiaoping and other party elders, especially during the political crises over the student movements of 1986 and 1989. Elders need not hold office; extraconstitutional arrangements allow "retired" officials to vote in "expanded meetings" of the Politburo and Central Committee.

Dittmer offers two new theoretical models that connect leadership configurations to policy cycles. First, leadership configurations fall along two axes: cleavage versus solidarity (distribution of agreement) and collegiality versus hierarchy (distribution of power). Four different patterns of leadership are possible: primus inter pares, disciplinary action, factionalism, and collective leadership. Second, economic cycles correlate to leadership styles: Economic booms favor the interests of reform-minded leaders and encourage greater toleration of mass mobilization, periods of retrenchment play into the hands of conservatives, and mass activism is treated more severely in the bust phase of a cycle.

Hong Yung Lee's detailed study of the Chinese bureaucracy finds permanent, limited, and generally positive changes. Professionalization of the Chinese cadre corps between 1982 and 1987 transformed it from revolutionary cadres recruited on the basis of political activism to a body of educated bureaucratic technocrats. These changes extend to the highest levels of the state and, to a lesser degree, party bureaucracy. An absolute majority of mayors, governors, and party secretaries now have academic training in technical fields or a specialization in economics. Lee argues that bureaucratic technocrats as a sociological type are more pragmatic, more supportive of reforms, and better qualified to manage an industrial society. At some point their policy preferences are likely to influence policy formulation and implementation, probably for the good of China.

Bureaucratic technocrats will not find it easy to become the political successors to the old generation. Careers spent as managers in specialized bureaucratic organizations rarely prepare individuals to act as "politicians" or leaders. Instead, successful bureaucrats develop a cautious work style, as job specialization narrows perspectives and limits personal connections. Even their education and training may isolate bureaucrats from the average Chinese. Because both of China's formal leaders, Jiang Zemin and Li Peng, epitomize the prudent work style and limited political base of the bureaucrat, Lee and Dittmer are skeptical that either can succeed Deng as paramount leader.

Recruiting better personnel has not overcome the structural problems of an unwieldy bureaucracy. Despite campaigns to cut bureaucracy and change the *yamen* (officious) mentality, bureaucratic offices and personnel multiply at a dizzying rate. Although some foreign businesspeople are impressed by the caliber of the Chinese bureaucracy, the majority of Chinese and foreigners complain about its lackadaisical style and overlapping jurisdictions. In one wag's words, the bureaucracy is "corrupt, gluttonous [i.e., bureaucrats eat out on public funds], lazy, and slow" (*tan, chan, lan, man*). Efforts to separate party and state are stalemated by the party's right to supervise government agencies and control personnel management.

Yet despite these caveats, Lee is convinced the modern civil service represents China's best hope for the future. The decline in ideology and collapse of party authority will continue despite the post-Tiananmen campaigns to reverse these trends. Because neither an army coup nor a democratic revolution from below is likely, bureaucratic technocrats are China's last good chance. Drawing implicitly on analysis of the experiences of Taiwan, Japan, and South Korea, Lee looks to economic development and a further strengthening of civil society as the requisites for ultimate democracy. Ironically, the necessary reforms to promote these changes, Lee says, require an interim stage of an "authoritarian regime with efficient bureaucratic administrators."

The concept of "civil society" has received much attention in recent works by China specialists and Eastern European democrats. According to Martin Whyte, civil society "involves the idea of the existence of institutionalized autonomy for social relationships and associational life, autonomy vis-à-vis the state." Civil society is also a precondition for democracy, for without it, formal democratic institutions can have little meaning. De facto civil society and associational life did exist in imperial China, but official norms have been consistently hostile to the idea of autonomous individuals or groups with inalienable rights. The brief flourishing of "seeds" of civil society in the late Qing and early Republic (1898–1927) were the consequence of the state's weakness, not its recognition of the legitimacy of these rights. Although the totalitarian impulse in Maoism negated the right to a free associational life, Whyte convincingly demonstrates how the reaction to Maoist absolutism encouraged the reemergence of civil society, a trend that has been strengthened by Deng's reforms. So overwhelming has been this impulse for a personal life that the party-state no longer possesses the capacity to suppress the rise of nonpolitical autonomous social groupings.

Whyte's explanation of the growth of autonomy in post-Mao China has been widely accepted; his assessment of its strength, however, is more controversial. In 1989, he argues, China had a more advanced civil society than the Soviet Union. The failure of democratic movements in 1989 was due to the staying power of China's first-generation revolutionaries and the strength of the army, not the weakness of civil society. The post-Tiananmen crackdown can only restrict rather than completely suppress the manifestation of civil society. Would-be hardliners hoping to turn back the clock will face grassroots resistance and the opposition of moderate elements in the leadership.

Andrew Walder's speculative essay is the first effort by the leading U.S. scholar of urban workers to analyze the origins of worker protest in 1989. Despite high levels of organizational control at the workplace in all socialist countries, only Poland has witnessed greater regularity of popular worker protest. Decisions by the Chinese leadership to seek popular support during factional struggles provided the opportunity for worker mobilization in the 1960s and the 1970s. During the 1980s, however, the cumulative impact of economic reform on Chinese urban workers increased their militancy.

To provide incentives for greater productivity, Chinese factories supplemented the standard base salary with piece rates and production bonuses. As bonuses increased as a percentage of wages, conflict on the floor over the setting of rates and quotas destabilized the patron-client relationship between managers and workers. After 1986, tensions generated by a system of remuneration that has been abandoned throughout most of the advanced industrial world were exacerbated by a decline in the growth of real income. The inflationary spiral of 1988–1989 terrified Chinese consumers unaccustomed to inflation or the idea that prices should determine the allocation of goods. Inflation also made workers more dependent on their bonuses. Because workers lacked appropriate means to adjudicate disputes and were locked into lifetime jobs, their resentment festered. When student demonstrations broke out in Beijing, factories sent delegations to participate in the protest marches and sit-ins. Despite the importance of universal discontent among all segments of the general population, especially over inflation and corruption, Walder believes that worker involvement represents something new in China: mistrust of the government and an anti-elitist working-class consciousness. Equally alarming from the government's point of view, worker alienation came after a decade of improving living standards; essential economic reforms that will attack the vested interests of China's urban workers have yet to begin.

The spectacular explosion of private business throughout China, according to Dorothy Solinger, has neither led to a civil society nor institutionalized the power of urban entrepreneurs. The decay of the hegemonic party-state allowed the emergence of new career patterns outside the formal state sector, but state domination—what Solinger terms the "monolith"—remains. Urban economic reforms in a mixed economy created a new category of business entrepreneurs who depend on bureaucrats for support. This is not civil society nor a ruggedly individualistic bourgeoisie about to fulfill its historic role as leaders of a bourgeois-democratic revolution. Instead, bureaucrats and merchants fuse in an ill-defined, multifaceted, symbiotic relationship that encourages preservation of the monolith. The state needs merchant capital and entrepreneurial skills to build the economy and generate state revenues; individual bureaucrats need the business sector to supplement personal income and employ relatives and friends. Because they cannot operate a business without political and financial assistance from officials, merchants are willingly co-opted. Reform-minded merchants who aspire to greater independence cannot forget that free competition would deprive them "of their special inside channels."

In his chapter on rural policy, Thomas Bernstein challenges conventional wisdom about the government's commitment to a permanent "decollectivization" of Chinese agriculture and eventual acceptance of peasant autonomy. It is well known that the state is the main supplier of basic agricultural inputs such as chemical fertilizer and fuel and is also the major purchaser of agricultural outputs. As is true of urban enterprise, new systems of economic management (the agricultural household responsibility system) have not eliminated bureaucratic microintervention nor ensured institutionalized legitimacy for private enterprise by privatizing land ownership. Negotiated contracts, grain quotas, administrative limits on hiring labor or renting land, and plain arbitrary interference guarantee that, despite freedoms granted to the peasant, the party-state still exercises a formidable influence.

China's impressive rural growth stands in striking contrast to agricultural performance in Eastern Europe. Yet in the policy area where reforms have enjoyed their most spectacular successes, the hegemonic party-state refuses to concede institutionalized autonomy or provide an unqualified commitment to the contract system. The failure to assure the permanence of the agricultural responsibility system discourages peasant investment in the land. Why, then, does the state shrink from offering such guarantees? In addition to harboring legitimate concerns about fragmentation of landholdings, Bernstein believes, conservatives are ideologically unwilling to abandon socialism as the ultimate goal. Despite the widespread tendency of Westerners to portray ideology as a "declining fringe phenomenon," ideology still plays a role in defining and legitimizing ultimate goals. Reformers as well as conservatives must defend market values as a means to promote ultimate socialism. This makes China's commitment to the household responsibility system "contingent." Tension between the values implicit in the means (markets) and the explicit ends (socialism) bedevils planners and peasants. The nineteenth-century dilemma of reconciling ultimate value with practical technique thus resurfaces in contemporary government rural policy.

For the first time since 1949, official ideology and norms no longer find a receptive audience among any segment of China's youth. Stanley Rosen's study of youth and public opinion emphasizes the limited appeal of values associated with "socialist civilization." Government attempts to resuscitate political commitment through compulsory political study are counterproductive, often alienating instructors and students alike. Attitudinal surveys of youth document the waning popular appeal of "politically correct" role models. Instead, personal goals emphasize material success and private achievement; altruistic behavior ranks near the bottom. Any campaign to mobilize youth confronts massive apathy, if not outright antipathy, toward official norms and political orthodoxy.

The reform program and readjustments of party ideology are partly to blame for this situation. By presenting itself as the promoter of modernization and higher standards of living, the party liberated itself from Maoist obsession with class struggle but made itself hostage to rising living standards. The modification of ideological orthodoxy to provide sanction for economic reforms muddied the distinction between capitalism and socialism. If in the primary stage of socialism it is appropriate to have higher levels of inequality, foreign investment, and construction of luxurious international hotels, the average person found it difficult to understand what makes socialism superior. Ideological campaigns to build modern normative values based on "socialist spirituality" or to combat "bourgeois liberalism" seem atavistic and self-contradictory.

As faith in Marxism waned, the regime appealed to nationalism and promises of improved living standards. Admiring accounts of wealthy entrepreneurs contributing to China's new prosperity conveyed the impression that "to be wealthy is glorious" but did not link this behavior to broader ethical and moral values. In a world just discovering the pleasures of consumerism and filled with uncultured, nouveau riche "operators," idealism and self-sacrifice seem slightly old-fashioned. After seeing the unfair advantages enjoyed by children of party officials, most Chinese conclude personal relationships (*guanxi*) are more important than merit.

Whereas the Communist party once stood as the symbol of integrity and self-sacrifice, it is now tainted by corruption and nepotism. Youth have a low regard for officially sanctioned forms of political activism and altruism; the party-state fears unsupervised youthful idealism might be directed against the government. Under these circumstances, youth are attracted to activism and party membership only to the extent they can help advance careers; otherwise they distract an individual from more important aims: good grades, money, and professional advancement.

The state's relationship to intellectuals is similarly strained. According to Merle Goldman, intellectuals are both beneficiaries and victims of reforms that prepared the ground for a civil society in the making. Repression has declined and working conditions improved, but intellectuals still find themselves caught in alternating cycles of "relaxation" and "tightening." The intensity of the cycles and the harshness of punishment is constrained by the state's need for intellectuals to help promote the Four Modernizations. The process of scientific modernization, building a modern economy, creating a modern culture, and upgrading administration requires granting specific categories of intellectuals enough autonomy to do their jobs. To encourage new thinking about reform, the government has funded a variety of research institutes and think tanks and has even tolerated a few that were privately financed. This atmosphere encourages intellectuals to place professional competence above adherence to ideological orthodoxy. Growing numbers of scientists, social science professionals, and apolitical writers seek freedom of inquiry, access to the outside, and conformity to international standards of professionalism. Moreover, the government cannot respond to these indirect and direct challenges to its monopoly of power by distinguishing between technical experts and nonscientific intellectuals. Memories of the Cultural Revolution and antirightist campaigns remind scientific personnel that they are not immune to the movements to repress nonscientific intellectuals. The growing autonomy of the intellectuals suggests a potential civil society in the making that cannot be checked without threatening scientific and economic modernization.

The emergence in the mid-1980s of "critical intellectuals" and new patterns of intellectual dissent was caused by the linkage between factional politics and intellectual currents. *Critical intellectuals* refers to a group of politically active intellectuals—such as Liu Binyan, Su Shaozhi, Li Honglin, and Yan Jiaqi—who openly advocated fundamental institutional and legal reforms, including freedom of speech and establishment of representative government. Most were rehabilitated victims of antirightist campaigns and the Cultural Revolution who had been recruited by Hu Yaobang in 1979 to help him revise Maoist policies. As Hu's intellectual brain trust slowly became alienated from the party, they moved beyond questions of party and ideological reform to the advocacy of a more open democratic society.

Goldman has earlier traced the first indication of Chinese concern for civil society back to Wang Ruoshui's denial that the party represents society. By 1986, intellectuals, journalists, and students all were talking about fundamental changes, including the establishment of checks and balances and a multiparty system. After Hu Yaobang's dismissal as party secretary in 1987, the critical intellectuals stayed on as advisers to Zhao Ziyang until he started promoting the theory of neo-authoritarianism.

Fang Lizhi's open letter on behalf of Wei Jingsheng, presented on January 6, 1989, launched a new round of political activism by intellectuals. Group petitions called for release of political prisoners and the establishment of human rights. The critical intellectuals now saw themselves as a Western-style intelligentsia. That spring they established direct contact with the students and merchants, completing the movement from talk to action.

Throughout history, Chinese intellectuals' sense of obligation to critique abuses of power has been balanced by the quasi-Confucian feeling that it is their duty to serve as advisers to the government. Feelings of patriotism, fear, self-interest, and duty discouraged dissenting intellectuals from adopting a stance of totalistic opposition. The recent willingness to attack socialist principles, advise student protesters, and, for those who fled abroad, join opposition movements is a watershed in the self-identification of Chinese intellectuals. The failure of the 1989 democratic movement showed many intellectuals that they needed to develop closer ties with other strata of society; it also forced them to abandon any lingering illusions about the nature of the political system.

Points of Departure: Reform and Repression

Reform stimulated the rise of societal groups, which then became alienated from official norms because the party-state failed to pursue even more vigorous changes. Most of these groups lack the capacity or motivation or both to initiate political movements on their own. These independent groups organized for political ends at critical moments when intra-elite factionalism created opportunities for expression of dissatisfaction. Meanwhile, the old political mechanisms of Communist China have atrophied to a point where they cannot resolve intra-elite differences, co-opt newly emerging social groupings, or convert alienated segments of the population. Insufficient to impose a solution, the residual power of the party-state is sufficient to suppress open expression of dissent. Thus decisive change or resolution of internal tensions remains unlikely until the party elders die.

The collapse of official ideology and appearance of a market mentality pose problems that transcend political issues. Consumerism and use of personal relationships for private gain have created a spiritual and ideological vacuum that has been exacerbated by Tiananmen. Groups, institutions, and ideas continue to evolve beneath the surface calm of post-Tiananmen China, but a new reconciliation between state and society is not yet in sight.

Political Leadership

The low level of leadership institutionalization and the inability of political structures to resolve intra-elite differences or open better channels between the leadership and the masses point to the continued deterioration of older patterns of governance. Because the chosen successors and bureaucratic technocrats may not be able to manage inherited political problems, the passing of the party elders will not automatically end political stagnation.

Dittmer provides convincing explanations both of how Deng made informal power the key to personal power and of the consequences, often negative, of the weakness of formal power. His interpretation breaks new ground by incorporating a nonstatic model of analysis but is still limited by the standard defect of conventional models of factionalism: Easily identifiable data, such as ties of military service, work experience, or school, provide imprecise clues as to political allegiance and policy preference. Similar methodological problems in inferring policy preference from background appear in Lee's chapter. Highly educated technocrats with engineering degrees, such as Li Peng and Jiang Zemin, favored suppression of student demonstrators; Hu Yaobang and Zhao Ziyang, neither of whom had a good formal education, were proponents of political liberalization and radical economic reform.

All levels of leadership have reached an impasse. Although informal power sometimes is a useful mechanism for resolving intra-elite differences, in contemporary China it has many dysfunctional features. It gives octogenarians a decisive voice in decisionmaking but allows them to evade responsibility for policy implementation and its consequences. Sharp intra-elite differences prevent party elders from serving as mediators. At the same time, formal leaders are constrained from pressing their own ideas or developing too powerful a political base.

It is not apparent whether the exercise of informal power originates purely as a product of Deng's tactical approach to politics, a stage in political development, or a lasting phenomenon. Political development normally implies a closer correlation between formal office and power, the development of leaders who can serve as political brokers, and the emergence of an impartial professional civil service. The new institutions described by Lee and Dittmer may eventually become centers of real power, but this process will not go smoothly, even after the party elders pass away.

Chinese succession arrangements have a tendency to break down, and both Secretary General Jiang Zemin and Premier Li Peng have limited political bases. Moreover, the cautious work style and narrow specialization of bureaucrats associated with the central ministries tend to dull political instincts. Some scholars believe China's future leaders are likely to come from the ranks of provincial and local party secretaries, whose responsibilities as political brokers provide broad contacts and hone political skills. They are also skeptical about the leadership potential of China's technocrats. First of all, technocrats are much more adept at making systems work efficiently than they are at transforming systems. Even if economic reform is a prerequisite for eventual democratic reform, fundamental political reform may be needed to make economic reform work. Furthermore, the institutionalization of a bureaucratic technocracy normally is possible only if civil service bureaucrats become politically neutral. Because Chinese bureaucrats have always regarded themselves as active participants in the political process, they may be reluctant to vacate old seats of power.

In short, the crisis of the Chinese political system transcends the immediate problems, as great as they may be, of finding successors to the aging leaders and resolving intra-elite disputes. Collapse of party authority and the inability of formal ideology to foster popular legitimacy or elite consensus have destroyed the old mechanisms of effective governance. At a time when long-term internal and external trends are unfavorable to the existing party-state, political power in China remains poorly institutionalized and heavily dependent on personal connections.

Civil Society and Social Structures

Since 1978 the old roles and relationships of the Maoist and early Deng era have been giving way to something new. This profound evolutionary transformation is caused by the breakup of the monolithic party-state and the establishment of new functional roles. The growing autonomy of society and its progressive alienation from official norms and structures point the way toward a civil society. The disagreement between Whyte and Solinger over whether a civil society now exists in China is less over facts than perspective: Are autonomous informal groups evidence of civil society or of "government indifference"?

Contributors with backgrounds in Soviet studies distinguish between a formal political opposition and private autonomy. The Soviets permit organized dissent and concede formal powers to society; China tolerates informal organization but bans formal organizations with political overtones. China's weakly institutionalized civil society may contain the seeds of a pluralistic society, but thus far it has been excluded from the public arena. Whyte acknowledges that "much of the new and autonomous activity depended upon the tolerance of the authorities," but he thinks the survival of civil society creates possibilities for a more democratic China.

According to Western European precedents, autonomous associational life leads to institutionalization of organizations and moves from private to public concerns. Market economies facilitate these trends by creating alternatives to state-controlled channels for services, institutions, and the flow of goods. The existence of market economies and civil society is not a sufficient condition for a pluralistic democratic society, but it may be a necessary condition. In turn, the behavior of specific social groups raises two crucial questions: Does associational life exist at government sufferance or is it institutionalized? Does the group's reaction to the protests of 1989 indicate political consciousness and organizational solidarity, or was it triggered by intra-elite differences and inflation?

Reform, according to Walder, caused a fundamental shift in worker attitudes epitomized by mistrust of the government and an anti-elitist working-class consciousness, but he admits his preliminary findings are based on fragmentary data. Some observers maintain that regional variations demonstrate that factional alignments within the elite decisively influenced worker responses. Workers at the Beijing Shoudu Steelworks, whose leaders had close ties to Hu Yaobang, joined the demonstrations in large numbers; in Shanghai and Wuhan, leaders supporting Deng Xiaoping purportedly bought off their workers. Either way, workers mustered the strength to go into the streets only after the system had begun to crack.

Popular resentment against inflation and corruption allowed students to establish contact with workers, but blue-collar workers were equally motivated by a mistrust of the government and feelings of empowerment associated with the demonstrations. Today this alienation remains, perhaps deepened by memories of Tiananmen and the impact of economic retrenchment in north China. It finds expression not in active protest but declining productivity and worsening quality control.

Solinger's rich depiction of the symbiotic relationship between merchants and officials is unchallengeable, but we cannot be sure whether this is a cyclical response to the breakup of the state, an interim stage in the evolution of an independent merchant class, or a permanent feature. One school of interpretation believes successful entrepreneurs eventually will disengage from the state and assert their independence, much as happened in Taiwan and South Korea. It cites Wan Runnan, the founder of Stone Corporation and supporter of the Tiananmen demonstrators, as a prototypical forerunner of an independent-minded bourgeoisie. The other school believes Chinese entrepreneurs operate in an insecure environment that is qualitatively different from the Taiwanese or Korean model. Lacking formal legitimacy, even the most successful companies need governmental connections, which leaves them vulnerable to bureaucratic pressure. Much of an urban merchant's property and resources is technically state property, for which the merchant holds a lease. Both officials and the local population are jealous of the special status of high-flying entrepreneurs and the profits of small shopowners (*getihu*). Official campaigns against corruption and nonpayment of taxes, as well as ideological movements to promote socialist values, muddle the distinction between legitimate profits and dishonesty. Corruption, nepotism, and diversion of funds are so entrenched that such practices may even affect the rate of inflation. The existing relationship is frustrating to officials and merchants, containing as it does a mixture of cooperative/supportive relationships and antagonistic/parasitic relationships.

Peasants did not participate in the 1989 demonstrations, but rural policy also confirms the critical distinction between de facto and institutionalized rights. Bernstein believes a vestigial concern for ideological orthodoxy inhibits the government from making a permanent commitment to maintain the agricultural responsibility system. The implication is that ideology still counts in Chinese politics, something previous China scholars have dismissed or treated as a dependent variable.

Orthodox Marxism still matters to Deng's generation but is not necessarily the driving force in agricultural policy. Because party elders think in terms of a dualistic framework of capitalism versus socialism, subordinates must define complex issues such as economies of scale as a choice between large-scale collective farming or small-scale private farms. In fact, China wishes to combine socialist-style equality and capitalist efficiency. The issue of ownership also masks a practical concern about what to do with operations formerly run by the community, such as health clinics, schools, and irrigation systems. Once again, the government confronts a fundamental contradiction between granting more autonomy to social groups to promote production and its reluctance to legitimize the consequences of such autonomy, especially loss of control.

Dissenting Groups: Youth, Students, and Intellectuals

Age, training, or temperament makes youth, students, and intellectuals more susceptible to dissenting viewpoints and political activism. In addition to the lagging pace of political reform, economic reforms adversely affected the status and economic position of all three groups, thereby contributing to their intellectual and spiritual alienation. Between 1986 and 1989, key groups concluded that China required changing political systems as well as changing leaders. Political repression during and after Tiananmen has hardened these views, creating an unprecedented level of dissatisfaction that finds expression in a variety of forms, from apathy to careerism to wrenching soul-searching about the origins of China's "failure."

The disaffection of youth has multiple origins, including lack of faith in the fairness of the system that controls them and frustration over an uncertain future that cannot meet their needs. Students also see themselves as the embodiment of the nation's conscience, inheritors of a tradition of student protest dating back to the May Fourth movement of 1919.

The core demands of the 1989 student-led protests ranged from redress of specific grievances to a broad assertion of certain democratic rights. Requests that government leaders respond to citizen concerns about inflation, corruption, and other abuses of power fall within the Confucian tradition of remonstrance by loyal officials. A more flexible leadership might have accepted them. Demands that the government recognize autonomous student organizations implied an institutionalized right to organizational freedom, albeit one limited to university campuses. By seeking independence from the hegemonic party-state, the students explicitly challenged the foundations of Communist rule. According to the Four Cardinal Principles—which Deng Xiaoping established in 1979 to guarantee the unquestioned hegemony of Marxism-Leninism, party leadership, socialism, and the proletarian state—Communist organizations alone possess the right to speak for the people.

Was the 1989 student movement influenced by critical intellectuals and advisers to Zhao Ziyang's faction? Did students advocate Western-style democracy, or did they have more limited objectives, such as student self-governance and an end to corruption? Student charges of moral turpitude obviously struck a responsive chord within other segments of the population. Nonetheless, the transformation of student protest from small, localized demonstrations to a citywide movement that echoed throughout the rest of the country was only made possible by the unique circumstances of 1989: intra-elite factional differences over the handling of crises and a popular backlash against inflation and corruption. Government indecisiveness, as well as the tactical support of intellectuals associated with government reformers, helped overcome fears of repression. Meanwhile, growing crowds added to youth's sense of empowerment.

Although intellectuals are often popularly regarded as unflagging advocates of democratic reform, their social roles and self-definition previously encouraged measured dissent, not open opposition and uncompromising activism. The activism after 1986 marks a watershed in the self-definition of many intellectuals, but the new orientation requires interpretation. Did intellectuals belatedly discover the need for fundamental change, or did they simply muster the courage to say in public what they had long thought in private? Were intellectuals in the forefront of the democratic movement, or did most intellectuals follow the lead of the students, and then only when the political atmosphere was favorable?

Factional politics played an important role in the activities of the critical intellectuals. Critical intellectuals became progressively more disillusioned with the party as the possibility of significant change faded. The 1988 television series "River Elegy" ("He Shang," literally, "the river dies young"), a biting allegorical criticism of Chinese culture, accurately captured this mood. Espousing an alliance between intellectuals and other social classes, "River Elegy" is often cited as evidence that intellectuals were becoming autonomous of the state. Yet parts of the series defended Zhao Ziyang's reform policies. There is a similar ambiguity about the role played by intellectuals during the Tiananmen demonstrations. Did high-level intellectuals with connections to Zhao—such as Bao Zunxin, Yan Jiaqi, and Wang Juntao—act as autonomous intellectuals or as partisan supporters of Zhao when they advised student leaders?

The despair many intellectuals felt is related to a real decline in status and standards of living relative to other classes in society. In an era of inflation and inadequate budgets for schools, faculty found that their salaries were falling further behind factory workers, who have access to bonuses. Equally distressing is the flight of students from the humanities and academic disciplines into "hot" disciplines, such as management and economics, which prepare students for jobs in growth areas of the economy. A sense of relative deprivation and lack of appreciation (not unknown to U.S. faculty) compounds the frustration of those already alienated by the state's turn from reform to repression.

Factors in Renewed Repression

The Declining Reach of the State

Reform altered the balance between state and society but did not eliminate the domination of the hegemonic party-state or open channels for expression of grassroots opinion. According to Ezra Vogel (*Canton Under Communism*), during its first decade in power, the Chinese Communist party completed a "political conquest of society," suppressing autonomous social forces and replacing them with the institutions of a monolithic party-state. Formal organization and ideology embodied in the Communist party and state organizations provided the basis for the reintegration of a nation disrupted by a century of war and revolution.

The primacy of political power in China never led to stable administrative structures typical of other Communist party-states. Mao's penchant for permanent revolution and disdain for experts inhibited the process of routinization. By shattering formal organizational authority, the Cultural Revolution introduced systems of personalized rule, or perhaps "feudal totalitarianism," that began with Mao and ran down to local leaders in the factories and communes.

The reach of the state was marginally tempered by grudging recognition of a few practical limits. After the disastrous Great Leap Forward, when millions starved to death, Mao reluctantly pared back the commune system to the natural boundaries of preliberation villages. Political control was relaxed to encourage economic recovery (1961–1965), although the reappearance of arranged marriages, religious festivals, and free markets in rural China alarmed party leaders, who soon suppressed these expressions of local society. In the end, politics took command whenever leaders wanted to launch mass campaigns. The wishes and desires of the average citizen were of account only as they affected the implementation of correct policy.

Because the collapse of the Maoist system altered the environment in which the Chinese party-state operated, politics ceased taking absolute command. Two years after Mao's death and Deng Xiaoping's victory over leftist extremists, the Third Plenum of the Eleventh Party Congress (1978) proclaimed socialist modernization to be the goal of the Chinese Revolution. For Deng and his followers, the trick was to repudiate the negative features of the Cultural Revolution and promote socialist modernization while retaining the structural and ideological authority of the party-state.

As victims of the Cultural Revolution, Deng Xiaoping and other first-generation revolutionaries understood the deficiencies of the Maoist system. Drastic modifications were required to prevent a second Cultural Revolution and to regain public confidence. They loosened state control over society, eliminating the most bizarre intrusions into private lives. Economic reforms generated high rates of growth and dramatic improvements in living standards. Ironically, these reforms eroded the structures of authority and legitimacy that made possible strong leadership despite grievous errors. Intra-elite unity also became more difficult to sustain. The coalition of senior leaders backing Deng Xiaoping began to quarrel over the scope and pace of reforms and the distribution of political power.

China has gone through repeated cycles of reform and retrenchment since the Third Plenum. Each ends with a conservative backlash against alleged "excesses," including partial reversal of policies, personnel changes (purges), and perhaps new ideological campaigns affirming Marxism. Policy cycles reflect the changing balance between radical and conservative reformers within the leadership, adjustments to cope with negative consequences of reforms, and a continuing debate over means and ultimate goals. What appears at first glance to be a single, overarching, repetitive cycle really consists of overlapping cycles that often, but not always, coincide with one another (e.g., the progressive phase of a cycle of economic reform may coincide with the repressive phase of the policy cycle on intellectuals).

Over the years, cycles have ceased to be a dependent variable because policymakers no longer exclusively control the inputs shaping the cycle. Decentralization of economic authority and increasing reliance on markets, for example, mean the investment cycle may not respond to changing official signals from Beijing. The high growth rates recorded by Guangdong Province in 1990 contradict Beijing's stated policy of retrenchment and moderate, stable growth.

Policy cycles cannot be separated from considerations of power among the elite. In addition to ideologically based factional differences and generation-based tensions between formal and informal leaders, there looms the issue of political succession. The continuing intra-elite deadlock and the advanced age of China's present leadership accentuates the paralysis of a political system already under stress.

A Resurgent Society

Thomas Meadows's classic phrase of a century ago that the Chinese are the most rebellious and least revolutionary of all peoples suggests a fundamental paradox in Chinese culture. Despite a heritage of violent peasant rebellions and more than a century of bloody revolutionary upheavals that cost the lives of millions, a substantial body of literature still stresses the Chinese propensity to submit to "proper authority." In the assessments of psychocultural experts such as Lucian Pye and Richard Solomon and in historical studies of failed movements for democracy, a common thread is the absence of a tradition of acknowledging the rights of individuals against the authority of the state.

The Leninist party-state claims total hegemony over society that exceeds the most extreme pretensions of the imperial Chinese state. Despite the declining reach of the state, the Four Cardinal Principles have, since the early 1980s, been presented as an unshakable affirmation of the party-state's moral obligation as the vanguard of the people to preserve its monopoly of power. The party's superior understanding of the laws of social development makes it the best judge of what is in the long-term interests of the people. Independent bases of autonomous power that may thwart the will of the party must be suppressed.

After 1949 the Communist party monopolized the agencies that controlled coercion, normative values, and remunerative rewards. Coercion, social pressure, monopolistic control over the economy, revolutionary mobilization, and appeals to patriotism enabled the party to achieve nearly complete control over all aspects of society and culture. Successive political movements further restricted the freedom of independent action. Collectivization of agriculture and nationalization of industry left citizens dependent on political authorities or work units for provision of basic necessities and services. Individuals were enmeshed by an array of mass organizations that intruded into every aspect of their lives. First-graders vied to wear the red neckerchief of the Young Pioneers, and their grandparents were grouped together in neighborhood associations. Most ubiquitous was the *danwei,* the work unit that employed most urban Chinese. Whether store, factory, school, or ministry, the *danwei* was so central to the life of urban Chinese that the first question asked of an individual (especially on the phone) was not "Who are you?" but "What is your work unit?" Work units allocated scarce housing, medical care, schooling, access to special goods, and the right to have a child. Even in selecting friends and choosing a marriage partner, the politically correct individual considered others' political consciousness and class backgrounds.

Intense politicization of personal relations and eradication of private interests in the name of revolutionary commitment reached its peak in the tumultuous years of the Cultural Revolution. The very extremism of the Cultural Revolution, its incessant denunciation of privatized behavior and its stubborn refusal to acknowledge human desire for private pleasure, bred a sharp reaction. Moreover, a decade of attacks on once honored authority figures and the disruption of the party organization badly damaged party prestige and authority. To regain popular support and ease the crisis of authority following Mao's death, Deng and his backers systematically contracted state interference in society and tolerated a variety of private activities, ranging from rock music to religion. Establishment of private channels for the purchase of goods and services additionally diminished dependence on official channels.

Twelve years of reform thus paved the way for the emergence of new social groups. Peasants once engaged in subsistence farming under the authority of the commune became independent farmers producing cash crops on their own fifteen- to thirty-year leaseholds, or rural entrepreneurs running brick kilns or small factories. Disinterested workers employed in monotonous state-run stores began to compete with a small army of private shopkeepers and peddlers. Youth whose reading had been limited to the works of Mao routinely listened to the Voice of America and purchased rock tapes from the West and Taiwan. Television, study abroad, and contact with tourists gave millions of Chinese access to information once monopolized by the state.

That China has experienced substantial liberalization and increased social autonomy is no longer contested. Even the most bitter critics of the post-Tiananmen regime are hard pressed to argue that there is a return to the days of totalistic domination of society and culture. The real question is whether liberalization and reform, even if the process resumes in a serious fashion, can give birth to a civil society independent of the party-state.

A Market Economy

Economic reforms have profound social and political consequences for China. On the one hand, they partially free large segments of the population from direct dependence on the party-state, thereby giving them a degree of autonomy. On the other hand, the state's continuing intervention in the economy creates conditions for indirect forms of dependency based on private arrangements and influence peddling.

Deng's strategy of incremental reform, adopted in 1978, was intended to create a constituency for reform by assigning first priority to changes that guaranteed quick returns. The most promising area was rural policy, a sector of the economy where the potential of several decades of heavy investment in rural infrastructure had been squandered by counterproductive policies of low prices, collective labor, and local grain self-sufficiency.

The spectacular gains of the early 1980s were made possible by a variety of policy initiatives—higher prices for farm produce, the lifting of restrictions on sideline production and cash crops, and greater emphasis on rural industry. Ending collective agriculture was only part of the story. Decommunization allowed the peasant household freedom to lease its "own land" and obtain the profits therefrom. Rural industry achieved growth rates as high as 35 percent per year, grain production rose by one-third, and per capita rural income tripled. Today the coastal areas of Fujian continue the frenzied construction of three-story farmhouses, and villagers near Guangzhou have erected magnificent arches in front of their villages to signal village pride and prosperity. Other provinces, such as Anhwei and Gansu, lag behind.

Rural reform also means that the party-state no longer has absolute control over the lives of the peasants. Millions of peasants from China's backward rural regions flock (illegally) to the cities as day laborers and to prosperous farming areas to work as hired hands. In fall 1990, an estimated 6 million nonresidents were in Guangdong Province seeking employment. Although the loosening of controls increases opportunities for many, the weakened enforcement of official guidelines on family planning, land usage, and compulsory education endangers once successful programs.

The agricultural household responsibility system also has its limitations. With average farm size only 0.6 hectare per family, farm mechanization and the introduction of expensive modern farm techniques will be difficult. Further privatization or even maintenance of the existing agricultural system does not assure the long-term investment essential for increased productivity. The government's anxiety to have grain production match population growth is partly a matter of economics and partly ideologically motivated. Whatever its economic wisdom, concern for grain production provides a convenient pretext for those favoring greater emphasis on a planned collective economy.

By autumn 1991 there was little indication that China could escape from this predicament. In the spring the government had experimented with alternatives to economically unsound, small family plots. One approach allowed farmers to expand their holdings by leasing land from other farmers. The alternative called for a "two-tier rural economy" that combined individual farming with collective access to agricultural inputs. Whatever the merits of the latter, the consequences were similar to those predicted by Bernstein. In some villages, leaders reportedly decided to reintroduce collectives. Farmers stopped investing because they feared losing their land and refused to believe the reassurances from officials.

In a situation in which the urban population working for inefficient state factories enjoys subsidized prices for certain goods and services (apartments in Beijing rent for as little as $1 per month, approximately the cost of a large bottle of Coca-Cola), reform of the urban economy requires unpopular sacrifices: higher prices and possible unemployment. Even during the first stages, when the real income of urban workers grew steadily, reform generated worker discontent rather than gratitude.

The impact of the post-1989 repression and economic downturn has further dampened worker morale. In Beijing sullen workers go through the paces with little concern for quality or efficiency. With 35 to 40 percent of state enterprises now reporting financial losses, the government faces equally unpalatable choices. It can reduce subsidies and end the "iron rice bowl," thereby endangering political stability; or it can seek greater political legitimacy by granting more political rights to workers, thereby raising the specter of a Solidarity-type labor movement.

The growth of a market economy and market values softens the boundaries between state and society. Previously Maoist ideals—self-sacrifice and proper political consciousness—restrained the open dispensation of favors by party officials and state cadres. Today's consumption-oriented society and mixed economy offer lucrative opportunities to exploit official positions for personal profit. Official assistance in obtaining access to capital, information, raw materials, and political protection is essential to most groups. Official involvement in private affairs alters the functions of the state and party elites, transforming them from "impartial" defenders of the public weal into brokers for special interest groups. Although the savings and loan scandal in the United States is a potent reminder that pork-barrel politics and corruption exist in all political systems, the separation between economics and politics is more pronounced in the West than in Asia. Civil service reforms intended to produce an incorruptible, Japanese-style bureaucratic corps could easily lead to Indonesian-style bureaucratic capitalism. Either way, the Communist party cannot survive in its old guise as the righteous guardian of political ethics and working-class ideals. Official corruption (*guandao*) and the privileges of the children of high-ranking cadres continue to undermine public faith in the party.

Entrepreneurs, intellectuals, and other new social groupings are torn between their perceived need for official backing and a yearning to assert their autonomy and self-worth. The inherent tensions in the present symbiotic relationship mean that interpenetration may be a transitional phase rather than a permanent condition. As long as they lack institutional legitimacy and official recognition, new groups will feel frustrated and resentful. Judging by what has happened elsewhere in Asia, we can see that the most likely scenario is their gradual movement toward an autonomous group identity and greater political independence. The separation between the state and economy/society, however, will probably be less apparent than in the West and the role of bureaucrats greater.

The End of Ideology

One of the most serious challenges confronting the regime is the diminished appeal of ideology and official norms to the population—and perhaps even to the elite. If the life of China's youth seems spartan and squalid in comparison to their U.S. or Taiwanese counterparts, a decade of economic growth and consumerism has given China's younger generation an adolescence filled with material benefits unimaginable to the previous generation. Most youth do not spend their evenings carousing on the town in bars and discos, but they are likely to possess tape recorders, wear more fashionable clothes, and occasionally eat out. Relaxation of political controls over culture allows them more opportunities to pursue their own interests, such as reading martial arts novels, listening to rock music, or playing mah-jongg. But just as U.S. youth in the 1960s were unmoved when defenders of the status quo pointed to progress since the Great Depression, Chinese youth take for granted the changes since 1976.

Since the Beijing massacre and the suppression of open political dissidence, the government has imposed stringent controls on even the most innocuous student activities. Memories of June 1989 and the intensification of public security precautions are sufficient to intimidate youth. Young people have retreated into passivity and despair about the future, made worse by the awareness that the "people's army" would use naked force against its citizens. Most notably in Beijing, this low morale adversely affects study and production. The current status quo leaves the government in a quandary: It has neutralized the threat of an insurrection by youth using measures that preclude mobilizing youth on the government's behalf. Anniversaries of past student movements, once celebrated by the Communist party, become a time to step up security. Officially sponsored norms alienate youth, yet adapting ideology to their concerns threatens to condone "bourgeois liberalism" or "pornographic influences." A new spurt of economic growth could conceivably create enough professionally rewarding jobs to provide some breathing room for the government. A meaningful reconciliation between state and youth, however, requires a better match between official and youth norms.

Conclusions

Formal Communist ideology, which has entered an irreversible decline, no longer provides a compelling basis for legitimizing the party-state nor offers normative values for organizing society. For the older generation who made the revolution, ideology is a universal truth and a determinant of fundamental structural change. In this vision the chiliastic struggle between Marxism and alternative systems of thought, whether Western liberalism or Confucianized traditionalism, pits absolute good against absolute evil.

In its Maoist guise, Marxist ideology was turned into a totalistic system of thought that, like ancient Confucianism, provided a unified basis for judging culture and aesthetics, public policy and private behavior, organizational life and personal relationships. Ideological atheism among all but first-generation leadership thus has multiple consequences for society, polity, and culture.

As the country rushes headlong toward modernization and consumerism, and with communism being abandoned in Eastern Europe, the value system of China is being reassessed. Because Marxist and Maoist ideals were associated with austerity and self-sacrifice, calls for public-service-oriented behavior and egalitarianism do not speak to the concerns of a population infatuated with the baubles of consumerism. The older generation's open disdain for the perceived hedonism of youth vividly adumbrates the ideological chasm between the generations. The deep antipathy students and intellectuals show toward official ideology, as well as the indifference of merchants and urban workers, illustrates the irrelevance of Leninism to resolving contemporary problems. Television programs recounting glorious victories of the past or atavistic campaigns to study Lei Feng evoke little popular interest. Some images of Mao Zedong and Zhou Enlai still appeal to youth, but often because they symbolize a time when China's leaders were uncorrupted by self-interest.

It is impossible to predict which values will emerge. Pluralism and other values associated with a civic society have yet to become fully accepted as legitimate goals. The heartfelt desire for liberalization and government for the people is not quite the same as a belief in liberalism and government by the people. The symbiotic relationship between entrepreneurs and the state, the state-oriented vision of the new bureaucracy, and the bonds that tie intellectuals to the state (although not necessarily the regime) are evidence that neither social autonomy nor a belief system legitimizing it has yet been institutionalized.

In the 1950s and 1960s, exponents of modernization theory argued that the prerequisites of Confucianism ran counter to those of modernization. Today scholars commonly treat ideology as a dependent value or as a mixed bundle of ideas that contains elements of both modernity and traditionalism. As a result, they view resistance to change as defense of privilege. In today's China, some party elders may be motivated purely by ideology, but much of the ideological resistance to radical reform masks defense of power and status—or sheer inertia. As many Chinese say, "The more you do, the more errors you make. Doing nothing is best" (*Duo zuo, duo cuo; bu zuo, bu cuo*).

In short, the old structures of power and ideology no longer have the same functionality as in the past. New structures and groups have usurped functions previously monopolized by the party-state. A weakened party-state remains strong enough to prevent people from blatant violations of official policy (with the notable exception of enforcing the single-child family policy in the countryside), but it can no longer actively manage society or elicit positive compliance.

The same is true for values. Many years ago, in *Confucian China and Its Modern Fate,* Joseph Levenson described how the changing context of nineteenth-century China altered the meaning of Confucian argumentation. What once had seemed self-evidently meaningful to the generation brought up in a Confucian China unexposed to the West had to be self-consciously defended on new grounds to a generation exposed to Western power and science. Whatever Lei Feng symbolizes to the older generation, the images and words no longer have the capacity to command the hearts and minds of the current generation.

No adequate channels for grassroots protest exist in China today. A major transformation is not imminent while the first-generation revolutionaries remain in power, but significant change is inherent in the situation China faces. China's involvement in the international community and its search for great-power status force the government to modify domestic policies. In order to maintain access to international credits and trade, especially annual renewal of most-favored-nation status by the U.S. Congress, it must make minimal concessions to human rights concerns and allow reporters to ask embarrassing questions at press conferences. The domestic scene also imposes a context that cannot be ignored: the rise of a bureaucratic technocracy, limited leadership institutionalization, autonomous private organization, coastal zones open to foreign influences, and the appearance of new social groupings. These seeds of potential change could blossom under the right conditions. But in June 1989 even the combined weight of massive popular discontent, the proreformist tendencies of important components of the party-state—including the party secretary general, the National People's Congress, some retired marshals of the People's Liberation Army (PLA), and much of the new bureaucracy—and active agitation by urban entrepreneurs, intellectuals, and students were insufficient to carry the day. Instead, the armed forces, acknowledging the informal authority of China's elders, crushed the most spontaneous expression of the Chinese people in the twentieth century.

The crisis of 1989 was made possible by a confluence of factors that exacerbated the prevailing mood of frustration and dissatisfaction: inflation caused by Zhao Ziyang's bungled attempt to promote price reform, corruption, declining growth rates, poor living and work conditions on campuses, and dissatisfaction with the slow pace of political reform. The enabling factor, however, was intra-elite divisions, which precluded a strong government response to the initial student protests, either through repression or by modest concessions. Given their obsession with "stability and unity" and their belief that political liberalization in Eastern Europe led to economic and political disintegration, the current leaders are unlikely to appeal to the public for support in factional struggles. As long as Deng Xiaoping or a sufficient number of the founding generation survive, the potential of the new institutions and groups to openly challenge the status quo will not be tested.

Determining how far China has moved toward a civil society depends, in part, on definition and perspective. Despite hesitant, ineffective movements to recentralize control and reassert the primacy of the party-state, there seems little prospect of successfully arresting the evolutionary trend toward privatization of behavior and acceptance of autonomous associations. Although entire sections of Chinese life and culture now seem off-limits to state interference on a de facto basis, the Chinese government has yet to acknowledge the de jure rights of civil society in a meaningful fashion. Social autonomy thus remains weakly institutionalized and confined primarily to nonpolitical activities. The stringent, almost paranoid controls on all types of group activity that have characterized official policy since June 4, 1989, can be seen either as proof of the weakness of civil society or the state's acknowledgment that civil society is emerging as a threat to state domination.

2

Patterns of Leadership in Reform China

Lowell Dittmer

Leadership has been one of the major strong points of the PRC's political system since 1949, clearly distinguishing the regime both from its immediate predecessor and from nearly a century of humiliating national weakness. This is true in the value-neutral sense that the leadership has been able consistently to implement its policies effectively, whether those policies have turned out to be well advised or not (a judgment that often depends on history and the observer's perspective). Thus in its first ten years in power, this new, revolutionary regime succeeded not only in rescuing an imperiled fraternal socialist country (the Democratic People's Republic of Korea) from otherwise certain collapse by staving off the mightiest power in the world (the United States) but also in transforming the domestic economy from its "half-feudal, half-colonial" form to socialist ownership under a comprehensive Communist authority structure. These changes were wrought in the context of an economic revival that is perhaps somewhat overstated in contrast to the abnormal trough reached at the end of World War II and the Chinese civil war (1946–1949) but is still impressive by any conceivable measure. It is true that toward the end of its first decade the leadership began to commit serious errors, such as the quickly aborted Hundred Flowers experiment (1957) or the more protracted Great Leap Forward (1958–1961), which contributed to a famine that killed more than 20 million people.[1] Yet that the leadership survived such debacles and in its tenacious self-confidence was even able to go on to commit similar blunders in the Great Proletarian Cultural Revolution (1966–1976) gives backhanded testimony to its strength.

There is little wonder that this should be so. Whereas the Chinese Communist party (CCP) has long decried a "cult of personality," nevertheless the party has consistently fostered a cult of *leadership.* Why did the party falter, as it often did, during its zigzag three decades of revolutionary war? Always, according to official histories, because of leadership errors. Success, failure, and the very survival of this band of desperadoes all depended on the quality of its leaders. Good leaders were assumed to be superior human beings, able to work harder and longer, suffer and sacrifice more without losing their comprehensive vision of the future salvation toward which all efforts must be focused. Potential leaders were selected very carefully for their conduct under fire or in a political campaign, then cultivated for years before acquiring leadership responsibility. And once they had so effectively acquitted themselves, it was expected that they would be obeyed "without question" by those following in their footsteps.[2]

If we try to infer the underlying reasons for the striking effectiveness of this arrangement, we find three factors preeminent. First, the human actors selected appear to be of exceptionally high caliber. This may be attributed not only to the competence of the cadre selection and training procedures but to the annealing impact of incessant intramural factional strife and extramural warfare, which had a Darwinian impact on the emergence of an unusually competent set of elites. Second, the Marxist-Leninist organizational structure seems inherently well adapted for effective leadership: The ideology provides a cognitive framework for goal selection and the channeling of appropriate means; the Leninist mechanism of democratic centralism ensures compliance. Third, indigenous techniques for building consensus and legitimacy, such as the "mass line," fostered broader participation in leadership and policy implementation than envisaged by classic Leninism. This third component, which is distinctively Chinese, typically has been incorporated into informal or makeshift arrangements rather than as part of the formal organizational apparatus.

The death of Mao marked the first serious challenge to the system that ensured the continuing existence of these conditions for effective leadership. The extinction of the original core leadership was of course merely a matter of time; the deaths of Mao himself, Zhou Enlai, Zhu De, and Kang Sheng in the same year (1976) marked the beginning of the end for first-generation revolutionaries. Repudiation of the Cultural Revolution shortly thereafter implied that quasi-wartime methods for "steeling" leaders could not be revived. Marxism-Leninism was sustained, both organizationally and ideologically, but the Cultural Revolution had severely damaged the party apparatus and left the country "deadened" (*mamuhua*) and disillusioned by endless paeans to Maoist ideology. The informal indigenous component of leadership selection, by contrast, had been given much freer play, but the impact by 1976 seemed to have been largely adverse, giving rise to rampant factionalism, the "backdoor" channel of constituency service, and the cult of personality. Even the gerontocratic, seniority-based promotion and lifetime tenure arrangements, against which the revolt of the young "revolutionary successors" had been mobilized, were only temporarily alleviated by the purge of the party and state leadership, leaving the underlying principles intact.

So far as leadership is concerned, the goals of the reforms inaugurated by Deng Xiaoping and his minions in 1978 were what Chinese typically called "complicated" (*fuza*). Retrospective examinations of the Maoist era, such as the document on party history issued by the Sixth Plenum of the Eleventh Party Congress in 1981, focused not on leadership weakness but on the flaws of excessive or unbridled personal power.[3] The task of reform was hence not so much to strengthen party leadership as to bring it under some sort of control. The means chosen to do this focused on institutionalization and the rule of law. This implied forswearing the indigenous component of leadership enhancement, which was increasingly perceived as a source of "corruption," and resurrecting Leninism. Yet it did not necessarily entail exclusive reliance on Leninist techniques. For some leaders, a reversion to the "golden age" prior to the Eighth Party Congress, when such practices were (somewhat sentimentally) believed to have held sway, was indeed the best of all possible worlds, but this older generation was increasingly upstaged by younger members of the reform elite who favored democratic techniques.

The stage is now set for an analysis of leadership and its reform during the Deng Xiaoping era. The actors sorted themselves out horizontally in terms of factional affiliation and vertically in terms of generations, arranging themselves by seniority into a gerontocratic pyramid. The new leadership structure fused Leninist and indigenous elements, the former influencing its constitutional and formal aspect, the latter shaping its more informal arrangements. These actors wished to reform this structure to permit greater stability, procedural regularity, and professional competence—but without losing the strength and popular legitimacy so long associated with CCP leadership that they had come to be taken for granted. I begin by examining the reorganization of the formal structure of leadership in which the reformers placed their greatest hopes; I then turn to changes in informal structure that were to have still greater impact on the actual evolution of leadership, notwithstanding the lack of a grand design.

Formal Reform

In the shadow of Tiananmen, the institutionalization of leadership in the PRC appears to have been an egregious failure. Before we dismiss this effort out of hand, however, it is only fair that we reconsider its achievements and shortfalls over the past decade.

It is more or less customary in China to inaugurate any major policy initiative with a campaign to win public opinion, including a thorough repudiation of the forces of the status quo that might otherwise impede the new policy. In the case of the reformers, their obvious target was radical Maoism as practiced during the Cultural Revolution. The campaign began under Hua Guofeng in the form of a critique of the Gang of Four and gradually became transformed under Deng Xiaoping's influence into an attack on radical Maoism and even on Mao's personal reputation. As conceived by reformist critics, the radicals were guilty of three main types of leadership abuse: a cult of personality, which involved the cultivation of reactionary superstitions among the masses; arbitrary personal tyranny, as displayed in a prolific variety of petty or gratuitously cruel episodes; and ideological dogmatism, as represented by the mass memorization of passages from the "little red book," persecution of many people for trivial or metaphorical acts of lèse-majesté, and a totalitarian suffocation of political dissent or indeed variety. Hua's campaign reached an initial high point in summer 1978 with a skillfully engineered program in support of the proposition (a quotation from Mao) that "practice is the sole criterion of truth," which undercut the religious worship of Mao and dogmatic adherence to whatever he said or did. Other major moves in undermining Maoist notions of revolutionary leadership were the public rehabilitation of thousands of victims or radical purges, the public trial of the Lin Biao and Gang of Four groups in summer 1980, and finally the document on party history passed at the Sixth Plenum in June 1981, which distinguished between Mao personally (who had committed errors with increasing frequency) and Mao Zedong Thought (now conceived as a collective intellectual construct). The implications of this campaign were that personal leadership is inherently dangerous and must be placed under institutional constraint.

The endeavor to do so was begun by Deng Xiaoping in a speech made and approved by the Politburo in August 1980. Deng opined that the overconcentration of power and the failure to develop a set of institutions had been the source of China's political difficulties in the past. For the sake of greater functional separation of powers (Deng even flirted at this time with the U.S. notion of checks and balances), he proposed to detach the government administration from the party, replace the cult of personality with collective leadership, and rejuvenate the leadership by retiring superannuated veterans, thereby making room for the recruitment of younger and better-educated leaders. These reform proposals were placed on hold in winter 1980–1981 because of a strong antireform backlash that came in the wake of a loss of government control over capital construction, budget deficits, and inflation. Yet reform discussion resurfaced in 1982, having a direct and visible impact on the structural reforms undertaken in the party and state constitutions adopted by the Twelfth Party Congress in September 1982 and by the fifth session of the Fifth National People's Congress (NPC) in November 1982, respectively. Because the state constitution actually seems to have been drafted earlier (though it was not finally approved until after the party congress), I will consider it first.

The state constitution strengthened the legislative apparatus with the addition of a feature of Soviet and Eastern European parliaments: functionally specialized committees separate from the Standing Committee, each with permanent tenure and its own staff. Mass participation had already been enhanced (in 1980) by introducing multicandidate elections to county-level people's congresses. In order to facilitate the turnover of elites, the constitution stipulated a fixed term of office (two five-year terms) for the prime minister, the president, and other top state officials (with the significant sole exception of the chair of the Central Military Commission, Deng Xiaoping). Further civil rights were extended to the Chinese citizenry, including equality before the law, freedom of worship, and protection against arbitrary arrest; the right to strike, however, was rescinded, and the practice of family planning was added to the list of citizen duties. The ministries and commissions operating under the State Council were retrenched, and the post of state councillor was introduced to facilitate the retirement of veteran cadres. The separation of powers between government and party administration was encouraged by proscribing anyone from holding leadership positions in both organs.

In the CCP, the chairmanship system (in which the party was led by a chair and a ranked series of vice-chairs, the first of whom was assumed to be heir apparent) was eliminated in the name of mitigating functional duplication, leaving the party general secretary as de facto leader of the CCP (and thereby bringing the Chinese leadership structure into closer structural conformity with Soviet and Eastern European models). The general secretary was, however, authorized to chair only the resuscitated party Secretariat, with power to "convene" meetings of the Politburo or its Standing Committee. Thus the general secretary's relative power and the concomitant possibility of a renascence of the personality cult was reduced. The Politburo, staffed by senior veterans, was consigned to a role as a board of directors and in fact began to meet less often; day-to-day implementation of policy devolved to the Secretariat. The Central Committee (CC) was divided into three concurrent (but not functionally differentiated) organs: the CC, the Central Disciplinary Inspection Commission (CDIC), and the Central Advisory Committee (CAC). The general secretary of the Secretariat, the chair of the Central Military Commission (CMC), the chair of the CAC, and the first secretary of the CDIC were all required to have concurrent seats on the Standing Committee, thereby composing its "natural membership." In addition to dispersing executive power somewhat more broadly, the constitution enhanced the discretion of the party legislature by stipulating that either there should be a "preliminary election" to draw up a list of candidates for formal election to executive organs or, if the preliminary election is omitted, the number of candidates on the name list should be greater than the number of persons to be elected.

In at least two respects, however, the party did not go as far as the NPC. Whereas the NPC adopted the system of permanent tenure of delegates, a reform intended to make the NPC a permanently functioning forum for legislative review, the party turned down an analogous proposal. And whereas the state constitution stipulated limits to the tenure of office for most government leaders, the party rejected any such limits on grounds that retraction of the principle of life tenure and adoption of relatively generous retirement provisions (via the advisory committees) would be sufficient to cope with the problem of protracted incumbency. Why the party has consistently remained more conservative than the state vis-à-vis structural reform probably has a good deal to do with its Leninist legacy, according to which the Communist party is the proletarian vanguard with a messianic historical mission that can brook no interference from the general population or democratic political institutions.[4] Unlike government bureaucrats, whose professional skills give them a more flexible employment outlook, party leaders are concerned essentially with the acquisition and exercise of power. Any retiree would not only be irreplaceable but might be exposed to some form of retribution.

In critical retrospect, the leadership institutionalization that impressed Chinese and foreign observers at the time was really quite limited. The pattern seems to have been guided throughout by political considerations. Thus the critique of late Maoist radicalism provided an opening for the insertion of Dengist pragmatism—which has turned out, with the addition of the Four Cardinal Principles in early 1979, to be no less politically restrictive. Elimination of the chairmanship system provided a convenient pretext for the removal of Hua Guofeng as chair of the party. Indeed, upon the demotion of Hu Yaobang in

January 1987, the Politburo was restored to its former position as chief locus of decisionmaking (by the Thirteenth Party Congress, in October 1987). The Secretariat once again was relegated to implementing Politburo decisions and overseeing the party apparatus.[5] By proscribing the constitutional concentration of power, the dispersion of formal power among executive offices and the trisection of the CC permitted informal power to be concentrated unconstitutionally, in the person of then vice-premier and CMC chair Deng Xiaoping. We find rather consistently that Deng's quest for the institutionalization of power has been compromised by the need to enhance his own power sufficiently to put his policies into effect.

But perhaps the biggest miscarriage was the elaborate retirement system, designed to eliminate gerontocratic tendencies and institutionalize succession arrangements to a second and third "line" of younger, better-educated leaders. This proved to be prohibitively expensive. At the highest level, retirees were offered pensions greater than their previous salaries. There were also a number of prominent exceptions. At the Thirteenth Party Congress, for example, Deng Xiaoping was permitted to retain his chair of the Central Military Commission. This then provided a precedent for others. At the first session of the Seventh NPC in April 1988, Yang Shangkun was appointed chief of state, Wan Li was appointed chair of the NPC Standing Committee, and Li Xiannian was appointed chair of the Chinese People's Political Consultative Congress. All of them, at ages eighty-one, seventy-one, and seventy-nine, respectively, should legally have been ineligible. As we shall see below, even those successfully retired or shunted off to "advisory" positions as state councillors or CAC members often prove to have more political lives than a cat.

In sum, the contribution of formal institutionalization to the evolving pattern of leadership has been modest and defeasible. The following points qualify this generalization only marginally for the present but may give greater grounds for hope in the long run:

1. Although this would require a much more ambitious analysis than is possible here, the attempt to rejuvenate the ruling apparatus has been more successful at lower (i.e., provincial, municipal, and county) levels than at the top. The incumbents of lower-level advisory committees are very much concerned with retaining their retirement privileges and if possible insinuating their relatives into positions of power, but they do not appear to be intruding into the decisionmaking process in the way that they do at the top. This is essentially because there is not as much power available at lower levels. After all, because China is a unitary rather than a federal system, the center retains final discretion. This means that the politics of retirement is controlled from

above, not on the basis of some collegial consensus: *Superiors* decide who should retire, as well as who should replace the retiring official. This leaves the retirees with little or no play in either retirement arrangements or subsequent policy decisions. The implication is that lower-level party and government organs may be more forthrightly reformist than those at the center.

2. The enhancement of the powers of the party and state legislative assemblies, however slight compared to developments in Eastern Europe and the Soviet Union, seems to have started a trend that may in the long run prove irreversible. Thus the use of the secret ballot and multiple candidacies at the Thirteenth Party Congress resulted in the unexpected retirement of five senior cadres, including Propaganda Department Chief (and leading critic of "bourgeois liberalism") Deng Liqun.[6] The NPC has gradually become more democratic and articulate, reaching a provisional high point at its seventh session (March 25–April 13, 1988): For the first time delegates were selected in multicandidate local elections, resulting in a high turnover (71 percent newcomers), and they expressed their opinions on inflation, corruption, low pay scales, Tibet, and so on in a rash of small-group meetings. Although all party candidates for executive office were overwhelmingly elected, not one was elected unanimously; in fact, there were hundreds of nays.[7] Though it is true that both the Thirteenth Party Congress and the Seventh NPC could be viewed as expressions of high-tide reform euphoria, even during the Fourth Plenum of the Thirteenth CC, convened to bless the results of the Tiananmen crackdown, more than fifty members and alternative members asked for sick leave or leave of absence, and the election of Jiang Zemin as Zhao Ziyang's successor passed with a bare majority of seven votes. Deng's personal motion made Zhao's dismissal from his last remaining governmental offices at the NPC Standing Committee meeting on June 29 a foregone conclusion, but three of the 132 Standing Committee members abstained and three failed to activate the voting mechanism.

3. Institutionalization has made some progress in the sense that meetings convene with greater openness and regularity than during the Maoist era. State Council meetings and those of the Standing Committee of the National People's Congress have become more frequent, for example, and they are usually publicly announced. This is also true for the CCP Politburo: Between the Thirteenth Party Congress and June 1988, the Politburo held nine publicly announced plenary sessions. The Thirteenth Party Congress in 1987 even announced a system of regular meetings of the Politburo, the Politburo Standing Committee, and the Central Secretariat, in an arrangement in which the Standing Committee will report regularly to the Politburo and the Politburo will

report regularly to the Central Committee.[8] More and more policy formulation must go through some sort of formal bureaucratic procedure, though personal ties can still find ways to prevail over procedure.

4. In contrast to the time when law was ignored and "bourgeois right" publicly denounced, constitutional legality now requires at least lip service. This was true even during the extraordinary crisis of Tiananmen. For example, on May 26, 1989, Peng Zhen, former chair of the Standing Committee of the NPC, gave a speech elaborately justifying the May 20 invocation of martial law in terms of constitutionality.[9] Yang Shangkun also felt the need to belittle the importance of the participation of nonmembers in the expanded Politburo Standing Committee meetings that decided to impose martial law on May 19 by pointing out that the crucial decision was made by a four-to-one majority of full members. (Two years earlier, in January 1987, objections had been raised to the analogous participation of seventeen "retired" officials in the vote to demote Hu Yaobang.) When Zhao's opposition to martial law was defeated in the Standing Committee of the Politburo meeting of May 19, he apparently sought to encourage Wan Li to return and convene the Standing Committee of the NPC, which was constitutionally authorized to rescind the declaration of martial law and even to discharge Li Peng, who had invoked it; some fifty-seven members of the Standing Committee signed a petition to this effect. The conservatives were sufficiently alarmed by this prospect that they prevailed upon Wan Li, who had obediently returned home early, to remain in Shanghai and "rest" until the smoke cleared.

5. Upon closer inspection, apparent violation of formal rules sometimes turns out to be technical conformity to those rules. For example, the party constitution was amended to permit Deng Xiaoping to retain his chairmanship of the CMC yet nominally retire from the Politburo.[10] Another example is the rule adopted at the time of Deng's resignation from the CC and the Standing Committee of the Politburo: In his televised May 16 talk with Mikhail Gorbachev, Zhao Ziyang indicated that "Comrade Deng's guidance was still needed in dealing with important issues. Since the Party's 13th Congress, we have always made reports to and asked for the opinion of Deng Xiaoping when dealing with most important issues."[11]

The implication of these points is that procedural legality has perhaps acquired a certain inhibitive effect on politics. But this effect is still very weak, and there is a discrepancy between public and inner-party (*neibu*) rules of the game, typically resolved in favor of the party. The principal reason for the failure of formal reform is that it was designed chiefly to inhibit what I call "bold" leadership—resorting to informal resources and techniques to reassert authority. Situations that demand

TABLE 2.1

		Distribution of Agreement	
		Cleavage	Solidarity
Distribution of Power	Hierarchy	Disciplinary Sanctions	Primus Inter Pares
	Collegiality	Factionalism	Collective Leadership

bold leadership are those in which the polity confronts unpleasant alternatives, conflict, and risks requiring a leap of faith. During the early stages of reform, sufficient consensus could be engendered on an anti–Cultural Revolution platform and on relatively modest initial reforms already experimented with during the post-Leap recovery. Bold leadership was not required; collective decisionmaking within formal institutional constraints sufficed. But during the later stages, particularly after reform was introduced to the urban industrial sector in October 1984 at the Third Plenum of the Twelfth CC, serious problems began to emerge—inflation, deficits, unemployment, unequal income distribution, cultural spillover—that could no longer be neatly blamed on radical predecessors. Splits developed within the reform coalition. Spontaneous mass protest resurfaced for the first time since the Cultural Revolution. Under these circumstances, formal constraints were swept aside, and a new leadership pattern emerged, fusing formal and informal elements.

Leadership Under Reform

The basic leadership configuration in post-Mao China may be conceived as a matrix that varies along two axes: the distribution of agreement and the distribution of power, as depicted in Table 2.1. What accounts for the variance along the two axes? Let us look first at the distribution of power. This is contingent upon two factors: formal office and the informal web of elite connections (*guanxi*) that Chinese refer to as one's "political base" (*zhengzhi jichu*). Formal position is the least important of these, and developments since 1986 have only underscored this fact. Previously, it was a necessary (not sufficient) condition to have a seat on the committees where decisions are made, but that is no longer the case. Formal position is still a prerequisite to building a base, but one may retain a base indefinitely without the position. Thus Deng Xiaoping, who was purged from all leadership positions following the first Tiananmen incident on April 5, 1976, still retained sufficient informal power to ensure a comeback.

A "base" consists of the circle of loyal supporters who may be relied upon to render aid when one's political survival is at stake and when associates based on one's current formal position are apt to be scared off. A base may be roughly gauged by whether it is wide or narrow, shallow or deep; an official with a network of cronies widely dispersed throughout the various functional and regional divisions of the civilian and military bureaucracies has a "broad" base; an official whose connections date from the party's founding or from the early recruitment waves (Jiangxi, Long March, Yanan) has a "deep" base (i.e., one may expect one's cronies to be highly placed, via seniority).[12] Having joined the party in 1924 and 1927, respectively, Deng Xiaoping and Yang Shangkun both have very deep bases; but their bases are also broad, including (in Yang's case) study in Moscow (linking him with the powerful "Returned Student" group), military staff experience, and a long incumbency as head of the General Office of the Central Committee. Until his appointment to the Politburo in 1979, the base of the younger Zhao Ziyang, who joined the party in 1938, was limited to the provincial level, seriously handicapping his career at the top. Li Peng began as a professional engineer after technical training in the Soviet Union and emerged as a central-level official only after 1980, when he served as vice-minister of the power industry, education, and water conservancy. He thus has a relatively narrow and shallow base that is somewhat compensated by his "princely" status (he is foster son of Zhou Enlai), from which he accrued connections with all the senior veterans. Jiang Zemin is a "helicopter" (the Chinese term for someone on the fast track) with a relatively narrow and shallow base who bounded (with Deng's grace) from the Shanghai Party Committee to the position of secretary general in 1989.

Members of a leader's base will expect timely help from their patron in promoting their careers, and the patron will depend on protégés to extend influence and provide an insurance policy. Thus an upwardly mobile leader will appoint as many base members as possible to formal bureaucratic positions from which their mutual needs can be served. Hu Yaobang was particularly energetic in appointing base members accumulated during his long chairmanship of the Communist Youth League (CYL), though he remained vulnerable to an attack from his own patron. The "petroleum faction" (*shiyou pai*), led by Yu Qiuli, Kang Shien, and Gu Mu, placed members "at various levels" in the State Planning Commission; the State Economic Commission; the ministries of finance, coal, chemical industries, and metallurgy; and the State Council.[13]

Whether the distribution of power in any given Politburo is hierarchical or collegial cannot be determined merely by examining the distribution of formal offices, which is in fact equal, everyone having only one vote; it is also necessary to compare members' bases. If one member's base is significantly broader and deeper than that of the others, the distribution of power may be assumed to be hierarchical, particularly if other members are part of the dominant member's base; if several members have comparable bases, a more collegial relationship may be expected to obtain.

Throughout the history of the Politburo, the "normal" vertical relationship among top leaders has been hierarchical and indeed monocratic, as indicated by the punctilious observance of protocol (who appears, who mounts the dais in what order, who speaks, who stands next to whom) in public ceremonies. Since the death of Mao, it seems clear in retrospect that only during the 1976–1978 period, when the succession was still in flux, did a collective leadership really exist. This collectivity came about because of the anomalous distribution of formal and informal power. As a result of his coup, Hua Guofeng had for the first time in CCP history managed to monopolize all formal leadership positions (namely, CMC chair, premier, and CCP chair), yet his informal base was both narrow and shallow. Thus he shared power with senior veteran Ye Jianying and, after their rehabilitation in summer 1977, Deng Xiaoping and Chen Yun, all of whom disposed of broad and deep bases.

Hampered by an assortment of policy disagreements and political rivalry, collective leadership soon degenerated into a relatively quiet form of factionalism. By dint of a lot of clever and plausible organizational engineering, Deng was able to remove Hua and his supporters from their leadership posts by June 1981 and assume de facto leadership without the corresponding formal status—although, as already noted, his constitutional reforms reduced and diffused formal executive power so that no one could challenge him based on office alone. He then concentrated on the appointment of his protégés to high positions from which they could effectively support him and began to move against other leaders whose bases made them potential rivals. These he maneuvered into "retirement" by endorsing the general principle of leadership rejuvenation and by simultaneously moving in the same direction, albeit at a somewhat slower pace. Thus at a CCP National Conference of Delegates presided over by Hu Yaobang in September 1985, 137 senior veteran high-level leaders resigned, including half a dozen Politburo members (e.g., Ye Jianying, Wang Zhen, Deng Yingchao). These resignations created vacancies for the conference to elect some 179 younger replacements. Although student demonstrations in December 1986 provided veterans with a convenient pretext for a counterattack, another breakthrough was made with the retirement of ninety CC members and eleven Politburo members at the Thirteenth Party Congress in 1987.[14]

Yet, as previously indicated, problems have remained. With the creation of advisory positions as an inducement to retirement, many of those "retiring" have simply moved to newly created posts. Thus the immediate effect of establishing advisory commissions was to increase the number of people attending CC plenums: Whereas only 318 people attended the Seventh Plenum of the Eleventh CC in August 1982 (297 CC members and alternates and 21 observers), early the following month a total of 631 people attended the First Plenum of the Twelfth Party Congress (347 CC members and alternates and 284 observers, most of whom were CAC members).[15] At the Politburo level, continuing participation of superannuated members on an advisory basis has had considerable impact. The campaign against "spiritual pollution" in 1983–1984, for example, was forced by strong attacks from the "second line" of retired cadres. In 1986, senior veterans began articulating their antireform views even before the demonstrations offered a suitable pretext to do so. Conservatives pushed through a resolution stressing "socialist spiritual civilization" at the September 1986 CC plenum, and Peng Zhen denounced Hu Yaobang's ideological laxness in speeches in October and November 1986. When Hu Yaobang became a legitimate target in January 1987, no fewer than seventeen officials came out of retirement to help decide on Hu's dismissal and on Zhao's appointment as acting party general secretary. One of them, Bo Yibo, actually made the case against Hu.[16] Although the reformers seemed to have regained the initiative at the Thirteenth Party Congress, when the reforms again ran into difficulty in mid-1988, these "retired" elderly cadres joined to criticize the reformers in the summer Beidaihe meetings that marked Party General Secretary Zhao Ziyang's first major setback. In spring 1989, of course, the gerontocrats led by Deng Xiaoping were to play a pivotal role in the decision to declare martial law and repress the demonstrators.

This has given rise to an anomalous situation in which there are two interlocking leadership groups, one based on formal position without real power, the other on informal bases without official responsibility. The latter consists of an informal group of octogenarians, many of whom hold positions in the CAC, some of whom have no formal offices at all.[17] One of the avenues through which they express influence is through consultation. The Secretariat and the State Council constantly consult with the elders on an individual basis. According to Zhao Ziyang, "Whenever there is a major issue, we go to Chen Yun, Li Xiannian, and Deng Xiaoping for advice."[18] Yet even in a culture steeped in filial piety, there is no guarantee that voluntary consultation will take place. Mao Zedong complained during the Cultural Revolution that "Deng Xiaoping has never come to consult me. From 1949 until now he has not come to consult me at all."[19] Consequently, other institutional mechanisms have been created to ensure that the elders retain the ear of those occupying formal office. One of these is the Central Work Conference, an ad hoc gathering that seems to have displaced CC plenums during the early 1960s, with nineteen meetings held between 1960 and 1966; its roster and agenda were flexible, controlled by the Secretariat.[20] But even formal organs can accommodate participation by nonmembers, in the form of the "expanded conference," which permits the chair to invite participants to attend meetings on a discretionary basis. Politburo discussions on major controversial issues have always been in the form of enlarged meetings. Attendance at the meetings that ousted Hua Guofeng, Hu Yaobang, and Zhao Ziyang, for example, was "packed" to ensure the outcome. Unofficial members are not permitted to vote, but party decisions on important issues are rarely decided by voting anyway, and the veterans express themselves with great self-confidence and authority in discussions.[21]

The relationship between the two groups is thus not collegial but hierarchical. This can be seen in that the "sitting committee" can overrule the Standing Committee on any given decision and may even discipline or purge its members if they happen to disagree. Unofficial members' authority is not only based on deeply entrenched habits of seniority but comes about because senior veterans exacted as their price for "retirement" the right to name their successors, who were then expected to remain loyal. Thus Yao Yilin was beholden to Chen Yun, Zhao Ziyang to Deng Xiaoping, Li Peng to both Deng Yingchao and Chen Yun, Hu Qili (later "adopted" by Zhao) to Hu Yaobang, and so forth.

Much as in the relationship between first and second "lines" during late Maoism, the second line functions as a board of directors, ignoring routine affairs and intervening selectively on key decisions of its own choosing. Though the elders may intervene at any time, as they did in January 1987 to demote Hu, the season and place that is more or less reserved for their input is summer at Beidaihe. This is a resort about 400 kilometers from Beijing where many senior cadres go for vacation, making it convenient for them to participate in expanded sessions of the Secretariat, State Council, or Politburo. Participants at the Beidaihe meetings of 1986 decided to reject several months' unprecedented agitation by reform-minded intellectuals and to postpone further reforms for the time being. Instead the meetings endorsed the idea of new campaigns to criticize bourgeois liberalization. The Sixth Plenum of the Twelfth CC then met in Beijing for only one day to approve the resolution. Two years later the decision to postpone further price reform and to divest Zhao Ziyang of his economic portfolio in favor of Li Peng also was taken at Beidaihe; it was later confirmed by the Third Plenum of the Thirteenth CC held in September 1988 in Beijing.

The distribution of agreement is less easily discerned than distribution of power. The latter is signaled in public displays of status, whereas the former is carefully veiled by rules of democratic centralism and inner-party struggle. If "primordial" and other patron-client ties remain meaningful in cementing vertical relationships, the horizontal distribution of agreement seems to depend more on how issues correspond to the material and ideal interests of the decisionmakers, at least at the highest level. The line of cleavage depends upon which issues happen to be salient at the time. Since the death of Mao, there has been an overall shift from ideological to political-economic issues, giving rise to somewhat more flexible alignments. Since elimination of the radical Maoists in 1976 and the departure of the last of the moderate Maoists in 1982, the leadership has divided itself into roughly three groupings:

Orthodox Leninists ("paleo-Maoists") hearken back to the "golden age" of Chinese communism before the Eighth Party Congress in September 1956. They not only reject democratically oriented political reforms in the party or government but criticize already implemented economic reforms for leading back to "capitalism." The "opening to the outside world," they believe, invites "spiritual pollution"; the special economic zones are neocolonialist enclaves. Among representatives of this point of view are retired party veterans such as Peng Zhen, Wang Zhen, Li Xiannian, and Bo Yibo, along with an indefinite number of their colleagues on the CAC. This group, however, appears to lack recruitment prospects among younger cadres and may fade away with the passing of its current membership.

Moderate reformers represent a line of continuity to the reforms introduced under Liu Shaoqi and Deng Xiaoping in the early 1960s. They strictly reject any form of democratization that might deviate from a single-party proletarian dictatorship, though they are willing to give at least lip service to a clearer division of labor between party and government. Their goal is "perfection" of the existing system rather than any fundamental departure from it. With regard to economic reforms, they adhere to the notion of the market as a "bird in the cage" of the plan—any expansion of private property or market activity must be strictly limited. However, they endorse existing reforms, such as the de facto decollectivization of agriculture or China's opening to the West. Among the supporters of this point of view are Jiang Zemin, Chen Yun (with reservations), and Wan Li. Although Deng Xiaoping took a somewhat more adventurous approach to economic reform in the past, supporting price reform in the spring and early summer of 1988, since Tiananmen he seems to have cast his lot with the moderate reformers. The so-called princes' party (*taize dang*) (children of high cadres) also generally subscribes to this point of view, which protects its vested interests.[22]

Radical reformers endorse much more sweeping marketization and privatization—such as complete price reform—than do conservative reformers. More significantly, they believe that reform cannot be restricted to the economic realm but must include politics. This means not only separation of party and government functions but some movement toward democratization and expanded human rights (just how much remains moot). Radical reformers include the late Party General Secretary Hu Yaobang; his successor, Zhao Ziyang; former Secretariat member Hu Qili; Vice-Minister Tian Jiyun; and presumably Li Ruihuan, a Politburo member and CC Propaganda Department chair.

In addition to these three elite opinion groups, there are three relevant corporate interest groups, all of which are assumed to be most sympathetic to the conservatives or the moderate reformers: the People's Liberation Army, whose instinctive support for law and order seems likely to be enhanced by their complicity in the June 3 crackdown; Qiao Shi's security forces, heavily reinforced since June 1989; and the state planning and ministerial bureaucracy, whose responsibilities have also expanded significantly. There are, however, also two more loosely organized functional interest groups whose sympathies in 1991 seemed to lie with reform: the intellectuals and the urban working class. This is so despite their reliance on fixed wages, which makes them acutely vulnerable to price reform.

Having examined the basic leadership structure, we turn now to the dynamics of change. There seem to be at least two types of change involved. The first is transitory, reversible change. The second consists of nonrecursive or secular change. The main form of transitory change to have affected leadership dynamics is a cyclical one in which the economic business cycle interacts with episodes of mass activism to create opportunities for elite conflict and purge. The business cycle goes through phases of vigorous expansion (booms) alternating with phases of retrenchment (busts). The main force pushing expansion has been the market, which encourages capital investment on the part of collective and private enterprises. It is the central planning authorities and ministries who have enforced periods of retrenchment, during which the collective and private sector is cut back and the planned state sector subsidized. The boom phase is obviously most favorable to the interests of the radical reformers, ceteris paribus, whereas a bust serves the interests of the central planners. In the course of the reform era, there have been three booms, very roughly calculated as the periods 1978–1980, 1984–1985, and 1988–June 1989, and three busts, in 1981–1983, 1986–1987, and June 1989–1990. Spontaneous mass mobilization does not coincide precisely with the business cycle but is nevertheless relevant to the political-economic dynamic.

Mass mobilization may take place either during booms or busts, depending on whether the issues on the national agenda arouse the students and other protesters. Whatever the stimulus for the movement, if it occurs during a boom there appears to be less likelihood of a sharp crackdown than if it occurs during a bust. Thus the Democracy Wall protest movement began in spring 1978 and lasted through 1980, arising in a boom and surviving with difficulty until a bust was deemed economically expedient, whereupon a harsh crackdown put the residual underground tabloids out of business. The fall 1985 student mobilization against the Japanese commercial invasion arose during a boom, was handled with kid gloves, and died a natural death by December. The student protest demonstrations of December 1986 and the democracy demonstrations of April–May 1989 both occurred during busts, and both were met with violent repressive tactics that included the purge of those leaders who supported the demonstrators or were considered insufficiently firm in repressing them.

There are several reasons for this variability of elite response. First, the radical reformers tend to have the upper hand during a boom, and they dislike cracking down on the students and intellectuals who make up their natural constituency. Second, a harsh crackdown is functionally inappropriate for economic reform and expansion, tending to have a chilling effect. During a bust, in contrast, the conservatives are riding high and have both pretext and opportunity to attack the reform constituency and purge the radical reformers for its excesses. Moreover, a crackdown is fully compatible with an economic retrenchment policy. The implication is that radical reformers are most vulnerable to purge when spontaneous mass activism arises during bust phases, whereas conservatives are most vulnerable during boom phases when mass activism is low. These relationships are depicted in Table 2.2. The lower righthand cell, consisting of low mass activism during a bust phase, seemed to characterize the Chinese situation toward the end of 1991.

TABLE 2.2

		Business Cycle	
		Boom	Bust
Mass Activity	High	Tolerance	Purge Reformers
	Low	Purge Conservatives	Chill

The major secular change in Chinese politics has been the waning of ideology, which has had profound and multiple effects on the leadership. This decline has come about for two reasons: On the one hand, the masses were generally exhausted by the rigors of ideological conformity in the absence of material payoffs in the wake of the Cultural Revolution; on the other hand, the Deng Xiaoping leadership deliberately undercut late Maoist ideology to introduce enough pragmatic flexibility to permit experimentation with various reforms (and to undermine Hua Guofeng's position). The primary drawback to this decline is that the leaders are bereft of a language through which they can appeal to the masses for the pursuit of collective goals. In the absence of such language and such goals, the masses tend to become totally absorbed in the pursuit of private material interests (*wang qian kan* in the Chinese pun).[23] Yet operational control of the material incentives through which the masses' interests could be manipulated has been decentralized or marketized in the course of the reforms, to the extent that the leadership feels a more or less acute sense of loss of control. During crisis situations, this tends to give rise to leadership panics.

The decline of ideology has rendered mass participation—at least the only type of mass participation that affords leaders a role as leaders rather than possible targets—infeasible. During the three decades of postliberation Maoist rule, mass participation took place exclusively through mass movements or campaigns. The ground rules were spelled out in the "mass line" (i.e., "from the masses, to the masses" and "out of struggle, unity"), which allowed a certain amount of tactical flexibility to accommodate local conditions and requirements but presupposed movement toward common objectives laid down by the central leadership. The existence of a common ideological language and value system in which everyone was painstakingly socialized made it possible to generate consensus on these collective objectives. Certain obvious alternatives (e.g., pursuit of private interests) were not even conceivable within that language and value system. The decay or discrediting (with the complicity of the reformers) of that language and value system makes it increasingly difficult to generate consensus on positive collective goals. Sending young people down to the countryside was quietly abandoned at the beginning of the Deng era, as were such programs as barefoot doctors and local medical facilities, off-season water conservancy construction projects, and worker emulation drives. The only campaigns launched under leadership auspices in the post-Mao era have been focused on essentially negative objectives, in which the masses would be enjoined to renounce certain of their own ideological failings—spiritual pollution, bourgeois liberalism, and other "ill winds" (*bu zhengzhi feng*). Negative ideological campaigns ran at cross-purposes to the logic of the economic reforms, which were all premised on appeals to material incentives. Whenever this contradiction cut into economic performance, the campaign had to be curtailed, sometimes after only a few months.

In the continued absence of elite-sanctioned channels for mass participation, entrepreneurs began to arise, usually from among the intellectuals, to lead mass movements toward independently targeted collective goals. This happened repeatedly, beginning with the famous Democracy Wall movement (1978–1980). District-level electoral campaigns in 1980–1981 were co-opted by certain young activists on behalf of nonsanctioned candidates. In fall 1985, students mobilized against the Japanese commercial invasions. The December 1986 demonstrations in support of reform and the April–May 1989 democracy demonstrations drew massive public support and provoked major splits in the leadership. Regardless of the intrinsic merits of such independently selected rhetorical goals, which often deviated only slightly from sanctioned objectives (e.g., the conservatives should have welcomed the xenophobic implications of the 1985 anti-Japan protests), the leadership was disturbed by the implications of the party's loss of its vanguard role to independent intellectuals. The conservatives objected because the protests were spontaneous, not because of what was said. In any case, slogans are interpreted from a paranoid perspective. Although leaders invariably defined grassroots initiatives as illegitimate and crushed them, such movements have, faute de mieux, repeatedly risen from the ashes.

In the wake of the latest and hitherto most emphatic repression of spontaneous mass mobilization, the leadership has attempted to regenerate the ideological language and value system of the Maoist era in order to define ideologically correct collective goals and preclude all spontaneous alternatives. But this language clashes at so many points with the thrust of the reform program as to jeopardize the program's credibility. The contradiction seems likely to force an eventual choice between a more definitive retrenchment of reform or the abandonment of the ideological revival. The leadership is at a crossroads, seeing only further social dissolution if the trend toward ideological secularization continues and a cold war with an alienated populace if it is forcibly arrested. It is a painful dilemma: Retrenchment of reform, on the one hand, might place the leadership on firmer organizational footing, but if economic growth bogs down, the situation could quickly become dangerous. Abandonment of the ideological revival, on the other hand, might imply surrendering all hope of leading the masses toward positive collective goals—at least within the existing conceptual framework.

Conclusions

The attempt to establish rational patterns of formal leadership via constitutional engineering clearly will have little bearing upon the current succession crisis—the eventual resolution of which will determine the future of the PRC. Formal structure seems to offer scant hope of either stabilizing elite conflict or providing some form of public monitoring or popular participation in the political process. The legislative institutions will survive, as they survived the Cultural Revolution, and certain of the limited reforms they have managed to institutionalize (e.g., permanent functional committees and multiple-candidate elections within the legislature) will endure. Multicandidate elections at the mass level have been eviscerated for the time being. The elaborate retirement arrangements designed to eliminate succession crises and rejuvenate the leadership are a notorious dead letter, at least at the top. To be sure, the conspicuous failure of such arrangements is likely to inspire future reformers to try again. The structural reform of the chairmanship system seems to have failed, in part because of an overcompensation for Maoism. The downsizing and dispersal of executive authority has permitted an informally based hierarchy to arise, no less arbitrary and authoritarian for having divested itself of official responsibility for its acts.

At the moment power remains informally based, albeit hierarchically structured. For as long as the present gerontocratic arrangement endures, it will function to reinforce the socioeconomic and political-cultural status quo that undergirds this hierarchy, particularly when it appears to be threatened from below. The most recent purges have severely attenuated the strength of the radical reformers, leaving Wan Li, Tian Jiyun, and perhaps Li Ruihuan as sole survivors amid the central leadership; at middle and lower levels, reformers appear to remain more numerous, attempts at a sweeping purge having apparently failed. Assuming that the foregoing depiction of the political-economic dynamics of leadership is correct, the radical reform faction should have another chance to regroup if and when the leadership opts to sponsor another investment boom, provided mass activism remains quiescent. This may, for example, occur if the current freeze qua economic slowdown deepens to such a degree that the leadership feels vulnerable to a possible Eastern European–style explosion.

The apparent death of ideology in China and the perplexed and intensely aversive elite reaction to its consequences place the entire future of reform in some question. Should this trend continue, the leadership's task becomes far more difficult. Without ideological legitimacy, the leadership must pay high "transaction costs" to implement its policies. If the regime continues to enforce a lockstep with stale ideas, inconsistent reforms may be expected eventually to wither in the dead grip of "adjustment" and "consolidation," giving way to a Chinese form of Stalinism. Yet if freedom is again granted to reassess the dominant idea system, the consequences are unpredictable and quite possibly volatile. The only way in which popular faith in the old legitimating ideology might conceivably be regenerated is through the rise of some vigorous, charismatic leader—another Mao—with all the attendant risks. Failing that, the long-term prospects of the current leadership arrangement do not appear rosy.

Notes

I wish to thank those who provided comments and criticisms on an earlier draft of this chapter, especially Arthur Rosenbaum, Haruhiro Fukui, and Richard Baum. For research support I am grateful to Bettina Schroeder, Guoliang Zhang, and the MacArthur Group for International Strategic Studies.

1. There is now ample documentation of the severity of the politically induced famine in 1959–1961; see, for example, Thomas P. Bernstein, "Stalinism, Famine, and Chinese Peasants: Grain Procurements During the Great Leap Forward," *Theory and Society,* 13:3 (May 1984), 339–377; Judith Banister, "Population Policy and Trends in China, 1978–83," *China Quarterly,* 100 (December 1984), 717–742; and Jurgen Domes, *The Government and Politics of the PRC* (Boulder: Westview, 1985), 38, 274.

2. Unquestioning obedience was associated with the discredited Liu Shaoqi and repudiated during the Cultural Revolution, but it was an authoritative part of party doctrine before that time and seems to have been reinstated with the official rehabilitation of Liu at the Fifth Plenum of the Eleventh CC in March 1980. It is no coincidence that this rehabilitation came at the same time as the

approval of a document on the strengthening and improvement of party leadership. See Siegfried Klaschka, *Die Rehabilitierung Liu Shaoqis in der chinesischen Presse* (Munich: Minerva, 1987), 99–121.

3. See *Resolution on Certain Questions in the History of Our Party Since the Founding of the People's Republic of China* (Beijing: Foreign Languages Press, 1981).

4. This may even be defended by comparison to bourgeois arrangements, wherein parties have been viewed as informal or quasi-private actors that may be allowed to regulate themselves. This does not take into account, of course, the much more authoritative role of the party in the Leninist single-party dictatorship.

5. *Renmin ribao* (People's daily, hereafter *RR,*) November 12, 1987, 2.

6. This even though Deng Xiaoping himself reportedly asked Zhao Ziyang to see to it that Deng Liqun was reelected: "It seems to me that the Marxist-Leninist level of comrade Liqun is high." Zhao thus personally nominated Deng Liqun for membership in the CC Politburo at the nomination meeting. But with the adoption of more democratic voting procedures, the nomination failed, along with that of four conservative veterans who were to become vice-chairmen of the CDIC. See Fu Liqing's article in *Ching Bao* (The mirror), Hong Kong, No. 126 (January 1988), 18–22.

7. *Foreign Broadcast Information Service, People's Republic of China* (hereafter *FBIS-Chi*), April 13, 1988, 28.

8. Chen Yizhi et al., eds., *Zhengzhi tizhi gaige jianghua* (Talks on political restructuring) (Beijing: People's Publishing, 1987), 44–45, as quoted in the insightful two-part article by Suisheng Zhao, "The Feeble Political Capacity of a Strong One-Party Regime: An Institutional Approach Toward the Formulation and Implementation of Economic Policy in Post-Mao Mainland China," *Issues and Studies,* 26:1 (January 1990), 47–81 (Part 1); 26:2 (February 1990), 35–75 (Part 2).

9. Peng pointed out that although Article 35 of the constitution permits demonstrations, Article 51 provides that in the exercise of freedoms and rights, citizens may not infringe upon the interests of the state, society, or collective or "upon the lawful freedoms and rights of other citizens." To underline this point, Peng added that Articles 2, 158, and 159 of the criminal law code provide that no one may use any means "to disturb the social order . . . or the people's daily life." He concludes that "the decision of the State Council to impose martial law in some parts of Beijing for the sake of upholding the dignity of the Constitution and preserving the social order, the order of production, work, education, scientific research, and the daily life of people in the capital is entirely lawful, necessary, and proper." "Peng's 26 May Speech," *FBIS-Chi,* 89–102, May 30, 1989, 24–25, as cited in Richard Wilson, "The Filial Ideal," paper presented at the conference, China's Search for National Identity, January 25–27, 1990, Princeton University.

10. *RR,* November 2, 1987; see Article 21 of the constitution of the CCP Twelfth Congress.

11. *Ta Kung Pao* (The impartial daily) (Hong Kong), May 17, 1989, 2. Although at the time Zhao made this remark it caused great consternation

because he seemed to be deflecting responsibility to Deng for the unpopular decision to invoke martial law, the arrangement was no secret, nor was this the first time it had been disclosed. In a July 1984 interview, Zhao first indicated that both the party Secretariat and the State Council looked ultimately to Deng, who held office in neither of these bodies; see A. Doak Barnett, *The Making of Foreign Policy in China: Structure and Process* (Boulder: Westview Press, 1985), 9. He made the same point in a public talk before Deng decided to retire at the Thirteenth Party Congress; see *Zhengming* (Contend), No. 122 (December 1987), 9.

12. See Lowell Dittmer, "Bases of Power in Chinese Politics: A Theory and an Analysis of the 'Gang of Four,'" *World Politics,* 31:1 (October 1978), 26–61.

13. Kenneth Lieberthal and Michel Oksenberg, *Bureaucratic Politics and Chinese Energy Development* (Washington, D.C.: Government Printing Office, 1986), 133.

14. The Politburo members involved were Deng, Chen Yun, Li Xiannian (former members of the Politburo Standing Committee), Peng Zhen, Yu Qiuli, Yang Dezhi, Xi Zhongxun, Hu Qiaomu, Fang Yi, Ni Zhifu, and Chen Muhua (alternate).

15. See Tony Saich, "Cadres: From Bureaucrats to Managerial Modernizers?" in Birthe Arendrup et al., eds., *China in the 1980s—and Beyond* (London: Curzon Press, 1986), 133.

16. *RR,* January 17, 1987, 1.

17. In estimated rank order of influence, these are Deng Xiaoping (born in 1904), former CMC chair; Chen Yun (born 1904), CAC chair; Yang Shangkun (born 1907), chief of state and first vice-chair of the CMC; Li Xiannian (born 1909), chair of the National Committee of the Chinese People's Political Consultative Conference (CPPCC); Wang Zhen (born 1908), vice-chief of state and a CMC vice-chair; Bo Yibo (born 1908), executive vice-chair of the CAC; Song Renqiong (born 1909), vice-chair of the CAC; Peng Zhen (born 1902), retired former chair of the NPC Standing Committee; and Deng Yingchao (born 1904), widow of Zhou Enlai, former Politburo member and former chair of the CPPCC National Committee.

18. Barnett, *Foreign Policy,* 11.

19. *Yumiuri,* January 8, 1967, as translated in *Daily Summary of the Japanese Press,* January 8, 1967.

20. Parris Chang, "Research Notes on the Changing Loci of Decision in the CCP," *China Quarterly,* 44 (October-December 1970), 169–195.

21. "Discussions within the party on important issues," concedes Deng, "have rarely used voting"; see *Deng Xiaoping wenxuan* (Selected works of Deng Xiaoping) (Beijing: People's Publishing, 1984), 290. A book written by a group of Zhao Ziyang's most important advisers states: "In the past, apart from elections within the party, we have rarely made decisions on important issues by voting. This has tended to result in discussions not reaching decisions or delayed decisions, and even allowing one or a few persons to make decisions." Chen, *Zhengzhi,* 44.

22. See "Chart of Present Hereditary Bureaucrats," *China Information,* 4:1 (Summer 1989), 64–69.

23. The term *qian* (forward, future) is similar in pronunciation to the character *qian,* representing money. "Look to the future" thus becomes "look to money."

3

China's New Bureaucracy?

Hong Yung Lee

Socialist China's bureaucracy has never approximated Max Weber's ideal type in terms of its environmental setting and internal structure.[1] In theory as well as in practice, there is no division of human activities into political, social, and economic spheres, and all political power is heavily concentrated in the party, which itself has been bureaucratized. Instead of a rational instrument for implementing policies, the Chinese bureaucracy has been the source of political power that decides even the "substantive rationality" defining what is good for society but is not accountable to outside forces. Even the internal structure of the Chinese bureaucracy has been a strange mixture; it was hierarchically organized with full-time cadres, but it lacked such other characteristics as impersonality, technical expertise, and political neutrality.

Neither does the Chinese model fit Karl Marx's view that bureaucracy either represents only the interests of the ruling class or else perverts the class relationship by presenting its own interests as universal interests.[2] During Mao's era the bureaucracy claimed to represent the working classes, but it had its own revolutionary goals—dictated by its own ideology—that frequently clashed with the interests of the classes it claimed to represent. The Maoist ideology in turn reflected the personal experiences and mentality of the revolutionary cadres, mostly recruited from the poorest rural population for their political loyalty despite their low educational level. This contrasts with Franz Schurmann's argument that Chinese Communist ideology was the manner of thinking characteristic of an organization, a systematic set of ideas that shaped individual behavior.[3] The revolutionary cadres acted as the political elite, but they had no vested interests in the society and owed their power, prestige, and income to the positions they occupied in the ruling structure. The Maoist political elite, therefore, continously attempted a total change of China, initating one political campaign after another and thereby undermining possible routinization and institutionalization of political process.

Because of the multidimensional problems of the Chinese bureaucracy, Harry Harding proposes to examine the bureaucracy in light of administrative, social, and political problems, and Kenneth Lieberthal and Michel Oksenberg suggest a case study of bureaucratic organization in decisionmaking processes.[4] Instead of looking at all these aspects of the system, I focus on three aspects of Chinese bureaucracy during the years of reform since 1978: the cadre corps that occupied the official positions of the bureaucracy, the structural dimension of the bureaucracy, and its personnel management system. How much has the Chinese bureaucracy changed in these three respects? Is China's new bureaucracy more efficient, less political, and better supervised by the politicians? What are the new bureaucrats' ideological orientations? Will they lead China to democracy or at least in a new direction? These questions have crucial bearing on China's future.

Rise of the Bureaucratic Technocrats

Since 1978, when the rehabilitated cadres shifted the regime's goal from revolutionary change to economic development, they found that the existing bureaucracy was unsuitable for the new task because the cadre corps was huge, old, poorly educated, and ossified in its ideological outlook. The regime therefore started bureaucratic reforms in 1982 to make the cadre corps revolutionized, professional, better educated, and younger and to streamline and rationalize the unmanageable bureaucratic structures.

The regime succeeded in replacing the existing cadre corps—or at least its leaders—with what I will call bureaucratic technocrats, many of whom are educated in production-related fields of the natural sciences and are specialists in bureaucratic organization. Because of an attractive retirement program, most of the senior revolutionary cadres stepped down. The process of elite transformation was nearly completed by the Thirteenth Party Congress in 1987, when almost all leading positions, from the highest level to the basic level, were filled by the bureaucratic technocrats. By that year, about 0.5 million young and middle-aged cadres had been promoted to leadership positions at the county level or above. This number is equal to the total sum of leading local *government* cadres or 10 percent of cadres holding rank in all government, party, and other organizations. Despite the tragedy of Tiananmen Square, the process of replacing the old leaders with the bureaucratic technocrats continues, as Jiang Zemin's rise to general secretary of the Chinese Communist party and chair of the Military Affairs Commission amply demonstrates. The success is largely due to the pragmatic and incremental strategy of changing the cadre corps step by step, level by level, and group by group.

The bureaucratic technocrats are by and large the postliberation generation who came of age in the new socialist China, the third generation—after the first generation, which joined the revolution before the Long March, and the second generation, which participated in the anti-Japanese war. The average age of the new leaders is below sixty. Except for the few still remaining in government positions, usually as chiefs of the central government commissions, the second generation has largely been removed from active duty.

Most of the bureaucratic technocrats have college-level educations, whereas only 4 out of every 1,000 Chinese in the general population have received a similar level of schooling. About half of the delegation to the Sixth People's Congress had college-level education, with degrees mostly in practical fields such as business and economics. In the Sixth Political Consultative Conference, the proportion of intellectuals increased from 16 percent to 40 percent.[5] They are not only from the best-educated groups in China but are also largely trained in scientific and technical fields. For instance, in 1987, 45 percent of ministers, 25 percent of secretaries, and 33 percent of governors were engineers. If one adds up the cadres with some experience in economics and management, the number of those whose specialty is production increases to 70 percent of the ministers, 32 percent of the secretaries, and 50 percent of the governors. Of the 166 mayors Cheng Li and David Backman surveyed, 64 percent were trained as engineers.[6]

Very few of the bureaucratic technocrats have an in-depth knowledge of economics and management—"soft knowledge" in current Chinese terms. For instance, among 5,000 leaders of large, state-owned enterprises, about 84 percent had career backgrounds in science and engineering, whereas only 11 percent of them had studied management. Moreover, in sharp contrast to the Maoist era, only a few cadres have experience in overall political leadership—5 percent of the ministers, 36 percent of the secretaries, and 21 percent of the governors. Virtually none of the leaders examined here had any significant experience in the field of propaganda. This graphically illustrates the lessening importance of a political career as the required background for promotion to top leadership positions.

Although we cannot assume that the new bureaucrats form a homogeneous group with a shared ideology and similar policy preferences, they are on the whole quite different from the revolutionary cadres in many aspects. First of all, the criteria used for selecting the bureaucratic technocrats are different from those used for the revolutionary cadres. The revolutionary cadres owed their positions to their ideological reliability, whereas the bureaucratic technocrats are promoted on the basis of their "ability." Currently, the political factor is not irrelevant, but if it does come into play, a candidate's commitment to economic development rather than revolutionary change is crucial. Ideological criteria such as an understanding of Marxism-Leninism, dedication to the mass line, or a willingness to sacrifice private interests are no longer used as indicators of political qualification. Even when a candidate's dedication to the "socialist principle" is examined, the term is broadly interpreted so as to include any principle that brings good fortune to the people, encourages productivity, or contributes to socialist goals.

In a sharp departure from the Maoist practice of stressing "virtue," the regime has used such objective and universal criteria as age, educational level, and professional competence to select the political leaders from the bureaucratic technocrats. However, universal, achievement-oriented criteria have not been uniformly applied to every qualified cadre; personal connections have also been taken into account, thereby resulting in "unprincipled universalism," in contrast to what Andrew Walder calls the "principled particularism" characteristic of Mao's era.[7] Because of the particularistic application of universal criteria, some social groups have benefited from reform whereas others have not.

Second, the bureaucratic technocrats are less committed to any political ideology—regardless of whether it is a broadly defined socialism or Mao Zedong's discredited thought—than the revolutionary cadres. Instead, they are rather critical of the existing ideology. Like their counterparts in Western Europe, if they have any common ideology, it is probably the simple pragmatism necessary to get the job done.[8] As pragmatists, they would resent the bureaucratic rules that have constrained their work in the past, and they view ideology not as dogma but as something to be flexibly interpreted for economic ends. Instead of the ideological solution that the revolutionary cadres tended to opt for, the bureaucratic technocrats will likely desire a structured and orderly environment, preferring technical and piecemeal measures to comprehensive political solutions to overcome China's problems.

Third, on the whole, the bureaucratic technocrats are more supportive of economic as well as political reforms than the retiring revolutionary cadres, although they are more committed to economic than political change. Many of them served in technical positions without influence, watching uneducated political leaders make arbitrary decisions. Some of them were frequently condemned as "bourgeois experts." Even those from the lowest class of preliberation China have diminished gratitude to the party because of their experiences with past political turmoil.

Fourth, the new leaders are more self-confident, less dependent on the party for guidance, urban oriented, forward- and outward-looking, and have minimal emotional ties to or understanding of the rural peasants. They have greater understanding of and better qualifications to deal with such prerequisites of an industrialized society as functional specialization, coordination of various parts, rational decisionmaking, and problem solving. At the same time, the new leaders also lack moral integrity and the commitment to the Communist code that the old revolutionary cadres possessed. In the eyes of old revolutionaries, this quality causes the widespread corruption and abuse of political authority for private gain.

Fifth, having spent most of their careers as technical staff in functionally specialized organs, they have accumulated very little experience in overall political works—which include administrative, propaganda, and mass works. Unlike the revolutionary cadres, who were urged to be good "proletarian politicians," the bureaucratic technocrats do not have backgrounds in energizing, representing, organizing, and mobilizing unorganized interests.[9] It seems likely, therefore, that those who have reached the highest positions of the Chinese bureaucracy—for instance, Jiang Zemin and Li Peng—will act more like coordinators, conciliators, and managers than like politicians, who tend to represent the interests of various social groups, develop long-term visions, manipulate symbols, and rally the support of the people. If one takes Li Peng as an example, his behavior so far resembles the bureaucrat rather than the politician. He has been conservative, cautious, submissive, and primarily concerned with immediate problems and piecemeal solutions in dealing with such issues as inflation, corruption, fragmentation of the bureaucratic authority, and student demands for democracy.

Last, the revolutionary cadres and the bureaucratic technocrats differ over a range of policy alternatives that are considered feasible. If an ideologically inspired policy option was a real alternative for the revolutionary cadres, it may not be so for the bureaucratic technocrats, whose primary concern is China's immediate and pressing problems. Criteria for judging policy options are different, too. The revolutionary cadres tended to view policy options in terms of their being morally right and wrong, ideologically correct and incorrect, whereas the bureaucratic technocrats, more concerned with specific problems than abstract ideals, will look at technical and administrative feasibility to select a final choice. They will evaluate even a political decision in terms of its actual outcome instead of its ideological value. In developing a range of policy options, each of which involves only different costs, benefits, and feasibilities, this way of thinking will make the bureaucratic technocrats more inclined toward compromising, bargaining, and negotiating than were the revolutionary cadres. This tendency will gradually change the basic rules of the Leninist party.

There are additional reasons to believe that the bureaucratic technocrats will be more prone to bargain and compromise among themselves. Given their political style and rapid rise in the past few years, it is very unlikely that any bureaucratic technocrat—including Jiang Zemin (whom Deng Xiaoping designated as his successor)—will emerge as an undisputable, paramount leader and come to exert as much real power and influence as Mao or Deng did. Moreover, the personal ties among the bureaucratic technocrats are much weaker than those of the revolutionary cadres. These two factors will compel the new leaders to rely more on formal procedural rules and to take a collective decision-making approach, which in turn will foster compromise and consensus building rather than confrontation. Of course, these factors can turn out to be decisive liabilities, keeping the bureaucrats from reaching any compromise and instead ending in division, stalemate, and immobility.[10] And any decision that is arrived at collectively will be less innovative and revolutionary than one made by a paramount leader. The collective decisionmaking process, however, would less frequently result in power struggles, purges, and counterpurges.

Streamlining the Bureaucracy

In sharp contrast to its success in changing the top echelon of the bureaucrats, the regime's effort to reduce the size of the cadre corps and to rationalize the administrative structure was a total failure. The overall size of the cadre corps increased from 20 million in 1982 to 21 million in 1983 and then to 29 million by 1988. Neither did the efforts have much impact on the age and educational structure of the overall cadre corps, simply because of the limited resources of educated personnel.

Failure is more apparent at the provincial levels and below. The regime originally authorized an average of 140,000 cadres for a province, but the actual numbers exceeded the ceiling by 23 percent as early as 1984.[11] The situation at the municipal and county levels is much worse. For example, Huyong County in Hunan reports that after reorganization its offices have increased from seventy-three to ninety and its personnel from 22,204 to 25,298.[12]

Dangers inherent in reforming any system are so apparent that some social scientists argue that a successful reform is far rarer than a successful revolution.[13] This is particularly true of any Leninist system in which various subsystems are tightly interwoven and no political means other than cadres are available to implement reforms—and these reforms are bound to threaten the cadres' powers and vested interests.

In addition, there are several concrete reasons for China's failure to reduce the size of the bureaucracy. First, the regime tried to trim the cadres without simultaneously modifying the overall bureaucratic structure and changing the interventionist roles of the party-state. To use a colorful Chinese phrase, the regime tried to remove the burning candles (in this case, the cadres) before abolishing the temple (the bureaucratic functions). On the contrary, the task and responsibilities of the local governments have been expanding as they address such modern issues as environmental protection, urban planning, social welfare, and managing the retired cadres. The economic reforms so far created call for new organizations to facilitate the flow of information and technology, to coordinate operation of the various agencies, and to consult with the increasingly diversified demands of society.

As a result, the local government felt two conflicting pressures—to reduce its bureaucracy on the one hand and to cope with its increasing responsibility on the other hand. Worse still, the continuing multiheaded leadership structure made it more difficult for the local government to keep itself within limits. "Every functionally leading organ as well as every local party committee wants the lower-level unit to set up offices that they regard as necessary." Or to use Chinese imagery once again, "If there is a Buddha at the upper level, there should be bodyguards at the lower level."[14]

In addition, the low-level bureaucrats have all the incentives to resist and evade the center's pressure to reduce the number of personnel and offices. Apart from the ubiquitous bureaucratic turf wars and difficulty in dismissing people from their jobs in China, each office finds inherent advantages in staying as large as possible. Generally, the size of each office determines its bureaucratic status—as a bureau, division, or section—which in turn determines political privileges, wage scales, and other fringe benefits for its cadres. During the reform period many offices elevated their status, thereby raising the salary grades for their cadres.[15]

Lacking legal effect, the organizational table (the document authorizing the structure of a bureaucratic unit) operates only as a soft constraint. The authority to set up a new bureau lies in the hands of the leadership one level above. As a result, "if the leadership [of an upper echelon] signs one memo, it becomes a charter for a new organization."[16] The official policy of fixing the structure of an organization but not fixing the total number of staff provided the bureaucrats with considerable leeway. In addition, the evasive tactics of bureaucrats at the lower levels (succintly captured in the popular phrase, "When you have a policy, we have a countermeasure") undermined the central leaders' attempt to reduce the bureaucracy.[17]

Another way cadres avoid the pressure to simplify the administrative organs is to set up a "corporation," which the regime encourages as a means of separating the administration from economic management. Distinguishing between the administrative units and independent "corporations" in terms of their functions, however, is difficult.[18] In some counties, one bureau uses two different names, reporting itself as a "corporation" to the upper level while using the name of "bureau" in dealing with subordinate units.[19] Even when the functions of "bureau" and "corporation" are unequivocally differentiated, the parent administrative units continue to control the corporations, which they set up with funding from their administrative expenditures. Even in the case where an independent corporation has operational autonomy, the authority over personnel management of its top-level leaders lies with the parent administrative unit.[20] As a result, most of the corporations—75 percent of them in the case of Jiangxi—operate simply as extended arms of the parent administrative units.[21]

The increase in the size of the cadres inevitably entails a rise in administrative expense. Since 1978 such expenditures have been climbing steadily despite the State Council's numerous orders to keep expenditures under 8 percent.[22] As China becomes more complex and industrialized, the need for specialized agencies will continue to grow. For instance, personnel in the judiciary is bound to expand if the regime is serious in making the judicial system more effective and independent. The transfer of internal security forces from the military to the local government has increased the total size of the cadre corps. Moreover, if the regime keeps up the practice of assigning college graduates and demobilized military officers to cadre positions, it will further contribute to the cadres' growth. Most important, the effort to separate the party from the government and to develop a clear hierarchical command structure aggravates the complexity of the bureaucracy. Before the reform, for instance, the county-level authorities had only two systems—the party committees and the government organizations. But now there are five different sources of authority: the party committees, the disciplinary committee, the government, the National People's Congress, and the Political Consultative Conference. As a result, according to the bureaucrats' own description, the bureaucratic structure is top-heavy, like an "upside-down pyramid."[23]

To summarize, administrative reform has not solved the structural problems of the bureaucracy. At the lower level, offices still stand like "trees in forests," with numerous layers, unclear responsibilities and tasks, and overstaffed bureaucracy. One Chinese scholar summarizes the result of the reform in the following way:

> Units that should be abolished are not abolished. On the surface units are merged, but internally the size increased. The original personnel are not reduced; instead, they are internally absorbed. People continue to make work, and, as a result, the seignorial and deputy positions are numerous. At the lower level the administrative units set up many "general corporations," "leading small groups," and "management offices."[24]

Some cynics argue that reform resulted in more work, more offices, more cadres, but fewer people actually working. On the whole it seems that the efficiency of the bureaucracy improved slightly but not in any meaningful way. The phenomenon of mountains of documents and seas of conferences—formalism and low-level efficiency—continue to characterize the Chinese bureaucracy. Many cadres still "spend a half day drinking a cup of tea, smoking a cigarette, and reading a paper."[25]

Changes in the Personnel Management System?

The various parts of any socialist system—including political, economic, and social systems—are tightly integrated, and changing any one part means simultaneously changing others. Similarly, the gigantic bureaucratic system cannot be modernized without overhauling the personnel management system, which in turn requires resolving the broader question of how to separate the party from the government and other functional units.

The party-state during Mao's era not only jealously guarded its prerogative over the personnel management of cadres but also exercised that authority in a highly centralized fashion without developing any meaningful classification scheme for the gigantic cadre corps. Superior organs two levels above a unit controlled that unit's personnel. Party committees and organizational departments managed all the cadre corps using political criteria. The personnel dossier system allowed the superior organizations to tightly control cadres under their jurisdiction; however, it disintegrated during the chaos of the Cultural Revolution.

Immediately after Mao's death, the regime initially tried to rationalize the personnel management system by first strengthening the authority of higher levels and then decentralizing control, restoring the party committee's authority over personnel matters. But all these attempts were made in piecemeal fashion with the knowledge that the party would directly manage all cadres. Consequently, the personnel management authority still remains too centralized and very rigid: Authority for recruitment is separated from personnel management, and managing personnel from managing affairs. It continues to be a closed-door system; each functionally leading organ and local party committee sets up its own system, and any horizontal coordination between the two is extremely difficult.

As I have already noted, the personnel management system cannot be changed unless the regime resolves the question of separating the party from the government and the administrative units from other functional units. But progress in this area was mixed even prior to the Tiananmen massacre of 1989. After the tragedy, the liberalization process came to an end.

In structural terms, the regime has separated the party from the government and other functional units. But how to separate their functions is not yet resolved. With regard to the party committee's functions at the lower level, numerous articles published in the official media suggest the following tasks: (1) supervising the implementation of the party line and policy, (2) leading ideological and political work, (3) managing the party's internal affairs, (4) making decisions on "important matters," and (5) managing the personnel matters of cadres.[26]

Assigning these functions to the party committee does not resolve the controversy. First of all, no one disagrees with the idea that ideological work belongs under the party committee's jurisdiction, but whether the party committee should concentrate only on ideological tasks is open to dispute. Limiting the party's main function to its own internal work, such as managing and educating its members, is not problematic. But a persistent question is whether the CCP, a Leninist ruling party committed to one-party dictatorship, can afford to restrict its activities to such a narrowly defined range.

The problem with the term *important work* (which is generally defined as "affecting the fate of the entire people") is that it does not specify how and who will determine which matters are the "important" ones in a particular case.[27] The highly centralized bureaucratic structure in China does not leave many "important matters" for the lower-level party committees to decide. Thus it is no surprise that after extensive debate on what constitutes "important matters," a county party secretary and magistrate decided to jointly consider all issues.

Authorizing the party committees to supervise government and enterprise units in the implementation of official decisions is not controversial. But it does not resolve the technical questions of what supervision means in concrete terms, how to supervise the operation of the government agencies and the enterprise units without taking over their tasks, and how much and what kind of power the party committees need for the supervision. Lower-level party secretaries insist that "without substantial authority, there is no way to supervise and guarantee that works will be done correctly."[28] Managers are also unhappy with the supervision: "If they trust secretaries and do not trust managers, it is better to make the secretaries managers."[29]

Despite the official policy of separating the party from the state, numerous investigative reports prepared by Chinese scholars after their fieldwork at the county level indicate that the party committees continue to dominate not only the executive organs but also the People's Congress and its standing committees—which theoretically represent all the people—through overlapping personnel. The turf fight is particularly fierce over economic issues, which make up 60 percent of government tasks. At the moment, whether a county party secretary makes a decision on economic matters largely depends on the individual's personal characteristics. Even the magistrates look to a competent secretary with high prestige to make all major decisions.

Moreover, the county party committees have not relinquished their prerogative over personnel management. According to an investigation by Chinese scholars, many county party committees manage all the "important leading cadres of the first-class organs and second-class organs" (and certain enterprises), or they handle all the leading cadres of the first-class organs but allow the personnel bureau under the magistrates to manage the cadres of the second-class organs.[30] Believing that managing cadres is their most important responsibility, the county party committees spend most of their time on personnel matters.[31] Although its authority over certain government cadres is constitutionally guaranteed, the People's Congress remains a rubber stamp.

The situation in the enterprise units is a little better than in the county administrative level, largely because of the gradual introduction of the manager responsibility system, which substantially weakened the party secretaries' power. Nonetheless, the new arrangement has not yet completely resolved the controversy over personnel management authority, despite the bitter complaints of the managers that the existing personnel management system constitutes the most serious obstacle to efficient management of the enterprise, more serious than the shortage of raw materials.[32] The reformers advocate authorizing the managers to handle all the administrative cadres, limiting the party committees' authority to the party cadres in order to make the authority and the responsibility of managers coincide and to enable them to exercise "uniform leadership with regard to production, management, and administrative management."[33] In contrast, the conservatives try to guarantee the party committees' influence in personnel matters. Understandably, the party has been extremely reluctant to completely give up its influence over cadre management, particularly when the party is relinquishing direct control over economic resources.

Although the manager responsibility system authorizes managers to control the middle-level administrative cadres, the authority has to be used in consultation with the party committees: "On the matter of using persons, managers should rely on the party committee, should rely on the masses. . . . The managers should listen to the opinion of the masses, and then decide."[34] In other words, the party committees have retained the authority "to observe the cadres, examine the political qualifications of candidates, organize discussion meetings, and carry out public opinion polls in order to provide accurate information to the managers."[35]

While the controversy over personnel authority was going on, Zhao Ziyang, newly elected to the post of general secretary, announced the regime's plan to gradually introduce a civil system in 1987.[36] According to one version of provisional regulation on the civil service system—which will be applied only to a mere 4.2 million employed in the government agencies out of the existing 29 million cadres—all the leading cadres who legally constitute "governments," ranging from the center to the county levels, and whose appointments require the approval of the People's Congress, will be classified as "political" (*zheng wu*) civil servants.[37] Regarded as policymakers, these political civil servants will be elected for fixed terms as specified in the existing constitution and in the organizational laws of local government, and therefore they lose "life tenure," although there are no laws limiting the numbers of terms that they can serve.

The rest of the civil servants are functional civil servants (*ye wu*), "the implementers of policy," who are further classified as either "administrative" or "specialized technical." Their selection will be made through "open, equal, and competitive" examinations. All those who pass the examinations are required to go through one year of training at the basic level. Only after a successful training period can they become regular civil servants.[38] Moreover, these civil servants are to be promoted grade by grade.

The provisional regulation, however, leaves the most crucial obstacle to creating an efficient personnel management system—the party's domination over the government—unresolved. For instance, it does not grant political neutrality, even to career civil servants. On the contrary, they are specifically required to demonstrate a certain level of "socialist consciousness" and to follow the "political leadership of the Communist party."[39] Another ambiguity in the regulation and the official writings concerns the party committee's authority over personnel matters; on the one hand the party committee will give up its prerogative over the cadres, but on the other hand it will continue to exert a substantial amount of authority over the political civil servants and "the important cadres."[40]

Despite these ambiguities, the mere fact that the regime has recognized the need to develop a civil service system indicates its willingness to end the Maoist practice of selecting officials through mass campaigns and on the basis of class backgrounds and, instead, to develop rational, efficient, and competent administrative bureaucrats. The term *civil servants* itself implies that the government officials are "public servants" who will manage public affairs as the guardians of public interests, whereas the term *cadres* refers to those with certain leadership qualities necessary to lead the masses in revolutionary struggle for social change. *Civil servants* also connotes a merit-based recruitment, whereas the cadre's role requires political skills and ideological consciousness.

When the civil service system is implemented, its impact will not be limited to the party-state's bureaucracy but will reach even social structures and the entire political process. As many studies of Western European bureaucracies have demonstrated, a merit-based recruitment of the administrative elite tends to offer undue advantage to the middle class.[41] As the emphasis in competition for government employment shifts to ability, the educational institutions become the jumping board for entering official positions. China's new educational policy of attaching priority to academic achievement and spending large amounts of the state budget for key schools will accelerate the stratification of educational institutions. Middle-class students have the advantage of entering better high schools and then highly competitive colleges from which they can land cadre positions.[42] Actually, middle-class values are more congruent with the role of the technocrats than that of the revolutionary cadres.

The state bureaucracy in this way will lose any claim to representing a broad range of social classes, but it can be responsive to society.[43] This nondemocratic characteristic will, however, be compensated when the regime steps up its effort to professionalize state employment. The rigorous training of the civil servants, the development of an esprit de corps, and a trend toward professionalization will make the administrative elite act more as guardians of the public interest than as representatives of their original middle-class backgrounds.

As the evolution of the Western European civil service systems demonstrates, creating an efficient state bureaucracy is the first step toward reducing the patrimonial power of the monarchy. In Prussia the absolute monarchy created a civil bureaucracy largely staffed by the landed aristocracy. As the bureaucracy gained power and status, joining the civil bureaucracy offered upward mobility for the newly emerging bourgeoisie. Meanwhile, by claiming to represent the public interest, the civil bureaucracy gradually became independent of the monarchy. Once the monarchy collapsed, it was replaced by elected politicians who supervised the administrative bureaucrats on behalf of the people, whereas the administrative structure began to resemble Weber's ideal type of bureaucracy, staffed by specialists and neutral to the political process.[44]

Which controls the party will maintain over the administrative bureaucrats and to whom the latter will be held accountable still remain in question in socialist China. Because in most non-Communist countries democratically elected politicians supervise the administrative bureaucrats, one may predict that the party leaders at various levels will act likewise. In other words, the party leaders will become political managers and power brokers.

Uncertain Future

The 1989 democratic movement drastically changed China's political atmosphere, leaving the future direction of bureaucratic reform uncertain. The official policy since the Tiananmen incident is not promising. The economic reforms are stalled. The regime has recentralized economic authority, adopted a tight monetary policy, and initiated a campaign to "improve the economic order and rectify the economic environment." Instead of implementing price reform, which even in the eyes of the liberal economists could not be carried out because of superinflation, the regime intends to perfect the contract system. On the whole, state planning has regained control of the economy, and the idea of privatizing the ownership system is officially condemned. Although these actions are publicized as temporary measures designed to "deepen the reform," many liberal economists publicly worry that without genuine reform China has no future.

The regime has reverted to repressive measures and attempts to strengthen the party's role by restoring the party core group in the government ministries and bolstering the party secretary's authority in enterprises. The regime has changed its position in favor of separating the party from the government; the current official view is that the party and government will not have separate organizational structures but will merely divide functions.

Attributing the student demonstrations to Zhao's negligence of ideological works, the regime has tightened up ideological control. Ideological orthodoxy is now emphasized; the regime vows to develop "socialism with Chinese characteristics" and more frequently mentions class struggle and warns against the dangers of the "peaceful evolution of socialism." In personnel management, the renewed stress on political criteria replaces discussion of a civil service system. College students are to be educated using "ideals, discipline and ethics, as well as Marxist-Leninist theories." They are required to be "steeled" in the rural areas or factories before assuming any cadre positions. Criticizing the practice of emphasizing only skill and ability, Li Peng insists that personnel management of cadres should pay more attention to political ideology, practical experiences, and leadership skills. As part of an attempt to reimpose ideological orthodoxy, Li Peng even plans to assign one political cadre, who will have a professional job title, to every 100 workers and staff members within an enterprise.

The current policy of slowing economic reform and reimposing political control through repression may work as a temporary measure to deal with immediate problems, such as information and social unrest, but it will not resolve China's basic problems. Particularly unworkable are the present efforts to control the party and Chinese people through ideological education. Ideological education proved to be ineffective during the thirty years of Mao's rule and again failed during the three years of the party rectification campaign. The social changes that China has experienced since 1978 are too great for such an archaic method to work: The Chinese people's expectations are too high, cynicism too deep, the society too complex and diversified, the regime's legitimacy too low, and the official ideology too incoherent and irrelevant for China's mounting problems. Most important, as *Renmin Ribao* (People's daily) concedes, reassertion of ideological orthodoxy clashes with avowed policy of reform and the open door. Zhao Ziyang's tolerance of ideological liberalization was not due to his personal preference but rather to prerequisites of economic development. So-called ideological confusion in China is not derived from neglected ideological works but reflects the very social values that the regime tried to promote for the sake of economic development. Moreover, the present coalition of bureaucratic technocrats, with such old ideologues as Deng Liqun and He Jingzhi (whom critical intellectuals hate), is unstable and will not last long.

Since the start of reform in 1978, the CCP has been undergoing subtle but irreversible changes. In order to lead China to economic development, the party found it necessary to raise the educational level of its members by co-opting the intellectuals. The party changed its recruitment policy: To join, workers had to have a senior high school education and peasants a junior high school education. At the same time, the party members' task was redefined in order "to help others get rich," but it soon became apparent that party members would rather enrich themselves first. As official corruption spread, the gap between the official ideology and actual policy widened, and the Chinese were swept away by the fever of becoming wealthy.

The Leninist party's claim to legitimacy based on socialist values lost moral ground in the eyes of many Chinese. To the critics, the party consisted of groups who used socialism simply to defend their privileged positions. Indicative of the party's demoralization and disarray, the student democratic movement enjoyed massive support from the citizens in Beijing, where 8 out of every 100 people are party members. The ongoing effort to investigate each member's behavior during the protest demonstrations has encountered difficulties, for the basic-level party leaders protect those who showed sympathy to the movement by turning big problems into small problems and small problems into no problems at all.

So where is China going? If the present policy is a temporary measure, how long will it last and how will it be changed? Is pluralistic democratization or a return to the Maoist system likely? Despite the historical significance of the change in the elite types, China's immediate future is extremely uncertain. Jiang Zemin and Li Peng at the moment face almost impossible tasks—consolidating their power base while regaining the people's confidence after the regime lost its popular mandate to rule, and reimposing socialist ideology while continuing economic reforms and the open-door policy. The only way to regain some legitimacy is for the regime to produce tangible results from economic development.

It is very unlikely that China will return to the Maoist system, which was the product of several accidental factors that are now nonexistent. Moreover, the bureaucratic technocrats are too sophisticated to subscribe to Mao's values of a simple life, hard work, self-sufficiency, and economic development by human labor. Even if these values continue to dictate policy choice, the bureaucratic technocrats will be less willing to blindly carry out policies made by the top leaders, as the peasant cadres previously did. They will be more inclined to use their own expertise and judgment rather than the structural legitimacy of the party organization to evaluate the validity of a policy. Even Deng Xiaoping warned against regressing: "China cannot possibly return again to the previous closed era."[45]

Although presently conflicts of economic interest between the central government and the localities and among the regions are intense and the central leaders' efforts at recentralization encounter stiff resistance, there is not much chance for China gradually to evolve into various autonomous regional governments, as it did during the warlord period of the 1920s. If the military sides with civilians, as was the case in Romania, it means internal splits within the military that will certainly confound the regional rivalry, and China may face a real danger of disintegration. The possibility of such a scenario is minimal, however, largely because of the limited ability of the provincial authorities to collaborate with one another. And it is unlikely that the PLA, with 3 million soldiers, will act as a unified group and join with democratic forces. Moreover, a long tradition of a unitary government, bitter memories of warlordism, and the inability of the military to run the economy without support from the technocrats and the population at large further reduce the likelihood for such an outcome.

A democratic revolution led by social forces outside the system, such as the Democratic China Front organized by some of the exiled critical intellectuals and students studying abroad, is also implausible, although not impossible. No revolution will succeed in China without the support from the workers and peasants, and the chance for democratic forces in exile—which are prone to split over the control of the movement as well as on crucial issues such as the means by which to achieve their goal—to coalesce with them appears to be very slim.

Nor is it likely that the ruling elite will allow the drastic democratization that is happening in Eastern European countries. The bureaucratic technocrats are not politically democrats. Given the technocrats' general orientation toward outcome rather than the due process of decisionmaking (to which the democrats attach paramount importance) and their aversion to uncertainty, they tend to be less sympathetic, if not openly opposed, to political democratization. The technocrats tend to see their mission as improving and perfecting the existing system because they possess narrowly defined technical knowledge (mainly related to formal rationality) that helps choose the best means once the basic goals of the society are agreed upon.

In fact, available evidence indicates that the bureaucratic technocrats are not enthusiastic about political democratization. Although some of them might have felt sympathy for the demands for democracy during the 1989 student movement, they did not actively participate in the mass demonstration or support Zhao Ziyang. For that reason, after the incident of June 4, Jiang Zemin praised the natural scientists for refraining from participation in the controversy: "Especially the scientists and technicians, who have undergone practical training and stood fast at the frontline of scientific research and production, have given a good account of themselves."[46]

The bureaucratic technocrats, as the products of new China, have benefited from the existing political system. Their memories of Mao, who mobilized the masses in the Cultural Revolution against his adversaries, are still vivid. In addition, they apparently believe that China presently not only lacks conditions for political democratization but also needs a strong state system in order to sustain economic growth. In fact, the examples of Taiwan and South Korea demonstrate that only when economic development has produced differentiated social groups and classes—including the middle class—with some independent economic and political resources will an authoritarian regime begin to pay attention to the political demands of such groups.

Indeed, some economic reforms appear to be mutually exclusive with political democratization. For instance, one may argue that price reform precludes political democracy. Free price setting will inevitably lead to inflation in socialist countries, where shortages of goods are normal phenomena. If price reform is combined with the privatizing of ownership, it will lead to the bankruptcy of many inefficient enterprises and an increase in the unemployment rate. Ownership reform may be incompatible with political democracy in the socialist countries, where a large segment of the working class is accustomed to egalitarian distribution and a guarantee of the minimum subsistence. Ordinary people want to continue to enjoy the socialist advantages and are not willing to pay the price for the risk that the market mechanism entails. If the workers have political power, they may form an alliance with the conservative forces to oppose economic reform and to prevent the economy from moving in this direction. Ownership reform demands legal stability and constitutional guarantees to ensure the long-term investment by the people. Property rights should be respected in such a way that ownership is not subjected to the changing moods of the majority in democratic procedures.

China, therefore, needs not only economic development but also further strengthening of the civil society—with more differentiated social groups' and classes' possessing not only functional autonomy but also economic resources independent of the state—in order to satisfy the prerequisites of a stable democracy. At the moment the main obstacle to the development of this process is the work unit (*danwei*) system. Although the regime recognizes that the unit ownership system has "refeudalized" the Chinese, the effort to change the organizing principle of society has not yet made much progress. The only way to change the system of work units is to introduce a market principle.

If the present policy continues indefinitely, it may lead China to what is known as "Brezhnev's syndrome"—a stagnated economy with a petrified bureaucratic regime. If there will be a change, it will be in the direction of what Zhao Ziyang originally advocated: the marketization of the economy and strengthening of a central authority staffed by experts rather than revolutionaries. Only such an authoritarian regime with efficient bureaucratic administrators will be able to push economic reform step by step toward marketization while effectively dealing with all the problems arising in the process of reform. Paradoxical as it may seem, China may need a strong and powerful political authority in order to create preconditions for a market economy and to overcome the resistance of those Chinese people who wish to preserve the benefits gained under the old socialist system and fear the risks of a full-scale market-oriented economy.

There are good reasons to speculate that China may move in this direction. First, when the next major leadership change occurs—probably following serious power struggles after Deng Xiaoping's death—the winners will be more liberal bureaucratic technocrats, with a better understanding of the democratic aspirations of the Chinese population and the importance of a market economy than those leaders they replace. The probability that the victims of the post-Tiananmen purge will eventually be rehabilitated, with or without Zhao Ziyang's return to power, is high.

Moreover, once departure of the senior revolutionary leaders gives a free hand to the bureaucratic technocrats in policy matters, the new leaders probably will more forcefully pursue the goal of raising the level of production rather than equalizing distribution, and raising efficiency rather than social justice. As they learn how to use macroeconomic leverage and improve their ability to control the economy in a time of crisis, the bureaucratic technocrats will be more willing to introduce market mechanisms and reduce the scope of the economic activities that the party-state regulates through administrative means. Li Ruihuan's defense of the present policy of recentralization, subtly different from Chen Yun's analogy of a bird cage, hints at the possibility of such change: "What we are trying to do is fly a kite, not set it free. When we are flying a kite, it is still controlled by our hand. We can have many ways to control it. Our controlling ability is expressed by how far and how flexibly we can fly it."[47]

Notes

1. H. H. Gerth and C. Wright Mills, *From Max Weber* (New York: Oxford University Press, 1958), 196–244.

2. For Marx's view on bureaucracy, see Shlemo Avineri, *The Social and Political Thought of Karl Marx* (New York: Cambridge University Press, 1968), 48–52.

3. Franz Schurmann, *Ideology and Organization in Communist China* (Berkeley: University of California Press, 1968).

4. Harry Harding, *Organizing China: The Problems of Bureaucracy, 1949–1976* (Stanford: Stanford University Press, 1981); Kenneth Lieberthal and Michel

Oksenberg, *Policy Making in China: Leaders, Structures, and Processes* (Princeton: Princeton University Press, 1988).

5. *Shehui Kexue Yanjiu Cankao Ziliao* (Reference material for studies in the social sciences) (Sichuan), 21 July 1985.

6. Cheng Li and David Backman, "Localism, Elitism, and Immobilism," *World Politics,* Vol. 62, No. 1 (October 1989), 64–93.

7. Andrew Walder, *Communist Neo-Traditionalism* (Berkeley: University of California Press, 1986).

8. Ezra N. Suleiman, *Politics, Power and Bureaucracy in France* (Princeton: Princeton University Press, 1974).

9. For the distinction between the politician and the bureaucrat, see Joel D. Aberbach, Robert P. Putnam, and Bert A. Rockman, *Bureaucrats and Politicians in Western Democracies* (Cambridge: Harvard University Press, 1981).

10. Li and Backman, "Localism, Elitism, and Immobilism."

11. *Jiaoyuan Cankao* (Teachers reference), April 15, 1985.

12. *Renmin Ribao* (People's daily), August 3, 1985.

13. Samuel Huntington, *Political Order in Changing Societies,* (New Haven: Yale University Press, 1968).

14. *Renmin Ribao,* September 6, 1985.

15. *Renmin Ribao,* October 10, 1983; August 16, 1985.

16. *Renmin Ribao,* August 7, 1985; *Jiaoyuan Cankao,* February 1, 1986.

17. *Renmin Ribao,* August 16, 1985.

18. *Hebei Congkan* (The Hebei collection), May 1980.

19. *Lilun Yu Shijian* (Theory and practice), June 1985, 18–19.

20. *Renmin Ribao,* March 16, 1983.

21. *Jianghai Xuekan* (River and sea journal), No. 4, 1984.

22. *Renmin Ribao,* March 7, 1985.

23. *Zhongguo Xingzheng Guanli* (Chinese administrative management), No. 3, 1987, 34.

24. *Lilun Yu Shijian,* June 1985, 18–19.

25. *Zhongguo Xingzheng Guanli,* 1978, No. 2, 5.

26. *Shaanxi Ribao* (Shaanxi daily), October 26, 1983.

27. *Hebei Ribao* (Hebei daily), October 21, 1982.

28. *Lilun Yu Shijian,* June 1985, 34–35; *Tianjinshi 1984nian Shehui Kexue Geti Diaoyan Chengguo Xuanbian* (Selections on the results of the 1984 social science survey in Tianjin), Vol. 11 (Tianjin: Tianjin Renmin Chubanshe, 1985), 411–427.

29. *Xuexi Yu Yanjiu* (Study and research), 1985, No. 11, 15–17.

30. *Jingji Yanjiu Cankao Ziliao* (Reference materials on economic research), April 25, 1980, 32–34.

31. Ibid.

32. Zhongguo Jingji Tizhi Gaige Yanjiusuo Conghe Diaochazu, ed., *Gaige: Women Mianlin De Diaozhan Yu Xueze* (Reform: The challenges and choices we face) (Beijing: Zhongguo Jingji Chubanshe, 1986), 137.

33. *Zhengzhixue Yanjiu Tongxun* (Newsletter on political studies), No. 4, 1983, 7–13.

34. *Zengdang Yu Jiandang* (Party rectification and party construction) (Liaoning), June 1, 1986, 30.

35. Ibid.

36. *Renmin Ribao,* October 31, 1988.

37. Tan Jian, ed., *Guojia Gongwuyuan Shouce* (Handbook of the national civil service) (Beijing: Shehui Kexue Wenxian Chubanshe, 1988), 7.

38. Ibid.

39. Ibid., 10.

40. Nie Gaowu, Li Yichou, and Wang Zhangtian, eds., *Dangzheng Fenkai Lilun Tanlu* (Explorations in the separation of party and state) (Beijing: Chunqiu Chubanshe, 1988), 17.

41. Suleiman, *Politics, Power and Bureaucracy,* 72–99.

42. Ibid., 79–92.

43. Ibid., 386.

44. Hans Rosenberg, *Bureaucracy, Aristocracy, and Autocracy* (Boston: Beacon Press, 1958).

45. *Foreign Broadcast Information Service, People's Republic of China,* July 17, 1989, 16.

46. Ibid., July 20, 1989. A Chinese scientist visiting the United States told me that only 5 percent of those employed in the Chinese Academy of Sciences (CAS) participated in the 1989 demonstrations for democracy.

47. *Daily Report,* September 20, 1989, 11.

4

Urban China: A Civil Society in the Making?

Martin K. Whyte

The contrasting fates of popular pressures for democratic reforms of the Marxist-Leninist systems of Eastern Europe, the Soviet Union, and China in 1989 merit consideration and analysis. To what extent was the failure of the Beijing Spring inevitable or at least very likely? Insofar as the odds against success of democratic reforms in China were greater than in Eastern Europe and the USSR, to what causes can this difference be attributed? Does the failure of the Beijing Spring represent only a temporary setback in an inevitable trend toward pluralism and democracy, or is this setback more a sign of the unsuitability of democracy to Chinese conditions? These are obviously very large and complex questions, and I do not claim to offer definitive answers here. However, by focusing on the question of the conditions affecting the emergence of a "civil society" in the People's Republic of China, I hope to be able to contribute useful ideas that are related to these "big questions."

What is meant by the term *civil society,* and why is this concept important? *Civil society* has been used in a variety of contexts in recent discussions of democratic reform, but the essence of the term involves the idea of the existence of institutionalized autonomy for social relationships and associational life, autonomy vis-à-vis the state. Thus the existence of a well-formed civil society implies a degree of separation in the relationship between state and society, such that much social life goes on without reference to state dictates and policies. In such a civil society, individuals have identities as citizens that are independent of whatever relationships they may have with the organizations and political categories established by the state and its leaders.

Although for the sake of simplicity I often refer to civil society as an either-or proposition, it should be obvious that in reality what is involved is a matter of degree. A minimal civil society would involve only a modest amount of autonomous social life, mostly confined to contacts within relatively isolated primary groups—in families and among workmates and close friends, for example. A more fully developed civil society would contain much broader social networks within which free communication could take place and that could support a rich variety of autonomous secondary groups—associations, clubs, unions, mutual-aid societies, and so forth.[1]

Much of the autonomous social and associational life that takes place in a civil society may be avowedly apolitical, involving activities such as bird watching, promotion of the opera, or the salvation of souls. Nonetheless, the existence of a well-formed civil society involves clear limits on the state's ability to control society and its constituent individuals. Dissident activity can thus find some protection within civil society, and an independent public opinion will emerge that both individuals and the state have to take into account. The term *institutionalized* used in the definition above implies fairly explicit, although not necessarily legal or constitutional, recognition by the state of the right and ability of the activities and organizations of civil society to proceed without substantial state interference or control. Such autonomy is never absolute, of course, and the state may restrict the activities of civil society in certain ways. For a civil society to exist, however, there must be a fairly predictable amount of autonomy within which grassroots associational life can operate freely.

Many of the debates in Eastern Europe that utilize the term *civil society* oppose it to *totalitarianism.* This latter term is now out of favor in Western social science, but it is still widely employed by commentators within Eastern Europe.[2] If we discard many of the specific meanings attached to *totalitarianism* in Western writings, such as that it entails mass terror and the atomization of all social life, and use the term simply to mean a concerted effort by party-state authorities to control as much of social life as possible, then considering civil society as an alternative to totalitarianism makes sense. Because a civil society implies fundamental limits on the power of the state to control society, Leninist political systems dedicated to a totalitarian program (in the limited sense defined here) will try insofar as possible to prevent or limit the emergence of a civil society.

The term *civil society* has been of central importance in the thinking and political strategies of Eastern European dissidents, particularly in Poland. This centrality reflects a conviction that democratic reform of Leninist political systems involves not so much the implementation of procedural elements of what is called "formal democracy" (e.g., direct elections, competitive parties, checks and balances, etc.) as the development of a social basis for pluralism and state-society separation. Or perhaps the existence of a civil society can be considered as the infrastructure or as a precondition that makes the development of formal democracy possible, with formal democracy, once established, serving to protect and expand civil society. In any case, the creation and strengthening of civil society is a central part of the democratic reform agenda. In Poland the arduous struggle to establish civil society despite the Leninist state occurred over years and despite setbacks, and the protection and intellectual ferment provided by an increasingly robust civil society formed an organizational basis for the Solidarity movement and for exerting pressure on the state, pressure that in 1989 contributed to a major dismantling of Poland's Leninist political institutions. In other Eastern European states prior to 1989, the regimes were generally more successful in blocking the development of civil society, although to varying degrees—less so in Hungary and perhaps East Germany, more so in Czechoslovakia and the Soviet Union, and fairly thoroughly in Romania and Bulgaria.[3]

In the momentous changes of 1989 in Eastern Europe, it seems obvious that much of the impetus for democratic reforms came from outside and involved both the withdrawal of Soviet support for hardliners and a sort of domino effect produced by changes elsewhere. In other words, outside of Poland, these changes did not constitute victory of a fully developed civil society over Leninist systems. Even in Nicolae Ceausescu's Romania, however, some autonomous social and political activity was visible prior to the climax of December 1989 (e.g., in letters of protest written to Ceausescu by former party leaders, in mobilized local support to protect Reverend Tokes in Timisoara, in the campus grumbling that led to the hostile shouting during Ceausescu's final public speech). In all cases, then, some pressure from below helped to precipitate the crises, and the existence of such pressure implies some autonomy for society. But in those cases where civil society had been prevented from developing beyond a minimal level, a major problem confronting the new leaderships of Eastern Europe is how to create and consolidate the civil society that is needed to provide a stable basis for a more democratic political order.

I am not arguing that a fully developed civil society has to exist in order for Leninist systems to be changed. Instead, I simply contend that whether before or after major changes in a democratic direction at the elite level, democratic reform involves the creation of the social basis for a more pluralistic society. To the extent that a civil society develops within a Leninist political system, it will produce pressure on elites for democratic reforms. If a civil society does not exist for reasons other than elite manipulation and suppression (say, because of an unfavorable cultural tradition or the weakness of conditions fostering associations beyond a family or village context), elites will not feel such pressure. If a civil society that would have developed has been actively suppressed by the party-state, elites may feel that they can conduct business as usual, but they may learn to their surprise and sorrow, as Ceausescu did, that a nascent civil society nurturing and spreading protodemocratic views lies just beneath the surface of official controls.[4]

China's Cultural Tradition and Civil Society

What does this extended discussion have to do with the People's Republic of China? Two issues deserve consideration here. First, to what extent were the historical traditions of China and the post-1949 evolution of institutions in the PRC such that they made the emergence of a civil society difficult, if not impossible? Second, regardless of whether such conditions were favorable or not, to what extent did a civil society emerge in reform-era China and play a role in the events leading up to the Beijing Spring of 1989? The answers to these questions will tell us something about the prospects for democratic reform in China.

Starting first with the question of the influence of China's cultural tradition and of the sorts of Soviet-style institutions adopted in the PRC during the 1950s, I would say that the picture is mixed, but on balance both sets of "contexts" worked against the emergence of a civil society in contemporary China. In terms of the historical tradition, this is not simply a matter of China's lacking a tradition of formal democracy. The basic presumptions of rulers in the late imperial period were that all individuals should be enmeshed in hierarchies and networks of mutual obligation and propriety, and that the state and its officials should establish and enforce a political-moral orthodoxy that would provide guidance for the entire social hierarchy. In this view individuals were seen not as autonomous and possessing inalienable rights, as in the Western liberal tradition, but as malleable yet fallible, capable of proper behavior only when subordinated to the correct group influence and orthodox indoctrination. Similarly, social groups were seen not as properly independent and competing to defend and advance the interests of their members but as small links in a vast social hierarchy that should be guided by official values. Indeed, in most periods independent associations even of literati were prohibited, and parties or factions (*dang*) were equated with selfish partiality, if not outright disloyalty.

Notions of privacy, autonomy, individual rights, and the virtues of free competition of individuals, groups, and ideas not only had no place in Confucian statecraft but were profoundly threatening. Emperors and officials did not simply administer but preached and provided moral examples in this conception, and failure to enforce orthodoxy and subordinate social groups to official values was seen as leading to chaos. In this cultural milieu there was no alternative source of moral guidance, no counterweight to state authority comparable to the church in the West. Nor was there a conception that law was an institution operating "above the state" to restrict the actions of emperors. China's imperial rulers shared with their Communist successors a totalitarian (in the limited sense defined above) vision.[5]

These fundamental assumptions did not provide a basis for emperors and their officials willy-nilly to proclaim as orthodoxy anything they liked and enforce their views without fear of constraint or opposition. Official orthodoxy was not rigidly fixed, and new dynasties and emperors devoted considerable energy to formulating revised sets of orthodox texts, incorporating new ideas and interpretations. They also devoted attention to devising new schemes to indoctrinate the public. However, in late imperial times these new formulations of orthodoxy were justified in terms of an effort to recapture the true essence of Chinese civilization. This justification of orthodoxy provided a basis by which thousands of officials and literati could critically judge the edicts and formulations of their rulers.[6] The training of Chinese intellectuals oriented them not to simple and total subservience to the emperor and the state but to loyalty to the basic values of Chinese culture as they understood them. Rulers who were seen as departing too far from these basic values in their actions and edicts could expect to receive a string of memorials from officials. In extreme cases officials and intellectuals were willing to engage in brave acts of protest to register their displeasure—resigning posts, directly challenging the emperor and thus courting death, or committing suicide. With few exceptions, though, these acts of protest were of individuals rather than of organized groups, and they were carried out within the rules of the system rather than against it. One might say they involved remonstration (of the ruler) rather than demonstration. Elite intellectuals did establish academies and study societies with a reformist bent in both the Ming and Qing dynasties, but these existed at the sufferance of the state and tried to work within the system, at least until near the very end of the imperial era.[7] Even when rebellions and attempts to overthrow the dynasty were mounted (usually by others rather than by intellectuals and officials), they invariably sought to establish a new orthodoxy that could bind society together.

What I have been sketching is a simplified overview of the late imperial conception of the state-society relationship in China, and I argue that this official theory was quite hostile to the notion of an autonomous civil society. But this is only the theory. What was the reality of social life in late imperial China? The reality was far different from the sort of feudal or quasi-totalitarian polity that these official ideas might suggest. The actual personnel and resources of the late imperial state were modest in relation to the huge and complex society that they were trying to oversee, and thus it was impossible to enforce compliance with official orthodoxy. Individuals had substantial autonomy in their daily lives, and a wide variety of groups existed at the local level—lineages, guilds, native place associations, religious sects, secret societies, literary clubs, and so forth. Much social activity at the grassroots level took place with little active regard for how it conformed to official orthodoxy. One might say that a de facto civil society existed in late imperial China.

However, even if this claim is accepted, it is clear that this was not a well-institutionalized civil society. The extensive autonomy of individual and group activity existed at the sufferance of the state and was not protected by legal or other guarantees. Groups were expected to pay homage to official values, and heterodox local groups or those which simply grew too strong were potential targets for official suppression. The very substantial autonomy of social life in late imperial times remained precarious, and no set of doctrines justifying the free competition of groups and ideas emerged. The existing de facto civil society did not provide fertile ground for interest groups or parties to emerge to press demands against the state.[8]

Seeds of Civil Society in Late Qing and Republican China

In the waning days of the Qing dynasty, trends were emerging that encouraged the strengthening of China's nascent civil society. Western impact fostered awareness and appreciation of Western legal systems, political parties, active associational life, philosophies of individual rights, and other component elements of Western civil society. Unpopular treaties forced on the dynasty triggered mass protest activity and the formation of new associations and political groups. New study societies, academies, and chambers of commerce and other occupational associations (*fatuan*) emerged, and their existence bolstered a conception of a public realm (*gong*) that existed between the official or state realm (*guan*) and the private (*si*). The downfall of the dynasty and the rise of a republican and avowedly democratic form of government in its wake (with elected assemblies and political parties emerging) followed by the weakness of central political institutions of the warlord era, produced a wide variety of such new and modern forms of grassroots associational life—trade unions, professional associations, political parties, independent newspapers and journals, local assemblies, literary clubs, and so forth. In the wake of the May Fourth movement, initiated in 1919, criticism of China's bureaucratic imperial tradition sharpened, and arguments in favor of freeing individuals from the constraints of orthodoxy and tradition were more frequently heard.[9]

In general the last years of the Qing dynasty and the first half of the twentieth century saw the growth of more elements of a civil society in China, particularly in urban areas. However, two themes of those years inhibited the full institutionalization of civil society. Throughout most of this period, national and regional leaders remained at best ambivalent and often downright hostile toward autonomous associational life and interest group activity. Chiang Kaishek's rule was characterized by an increasing turn away from liberal or pluralist notions to a renewed authoritarianism, and pressures and threats against the new forms of associational life increased.[10] Even though the Nationalist regime was too weak to exert effective control over most grassroots associational life, the autonomy of the groups that did exist remained precarious, with official repression always a threat.

The second inhibiting feature involved the way in which the ideas associated with democracy in the West were altered as they were embraced by China's twentieth-century "liberals." In that process, basic parts of pluralist doctrine—that individuals have rights and interests that may conflict with those of larger groups and even the state, and that state power needs to be checked in order to secure the liberty of individuals—were deemphasized or ignored. Democracy was interpreted first and foremost as a means to make the government stronger so that China could hold its own in the world again. Democracy was seen primarily, then, as a way of increasing citizen involvement and participation, thus ending social fragmentation—what Sun Yatsen had called the "sheet of loose sand" that characterized Chinese society—and producing a population united behind the government. This slant is understandable, given China's cultural tradition and the weakness of the state throughout the previous century. Nonetheless, this interpretation meant that the primary goal of democratic reformers in the Republican period was promoting state strength, not safeguarding the rights and autonomy of individuals and groups.[11] In this environment it became all too easy to restrict or abandon democratic measures if they seemed to threaten the ability of the state to unify society.

Changes in Chinese Society in the Maoist Era

The fragile progress made in developing civil society in the Republican period was wiped out by the changes introduced by the Chinese Communist party after 1949. Pluralist ideas were rejected as part of a bogus "bourgeois democracy," and Marxist-Leninist ideas and organizational devices were grafted onto Chinese roots as the basis for the new order. These Marxist-Leninist ideas were, in fact, highly resonant with imperial Confucianism.[12] In the organizational system adopted from the Soviet Union, just as in Confucian statecraft, there should be one official set of values (now termed an ideology) proclaimed and enforced over all of society. Autonomy and rights for individuals and groups were not recognized. All individuals should subordinate themselves to the groups in which they operated (now referred to as "collectives"), and all groups should be subordinated to the policies and goals of the party-state. Proletarian democracy was proclaimed, but this meant officially managed and controlled mass participation within the system, with no rights to avoid participating, much less to organize separately from it or against it.

Although the basic assumptions of "Maoist statecraft" were strikingly similar to those of the imperial era, so that Leninism reinforced tendencies embedded in official Confucianism, there is one vital difference. In practice the CCP leaders had the will and the organizational means to enforce their new orthodoxy over all of society in a way that their imperial predecessors could never have imagined. The fragile independent forms of organizational life that existed in 1949 were coopted or suppressed. New "mass associations" and grassroots social-control structures were built that controlled the lives and manipulated the psyches of ordinary citizens as never before. The limited tolerance of disengagement and private thought that existed even in the quasi-totalitarian imperial era disappeared. Indeed, it could be argued that the Maoist state implemented a form of grassroots social control that was even more thorough than in Stalin's Soviet Union, a form producing an extreme degree of dependence of individuals on the agents of state power.[13]

I do not wish to claim that the totalitarian impulse in Maoist China produced a totalitarian reality—an ability of the state to totally control the thoughts and actions of every citizen. That was very far from being the case. In kin groups, among friends, and in other grassroots groupings, people retained considerable ability to escape from political controls and even grumble about their social order to close associates. Periodically these sentiments erupted to the surface in forms such as work slowdowns and even isolated strikes. However, very little of a civil society existed, as such pockets of autonomy and grumbling were small and confined and did not provide a basis for the formation of independent organizations, broad sharing of views and grievances, or the emergence of a coherent public opinion.

Seeds of Civil Society in the Late Mao Era

I have argued in the preceding pages that Chinese tradition was quite hostile to the emergence of civil society and that the weakly institutionalized forms of autonomous associational life that existed in late imperial times and developed further in the Republican period were snuffed out after 1949. If, as I claim, a civil society is an important element in creating a democratic society, the background conditions in contemporary China would appear to be quite inauspicious. Yet there are unmistakable signs of a revived civil society in the post-Mao era. How are we to explain the reemergence of civil society in such unfertile soil?

I would argue that the reemergence of elements of a civil society was set in motion by developments in the late Mao period. Curiously enough, it was the most extreme period of Mao's attempted strait-jacketing of his population, the Cultural Revolution, that sowed the most important seeds of this new trend. On the surface, the Cultural Revolution appeared to be a time when the small remaining areas of individual and group autonomy were being eliminated. Even trivial popular customs, such as bird raising, enjoying traditional operas, and the worshiping of ancestors, were apparently wiped out in favor of mass catechismal study of Mao's quotations and obligatory attendance at "revolutionary operas." However, despite such appearances, several important trends during the Cultural Revolution contributed to the revival of civil society afterwards.[14]

First, the antibureaucratic thrust of the Cultural Revolution and the revelations aired then about abuses of authority, elitism, and corruption among officials had a dramatic impact on the population, particularly on young participants in Red Guard struggles. The previous tendency to conflate feelings of nationalism, loyalty, gratitude toward the party, and respect for superiors and officials was ended, and people were encouraged to trust Mao and his ideas but to distrust all other authorities. The effect of these developments was not only to encourage suspicion of authority figures but also to make young people think that, when armed with the proper ideas (drawn from Mao, of course), they could distinguish political good from evil themselves, without relying on the "line" laid down by local party secretaries or higher-level officials. The spirit of the times encouraged them to dare to act and be heroic and bold, to "go against the tide," and to "doubt everything."[15] Even when Mao tried to put the genie back into the bottle by reining in the Red Guards and sending most into exile in the countryside, this spirit of suspecting authority and relying on one's own thinking ability was not lost. In fact, it may have been strengthened among many rusticated Red Guards by their isolation in the countryside and by their feelings that Mao had abandoned them and ruined their lives.

This ideological change was accompanied by important alterations in the organization of Chinese society. Particularly important was the immobilization of the party, mass associations, and most other official organs except the army. For an extended period of time during the Cultural Revolution, this situation released individuals from day-to-day control by their bureaucratic supervisors and enabled them to act and think much more autonomously. The most extreme manifestation of this new autonomy involved Red Guards' traveling freely around the country, forming a bewildering variety of groups and factions, and engaging in pitched battles with factional enemies. But for the ordinary population as well, the Cultural Revolution meant much more autonomy, with opportunities to escape from the previous routine of regular political study and mutual criticism and enjoy increased leisure time, share rumors with friends, and reflect on the worrisome chaos that surrounded them.[16]

A third development that helped prepare the way for the reemergence of civil society was the traumatic personal trials experienced by so many during the Cultural Revolution. These trials varied across individuals and groups, from a growing sense of abandonment and treachery felt by radical Red Guards; through the bitterness of bureaucrats, intellectuals, and others at being made victims of Cultural Revolution struggles; to the anxieties of many bystanders and nonparticipants who saw the fragile predictability of their lives destroyed. Even urbanites who were not centrally involved often experienced painful episodes during those years—for example, as their children risked their lives in Red Guard struggles, as cherished family possessions had to be destroyed to escape Red Guard wrath, or as parents died and could not be given proper funerals and burials. These kinds of traumatic experiences, although not universal, caused many people to abandon their former trust in the paternalistic benevolence of the system. Traditional feelings that politics and the state were treacherous "tigers" to be avoided at all costs resurfaced, and such sentiments contributed to a popular desire for forms of association independent of state control.

In the years after 1969, Mao and his radical followers tried to reconstruct the social-control system and even to make it more penetrating and cohesive than the pre-1966 version. However, severe damage had been done to that system, and popular cooperation was more grudging and problematic than before. Indeed, in the early 1970s various trends and policies—the continued exiling of urban youths to the countryside, the mysterious demise of Lin Biao, stagnating living standards, and the mass rehabilitation of targets of the Cultural Revolution (who often had to work alongside those who had been responsible for their victimization)—prevented the restoration of social cohesion and faith in the system. Growing signs of popular discontent and even of group action to express that discontent were visible in Mao's final years—for example, in the protest statement posted by the Li Yizhe group in Canton in 1974, the industrial strikes of 1975 in Hangzhou and other cities, and, most notably, in the Tiananmen "incident" of April 1976.[17] It was increasingly apparent that, underneath the surface of Maoist controls, Chinese society was riven with unorthodox thinking and group activity. These formed the basis for the reemergence of elements of a civil society when, in the post-Mao era, more favorable conditions arose.

Civil Society Emerges in Reform-Era China

After Mao's death in 1976, China's new leaders recognized the authority crisis they faced. They instituted a variety of changes designed to defuse that crisis. The changes they introduced, however, had decidedly mixed implications in terms of that elite's ability to manage and control the population. On the one hand, many of the most serious sources of popular discontent were dealt with directly and at least partially alleviated. On the other hand, the changes introduced facilitated the further emergence and consolidation of elements of civil society in urban China, a trend that inevitably presented a challenge to the power of the post-Mao party-state.[18]

The specific measures introduced by the post-Mao leaders in their effort to relieve political tensions are fairly familiar. They declared that the class-struggle campaigns were over; they rehabilitated thousands of victims of previous campaigns dating back to the 1950s; they dismantled the class-origin label system used to stigmatize large numbers of families for more than two decades; they terminated the campaigns of sending urban youths to the countryside and allowed millions of previous rusticates to return to urban areas; they restored pre–Cultural Revolution incentive systems, bonuses, and raises and stimulated competition for higher income; they revived the earlier system of competitive, exam-based entrance into universities and rapidly expanded college enrollments; they instituted reforms designed to make food and consumer goods more widely available; they initiated a housing construction boom to relieve the incredibly cramped urban housing situation; they relaxed the Maoist controls that impoverished cultural life, opened China's doors to foreign contact and influence, and allowed a much wider range of options in literature, art, music, religion, and popular culture; and they provided new opportunities for criticism of the inhumanities of the Maoist era and even, in some cases, of the negative tendencies existing in the reform era.[19]

Such changes, as already noted, did much to relieve the tensions of the Mao years and to earn popularity for the reformers and their policies.[20] Yet they also set in motion changes at the grassroots level that would complicate the job of the reform-era leaders. As the party-state stepped back from the effort to totally program all of social life, the opportunities for urbanites to express their views more freely and to participate in the formation of public opinion increased. Much of the post-1978 revival of autonomous associational life took an apolitical or even antipolitical form (i.e., emphasizing the desire to escape from politics)—for example, revivals of pet raising and other hobbies, renewed enthusiasm for the martial arts, seeking salvation through religious worship and pilgrimages to sacred sites, and so forth. In a society in which politics had for so long "taken command,"[21] however, even avowedly apolitical activities had an unavoidable political import, constituting rejection of the close ideological tutelage and controls of the Mao period. The reformers contributed to this spirit by encouraging critiques that stressed the stultifying effects of Mao-era controls. In so doing they lent legitimacy to the public hunger for autonomous and protected social lives.

Not all of the new types of urban social activity took the form of escapes from political involvement, though. The repudiation of the Cultural Revolution, the initiation of the open-door policy, and the sense of national crisis contributed to an atmosphere reminiscent of the May Fourth movement. Just as in that earlier era, the air was filled with debates over ideas and programs that could heal the wounds and make China a dynamic force in the world. Many participants in these debates looked outside of China to Western ideas and institutions for inspiration, whereas others countered with ideas drawn from China's own complex cultural heritage. Even though the authorities periodically put a damper on these debates by renewed efforts to exert central control (and to denounce the dangers of spiritual pollution and bourgeois liberalism), these conservative interludes were followed by new waves of debate and criticism that went beyond anything that had been heard before. Thus despite periodic setbacks, the range of alternative and often highly critical ideas that found a hearing increased over time.

In the liberal phases of these swings of official tolerance, the fruits of the seeds of civil society sown in the late Mao era were clearly visible. The rehabilitation of thousands of victims of earlier campaigns and the return of many to positions of prominence provided new and not easily intimidated opinion leaders. Although many former rightists, rusticated Red Guards, and "capitalist roaders" preferred to avoid trouble and enjoy their restored lives quietly, others saw their bitter experiences and years in political limbo as having provided them with authority to speak out about what changes China needed. The many individuals of this type who regained positions as teachers, writers, journalists, and researchers found ready audiences for their views among the younger generation and among disenchanted urbanites in general. Images spread of both Maoist and post-Mao China as a hidebound, quasi-feudal order in which popular initiatives were stifled in the interest of maintaining elite controls and privileges. Such images were reinforced by increased contact with the outside world and with both the alternative political orders and critiques of Leninist systems that flourished there.[22]

Official reform-era condemnation of the excesses of Mao-era politics made it difficult to use local party secretaries, propaganda officers, and the like to restrict and control the formation of popular attitudes. Studies show, for example, that among students distaste for mandatory politics courses and for political study in general mounted, that individuals assigned to lead such activities felt they had little authority and many headaches, and that as a result these rituals became increasingly superficial or were diverted to other topics.[23] Changes in local leaderships to replace "reds" with "experts" did not resolve the control problem, as this shift weakened still further the power of those in charge of political life in grassroots units but did not induce critical opinion leaders or their audiences to forget political issues in order to concentrate on work and professional advancement.

By providing greater latitude for social association and public expression, the authorities made it possible for views to be voiced and shared that went beyond what they intended. In this atmosphere, more and more people recognized that they were not alone in their feelings of discontent, and the brevity and ineffectual nature of the conservative phases (prior to 1989) fostered increasing confidence that things had really changed, so that a citizen could raise fundamental criticisms of the system without getting into serious trouble. In this new political atmosphere, critical views not only of the Mao era but also of reform policies and tendencies began to accumulate.

It would be a mistake to suppose that all of this popular grumbling involved a desire for more rapid and thorough reforms. Many elements of the population felt threatened by the loss of security and by the new inequities spawned by even partial reforms and were anxious about the loss of moral cohesion they perceived around them. For such groups, the new tolerance provided opportunities to raise conservative criticisms of reform policies.[24]

A number of escalating problems (inflation, elite corruption, etc.) added to popular discontent in the 1980s. One other crucial new element fostering the emergence of a civil society in urban China was the growing conflict within the elite. The movement toward increasingly fundamental criticisms of the system occurred within the reformist wing of the elite as well as among ordinary urbanites, and, as a result, critics who penned biting commentaries and heterodox proposals found that they could find patrons at the top who could get their views spread and provide protection. No longer did such radical views have to be whispered among family and close friends—now they might result in a series of publications, form the basis for a television series, or even appear in the *People's Daily.* The publication of highly critical views in official sources encouraged others to overcome their hesitation and join in the debate, and some of China's top leaders seemed to listen to, and be influenced by, these increasingly radical critiques.

The radical views aired in the late 1980s took a variety of forms, including advocacy of privatization of the economy, the virtues of bankruptcy and unemployment, and the need to eliminate party controls over literature and the arts. For my purposes, one of the most interesting developments was the appearance of articles stressing the need to encourage the development of elements of civil society. For example, a number of articles appeared discussing the virtues of interest groups and arguing that they would have a beneficial rather than harmful effect on the political order. One such article concluded, "China's reform is a special social project, which is so complex that it cannot be conducted flawlessly in tailor-made conditions. . . . We must recognize the existence of different interest groups which conflict and converge, and realize that in the end that very multitude of interests constitutes the general social interest."[25] Another article that appeared near the onset of the Beijing Spring pointed out, "'Reform and opening' inevitably brings with it the pluralization of interests and the pluralization of demands, as well as the rapid development of nongovernmental organizations."[26] The need for a rule of law and an independent judiciary to provide protection for individuals and newly emerging autonomous associations was another prominent theme at this time.

From a situation in which elements of civil society began to emerge at the grassroots level in spite of official hostility, a new picture was created in which relatively autonomous group activity was not only tolerated but even actively promoted and praised by some intellectuals and elements in the leadership, who saw autonomous associations and interest group activity as unavoidable and positive features of any modern society. As one enthusiastic commentator put it, "Socialist society should be a garden with a rainbow of colors; it should be a sparkling period in which human talents massively burst forth."[27] A few such discussions explicitly used the term *civil society* (*gongming shehui*) and made unfavorable comparisons between the Chinese and Western traditions in this regard.[28] In general, the sorts of arguments in favor of autonomous associational life that developed in Eastern Europe and elsewhere began to be raised in China.[29] However, this was not the only or even the dominant theme in discussions of political reform. Opposed to these sorts of pluralistic arguments was advocacy of a "new authoritarianism" for China, and the latter arguments were reportedly encouraged by Zhao Ziyang.

The logical culmination of this changing scene was the emergence of avowedly autonomous formal associations after the mid-1980s. In the Mao era, as noted, there was little possibility of autonomous organizations' existing, even if they were apolitical, and the populace was regimented by a sparse number of official organizations and mass associations. In the post-Mao period this situation began to change. First, there was a flowering of new (or revived) associations of a bewildering variety—professional associations, literary societies, recreational clubs, academic research institutes, foundations, think tanks, and so forth. Sometimes these could be quite specialized and rather unusual. For example, colleagues and I were amused to hear in 1980 that a Society for the Study of Hair-covered People had been founded in China. Some other organizations are revived relics from the pre-1949 period. For example, a number of craft guilds have recently been formed under the sponsorship of the All-China Federation of Industry and Commerce (itself a revival from the pre–Cultural Revolution period).[30] Similarly, the YMCA is once again operating in China, as is the Chinese Industrial Cooperative Association, a revival of the organization established by New Zealander Rewi Alley in the 1930s. Still other independent organizations are direct products of the economic reforms, such as the new private companies, schools, scientific research institutes, and polling agencies.[31] Intellectuals have taken the lead in advocating and establishing autonomous associations, but entrepreneurs, craftspeople, and many other urbanites have taken advantage of the "political space" created by these efforts to begin forming their own organizations.

Initially, most of these organizations took a fairly familiar, mass-association form, with official registration and supervision provided by designated arms of the party-state. However, after a few years this situation began to change. New organizations were established by popular initiative—organizations that were avowedly and quite self-consciously autonomous and that spurned attempts by the relevant official agencies to control their operation and activities. Many of these new associations were local, but some were national in scope and had attached publishing houses and other devices available to spread their views. Examples of new organizations with various degrees of autonomy from the state would include the Stone Institute of Social Development (established by the Stone Computer Company), the Capital Iron and Steel Legal System and Social Development Research Institute, the Asia Institute established under the Shanghai Academy of Social Sciences, private universities such as Ningbo University (established with funds from Hong Kong shipping magnate Y. K. Pao), the Oriental Cultural Foundation (affiliated with the Shandong Academy of Social Sciences), the Qinghua University Alumni Foundation, the International Art Foundation (established by artist Wu Xuoren), and of course the organizations that arose during the Beijing Spring, such as the Beijing Autonomous Students' Union and the Capital Independent Workers' Union.[32] According to one press account, by 1989 there were 1,000 such autonomous associations operating nationally and 100,000 at the local level.[33]

My first encounter with these new organizations occurred during summer 1986, when I was invited in Beijing to speak to something called the "Cultural Academy" (*wenhua shuyuan*). I was surprised to find about 300 people arriving to hear my talk and to learn that they had come from schools and colleges, as well as newspapers, television stations, and mass associations in various parts of the country. The leaders of this organization were quite amused when, in the banquet that was the reward for my ordeal, they saw my puzzlement at the negative replies they provided to a whole series of questions from me about registration and supervision from the party, Ministry of Culture, and other official agencies. Not all of these new associations had the formal structure of the Cultural Academy. During the same period a large number of "cultural salons" sprang up in which intellectuals, students, and others debated the problems of China's cultural tradition, much as their May Fourth–era predecessors had done.

Many of the new organizations saw their autonomy simply as a way of fending off controls from the state so that they could engage in their activities in peace. However, the intellectuals and students who predominated in these organizations were heirs to a tradition that obligated them to serve as the moral consciences for their society. This legacy impelled them to formulate ideas and activities for the reform and improvement of China, and inevitably many of these ideas and activities came into conflict with the CCP's claim to be the guardian of China's destiny. These new associations may not have become interest groups, in the narrow sense of organizations designed to extract from the government changes favorable to their membership, but many of them were increasingly functioning as pressure groups, and they were seen as such by the CCP. The months leading up to the events of the Beijing Spring saw petitions drafted in support of the release of imprisoned Democracy Wall activist Wei Jingsheng, the planning of an anniversary conference to analyze the 1957 antirightist campaign, and many other initiatives that Deng Xiaoping and other leaders found threatening.[34] After June 1989 the leadership accused the campus cultural salons of stimulating and planning the student demonstrations and blamed the Stone Institute of Social Development and other new associations with providing financial and organizational support to the demonstrators.

By the end of the 1980s, a combination of official tolerance, increasing acceptance of pluralist ideas, and the mushrooming of a variety of forms of autonomous grassroots social activity in urban China provided the basis for a full-fledged public opinion to arise. Observers increasingly remarked that popular moods that were not created or controlled by elites were more and more palpable. The open door fostered enthusiasm in China for the related arts of advertising, public relations, and public-opinion polling, and a large variety of new agencies became involved in taking the popular pulse. The authorities became concerned with how to handle and react to public opinion and how to gain control over it. Despite the leadership's instinctive Leninist impulse to mold public opinion, evidence from Chinese opinion polls showed a rising level of unorthodox opinions and declining faith in the system toward the end of the 1980s.[35]

By 1989, I am suggesting, a cumulative process was under way that was fundamentally changing the nature of the state-society relationship. A cowed and dependent population whose criticisms of the system could be bottled up and suppressed had given way to a lively scene in which urbanites were increasingly caught up in communications and associations that were at least substantially independent of the party-state. In other words, a nascent civil society was emerging and consolidating. I have also suggested that this trend was occurring despite a cultural tradition and a set of post-1949 organizational practices that were designed to prevent civil society from developing. This nascent civil society was fueled in part by the reform policies fostered by Deng Xiaoping but also, paradoxically, by the democratizing effect of the Cultural Revolution.

To be sure, there were still very important sources of weakness in this newly revived civil society of urban China. Much of the new and autonomous activity depended upon the tolerance of the authorities, for there were still no well-institutionalized legal or other guarantees protecting civil society from the state. Most urbanites remained highly dependent upon their work units and quite reluctant to engage publicly in heterodox activities. China's entrepreneurs and peasants did not enjoy the well-entrenched private property rights that gave the bourgeoisie such autonomy in the West. Furthermore, the influence of China's cultural tradition was still strong, and many urbanites worried that the bewildering array of new organizations and ideas was weakening China's moral and political cohesion. Many still held to the traditional view that interest groups and factions were selfish and divisive and therefore bad. Some even yearned for the enforced unity of the Mao era. In spite of these sources of weakness, I would say, the elements of an emerging civil society in urban China in the late 1980s compare favorably with those in Eastern Europe—to be sure, they were weaker than their counterparts in Poland and perhaps in Hungary and East Germany, but they were fairly comparable to the level of autonomous associational life in the Soviet Union and Czechoslovakia and probably stronger than such phenomena in Bulgaria and Romania.[36]

The most clear evidence of the strength of these new elements of civil society is to be found in the developments of the Beijing Spring itself and in the comparable movements that emerged in cities and towns all across China. In a brief span of time, new organizations emerged, large parts of the urban population detached themselves from official organizations to give support to the demonstrators, a vibrant and highly critical public opinion found voice, and the populace resisted all of the traditional social-control efforts of the state for weeks, until their independence was crushed with massive force of arms.

The observations presented here lead me to argue that the failure of the Beijing Spring to push the system toward fundamental democratization was not due to the weakness of elements of civil society in China as compared to those in Eastern Europe. Those elements appear to have been growing robustly, in spite of the generally unfavorable Chinese cultural and historical context. Rather, the differing outcomes were the result of the existence of other elements in the Chinese case—for example, a core group of original and still powerful revolutionary leaders who were not dependent upon Soviet support, who had confidence in their ability to ride out any internal and international criticisms, and who did not hesitate to use military force against their own people. If this observation is correct, then the failure of the Beijing Spring does not provide compelling evidence for the view that democracy is simply unsuitable to Chinese conditions.

Conclusions: The June 1989 Crackdown and Beyond

I have suggested that the emergence of civil society is an important element in the democratic reform of Leninist systems and that, despite a largely unfavorable historical context, elements of civil society were growing rapidly and strengthening in the reform era prior to 1989. Those trends contributed to the series of student demonstrations that broke out in 1985, 1986–1987, and most spectacularly in 1989. That the 1989 demonstrations were not confined to students but ended up including sympathetic intellectuals, workers, cadres, and urbanites in general and that the events in Beijing were copied in hundreds of cities throughout China may be attributable in part, at least, to the broad spread of autonomous social activity in the interim. In the wake of the violent suppression of these most recent demonstrations, what can we say about the prospects for a renewal of the democratic reform impulse in China?

On a number of grounds the situation appears to look rather bleak. The conservative victors of the elite struggle that erupted during the Beijing Spring have taken a number of measures designed to check and reverse the emergence of civil society. They have arrested large numbers of liberal-reformist opinion leaders and are trying to intimidate the rest. Certainly the harshness of the crackdown demonstrates vividly to the public that the institutionalization of autonomous associational life and freedom of expression that appeared to exist was ephemeral. Some of the independent groups that emerged prior to or during the demonstrations (e.g., the Beijing Autonomous Student Union and the Stone Institute of Social Development) have been banned or emasculated, and new sets of regulations and registration procedures have been introduced in an effort to bring under some degree of official control all such organizations that remain. Large numbers of magazines and publication series have been closed, and wholesale purges have altered the editorial boards in many parts of the mass media. A wide range of ideas and cultural products of the period prior to the crackdown have been subjected to denunciation. Advocacy of the virtues of privatization, interest groups, and alternatives to Marxist theory is now dangerous. Political study rituals have been beefed up throughout society, with college students subjected to especially intensive doses, in some cases as part of a temporary stint of "remolding" in a military academy.[37] In general many of the time-honored (or shopworn, depending upon one's point of view) ideological control devices of the Maoist era have been dusted off and put into service again. Even that paragon of competitive selflessness, Lei Feng, is supposed to be the object of study and emulation once more. Finally, in justifying their crackdown, the conservative leaders have appealed directly to popular fears of "turmoil" and "chaos" and have argued that all individuals and groups need to submit to party authority if these dangers are to be avoided. It is not impossible to turn back the clock and suppress an emerging civil society, as developments after 1949 showed, and this seems to be what the conservative leaders are trying to do.

However, balanced against these ominous signs are indications that this effort to suppress civil society has been only partially successful. To some extent this lack of success can be attributed to the robustness of the elements of civil society that had emerged prior to 1989. Reports from China indicate that there is a great deal of superficial going through the motions in this tightening of political controls, especially outside of Beijing. Many local authorities are protecting and making excuses for their personnel, whether because of active sympathy or fear of antagonizing subordinates in general. The sort of enthusiastic participation of mass "activists" in enforcing the party's will that was visible in the 1950s and 1960s seems to be hard to find today. In fact, some individuals who have cooperated in the crackdown too eagerly, such as by turning in individuals on the "most wanted" list, have been subjected to harassment and retaliation. In this sort of situation, many individuals apparently are not all that intimidated and continue to express critical views, at least among close friends and associates. (Indeed, among some, the harshness of the crackdown may have produced more anger and determination not to be silenced.) When the crude and tired nature of the slogans of the conservatives is considered as well, it is understandable why official orthodoxy is not meeting with much success in stamping out grassroots heterodoxy.

The limited nature of the retreat of civil society is also influenced by the less than total nature of the crackdown. Despite the considerable coercion involved and the return to Maoist slogans and practices, to date we do not see a total effort by the conservatives to turn back the clock and eliminate all of the changes unleashed. Rather, they claim they want to restore their political hegemony while retaining the open-door policy, private enterprise, market reforms, and a policy of "letting 100 flowers bloom" in cultural and intellectual life. Perhaps this mixed message should be attributed not to restraint but to divisions within the leadership, with surviving proreform forces' helping to stay the hand of those who would like to see a fuller return to the practices of the Mao era. But whatever the reasons for this approach, it is internally contradictory. As Stanley Rosen observed,

> The imperatives of economic reform are creating an increasingly heterogeneous society, which is marked by decentralization, rampant commercialism, privatization, even internationalization, all contributing to the loss of social control by the state. . . . The party is seeking to unify public opinion and harmonize interests, politically and ideologically, at a time when economic and social forces are pulling society *away* from the state.[38]

As China entered the 1990s, there was some restriction in the scope of civil society in urban China, but a situation far short of the suppression that characterized the Mao era. It appeared that a substantial amount of independent social life and sharing of heterodox opinions continued at the grassroots level, providing the basis for rapid revival of autonomous activity and perhaps even new rounds of mass demonstrations if the political situation should permit it—possibly as a result of Deng Xiaoping's death or a sharpening of elite conflict at the center. Still, it is clear that civil society has not been fully institutionalized in contemporary China and faces an uncertain future. A vigorous group of conservative leaders might be able to draw on their cultural legacy and the organizational practices of the Mao era to more fully suppress the remaining elements of civil society. However, to do so they would have to be willing to abandon most elements of the economic reform program and use harsh measures to command a return to the penetrated and officially mobilized society of the Mao era. I doubt that the current leadership, or any coalition that might succeed it, would have the vigor or internal cohesion to carry out such a fundamental shift. Thus on balance, and in spite of the negative influence of the historical background and the crackdown policies, there is some basis for optimism that a nascent civil society will survive to provide potential for a more democratic China in the future.

Notes

1. My thinking on these matters has been influenced by the ideas and written works of a number of colleagues, and particularly Donald Munro and Michael Kennedy. Some theorists exclude the family and other primary groups from their definitions of civil society, which focus only on secondary groups or associations. There is a rich literature stressing both the trend in modern societies toward the proliferation of secondary groups that bring together people from diverse backgrounds and the importance of such associational life for a democratic political order. See, for example, Emile Durkheim, *The Division of Labor in Society* (New York: Free Press, 1964; originally 1893); Alexis de Tocqueville, *Democracy in America* (New York: Knopf, 1945; originally pub-

lished in two volumes in 1835 and 1840); Edward Laumann, *Bonds of Pluralism: The Form and Substance of Urban Social Networks* (New York: Wiley, 1973).

2. See the discussion in Jacques Rupnik, "Totalitarianism Revisited," and Mihaly Vajda, "East-Central European Perspectives," in John Keane, ed., *Civil Society and the State* (London: Verso, 1988).

3. These distinctions are impressionistic rather than based upon detailed information and systematic analysis. My ignorance about these countries, particularly Romania and Bulgaria, is so substantial that there may have been a variety of autonomous social activities in these countries that I am not aware of. Michael Kennedy has pointed out to me that within the Soviet Union there were important variations in this regard, with the Baltic republics the site of growing autonomous associational life when other republics were still relatively quiescent. Subsequently, such activity spread widely in other parts of the USSR. See the discussion in Gail Lapidus, "State and Society: Toward the Emergence of Civil Society in the Soviet Union," in S. Bialer, ed., *Politics, Society, and Nationality Inside Gorbachev's Russia* (Boulder: Westview, 1989); S. Frederick Starr, "Party Animals: Pluralism Comes to the U.S.S.R.," *New Republic,* June 26, 1989, 18–21.

4. This discussion assumes that dissident activity spawned within such nascent civil societies will favor democratic reforms. However, the events since 1989 in Eastern Europe show that a variety of nationalist/populist movements may also flourish within a nascent civil society. The extent to which these latter tendencies may win out over pluralist/democratic sentiments and eventually threaten or restrict civil society is the focus of considerable debate among authorities on Eastern Europe. See Timothy Garton Ash, "Eastern Europe: Après le Déluge, Nous," *New York Review of Books,* August 16, 1990, 51–57.

5. See Donald J. Munro, "One-Minded Hierarchy Versus Interest Group Pluralism: Two Chinese Approaches to Conflict," unpublished paper. The generalizations offered here involve some oversimplification and the blurring of variations in time and space. A more detailed treatment is not possible in the space available here. See some further discussion in a related paper of mine: Martin Whyte, "State and Society in the Mao Era," presented at the Four Anniversaries China Conference, Annapolis, September 1989.

6. The inertia provided by this form of justification of revisions of official orthodoxy was one of the major factors impeding the ready acceptance of Western ideas and values in modern China.

7. See the discussion in Frederic Wakeman, "The Price of Autonomy: Intellectuals in Ming and Ch'ing Politics," *Daedalus,* 1972, 101:35–70. See also Merle Goldman, *China's Intellectuals: Advise and Dissent* (Cambridge: Harvard University Press, 1981); Jerome Grieder, *Intellectuals and the State in Modern China* (New York: Free Press, 1981); C. Hamrin and T. Cheek, eds., *China's Establishment Intellectuals* (Armonk, N.Y.: M. E. Sharpe, 1986).

8. Theorists such as Max Weber and Jürgen Habermas have written about conditions in the West that helped to facilitate the rise of both civil society and modern democratic polities. They typically mention such preconditions as a well-developed rule of law, private property rights, a national market, an

open stratification system, urban autonomy, mass education, competing bases for power among elites, and a large middle class. Some of these conditions existed in late imperial China (an open stratification system, private property rights, a national market), but others did not.

9. For studies of these developments, see William Rowe, *Hankow: Conflict and Community in a Chinese City, 1796–1895* (Stanford: Stanford University Press, 1989); William Rowe, "The Public Sphere in Modern China," *Modern China,* July 1990, 16:309–329; David Strand, *Rickshaw Beijing: City People and Politics in the 1920s* (Berkeley: University of California Press, 1989); and David Strand, "Protest in Beijing: Civil Society and Public Sphere in China," *Problems of Communism,* May-June 1990:1–19.

10. The New Life movement Chiang launched during the 1930s was a clear if ineffective effort to draw on the Confucian tradition by announcing detailed rules for polite behavior and trying to popularize and enforce these at the grassroots. More blunt methods were also used in the effort to control society, with organizations and publications banned, disliked leaders and intellectuals arrested or assassinated, and individuals pressured to join associations controlled by the Nationalist party. Lest we forget, that party was transformed into a Leninist organization during the 1920s, when Sun Yatsen was still the party leader.

11. The best discussion of these developments is Andrew Nathan, *Chinese Democracy* (Berkeley: University of California Press, 1985).

12. See also the discussion in Whyte, "State and Society in the Mao Era."

13. The particular organizational means by which this was done have been described in my previous work and are summarized in the paper referred to above, "State and Society in the Mao Era." Suffice it to say here that in the Soviet Union the existence of more of a market for labor and consumer goods and a less vigorous effort to penetrate and control all grassroots groupings and indoctrinate their members left more leeway and autonomy for ordinary citizens than existed in China. See also the discussion in Andrew Walder, *Communist Neo-Traditionalism* (Berkeley: University of California Press, 1986).

14. Here when I refer to the Cultural Revolution, I mean the period of mass struggles that lasted from 1966 to 1969, rather than the entire period up until Mao's death in 1976.

15. The Cultural Revolution's transformation of youths from obedient and respectful students to bold challengers of authority figures is described in Ronald Montaperto, "From Revolutionary Successors to Revolutionaries: Chinese Students in the Early Stages of the Cultural Revolution," in R. Scalapino, ed., *Elites in the People's Republic of China* (Seattle: University of Washington Press, 1972).

16. Even many victims of the Cultural Revolution experienced extended periods of time in relative isolation—not self-chosen, to be sure—during which they had the opportunity to rethink their lives and to reflect on what was wrong with their society.

17. These events and the general tension leading up to Mao's death are described in a number of sources. See, for example, Roger Garside, *Coming Alive* (New York: McGraw-Hill, 1981).

18. Only the trends affecting urban China will be dealt with in any detail here. In rural China there are clear signs of more autonomous associational life reviving as well, but in distinctive forms, including secret societies, religious sects, and lineages, for example. Because these rural trends did not play a central role in the events of the Beijing Spring, I will not deal with them here.

19. The outstanding example of such social criticism is in the writings of Liu Binyan. See his translated collection, Perry Link, ed., *People or Monsters?* (Bloomington: Indiana University Press, 1983). Liu is, however, only the most visible of the many critics of the system who had their voices heard in the post-Mao period. For further examples, see the collection edited by Geremie Barmé and John Minford, *Seeds of Fire: Chinese Voices of Conscience* (New York: Hill and Wang, 1988). Of course, official tolerance of such criticism fluctuated: Liu was expelled from the party in 1987 and now resides in the United States, and many other critics were arrested after the June 1989 crackdown.

20. For those closely associated with the practices of the Mao era, these changes were obviously a source of anxiety and anger rather than relief.

21. It should be noted that the term *politics,* as used in such Mao-era slogans as "politics takes command," means something quite different from what it does to Americans. What is involved is not the competition of opposed groups and parties but concern for imposing the official political-moral orthodoxy on all groups and activities.

22. The West was not the only source of such images and critiques. Awareness of political changes in places like the Philippines and Taiwan had a dramatic impact on the thinking of critics and reformers, and dissident works from Eastern Europe enjoyed some circulation in China as well. For example, Milovan Djilas's classic work, *The New Class* (New York: Praeger, 1959), with its damning critique of party bureaucrats in Leninist systems as worse than the capitalist bourgeoisie, was translated and circulated internally. Eventually some intellectuals mounted comprehensive critiques of Chinese society and history and unfavorable comparisons with the West, as in the influential writings of Jin Guantao and the documentary television series he helped make in 1988, "River Elegy." See Daniel Kane, "Jin Guantao, Liu Qingfeng, and Their Historical Systems Evolutionary Theory," *Papers on Far Eastern History,* No. 39, March 1989, 45–73.

23. On these problems, see Stanley Rosen, "Political Education and Student Response: Some Background Factors Behind the 1989 Beijing Demonstrations," *Issues and Studies,* 1989, 25:12–39.

24. I have tried to spell out the nature and sources of these differing responses in more detail in Martin Whyte, "Social Sources of the Student Demonstrations," in Anthony Kane, ed., *China Briefing, 1990* (Boulder: Westview, 1990).

25. Luo Rongxing, Zhu Huaxin, and Cao Huanrong, "Different Interest Groups Under Socialism," *Beijing Review,* No. 48, November 30–December 6, 1987, 18.

26. *Renmin Ribao* (People's daily), April 17, 1989, 8; see also *Renmin Ribao,* May 31, 1989, 5. These references were brought to my attention by Susan Whiting.

27. *Renmin Ribao*, overseas edition, May 17, 1988, 2, cited in Munro "One-Minded Hierarchy."

28. See Liu Zhiguang and Wang Suli, "From 'Mass Society' to 'Civil Society,'" *Xinhua Wenzhai* (New China digest), No. 119, 1988, 9, cited in Strand, "Protest in Beijing."

29. See, for example, *Foreign Broadcast Information Service, Daily Report: People's Republic of China* (hereafter, *FBIS-Chi*), March 28, 1989, 34; April 6, 1989, 29.

30. See *FBIS-Chi,* December 7, 1989, 32.

31. See the discussion in Marc Abramson, "*Minban* Science Firms in China," *China Exchange News,* 1989, 17:12–17.

32. The degree of autonomy from the state of such organizations, in terms of both funds and administrative control, varied widely, and perhaps few could be regarded as entirely independent.

33. *China Daily* (Beijing), September 2, 1989, 4.

34. For a discussion of some of these activities, see Andrew Nathan, "Chinese Democracy in 1989: Continuity and Change," *Problems of Communism,* September-October 1989, 16–29.

35. These trends, and the increasing importance of Chinese public opinion in general, are documented in Stanley Rosen, "Public Opinion and Reform in the People's Republic of China," *Studies in Comparative Communism,* 1989, 22:153–170. The emergence of a public opinion that is constructed through popular debate and discussion rather than imposed by governmental decree and indoctrination is a key development stressed in writings on the rise of civil society in the West. See Jürgen Habermas, *The Structural Transformation of the Public Sphere* (Cambridge: MIT Press, 1989; originally published in German in 1962).

36. Of course one factor that sets the Chinese case apart from the Eastern European examples is that China is still overwhelmingly a peasant society. Perhaps this makes it more likely in China than in these other socialist states that an average member of the population will be untouched by civil society activity. As I mentioned in note 18 above, some autonomous associational activity was visible in rural China in the 1980s, but it took different forms from that erupting in the cities, and peasants and peasant organizations played very little role in the events of 1989.

37. One postcrackdown statement described the cultural influences that had to be rooted out as follows: "Some young students worshipped Sartre, Nietzsche, Freud, James, and even Hitler," *FBIS-Chi,* August 30, 1989, 14.

38. Rosen, "Public Opinion and Reform in the People's Republic of China," 169. I should note that Rosen offered this observation before the crackdown, and he might not want to associate himself with my view that much the same situation still holds in the wake of the crackdown.

5

Urban Industrial Workers: Some Observations on the 1980s

Andrew G. Walder

The connection between social structure and politics in the People's Republic of China has long been enigmatic. Consider what is probably the most firmly grounded comparative observation about postrevolution Chinese society: that it has one of the most thoroughly organized and effective systems of grassroots social control in the world. Under Mao, the state was willing and able to control the movements and monitor the behavior of individuals to an extent unparalleled even in the socialist regimes of Eastern Europe. Yet despite this impressive network of control, China has long stood out from the socialist regimes of Eastern Europe—with the one exception of Poland—in the regularity of large-scale popular protest, many instances of which have marked decisive turning points in the nation's political course. The many Red Guard and Revolutionary Rebel movements of the Cultural Revolution are only the most famous examples. They were preceded by the student and worker strikes of 1957, and they were succeeded by major protest movements and recurring strikes from 1974 through 1976, the Democracy Wall movements in Beijing and elsewhere in 1978 and 1979, the national wave of student protests of 1986–1987, and of course the popular protests in Beijing and scores of other cities from April through June 1989. How could a society so minutely organized and monitored at so many critical historical junctures be so active and contentious?

This paradox is partly explained by another distinctive feature of Chinese politics: China's leadership factions have turned regularly to popular protest as a resource in their internal conflict and competition. This fact separates China's recent political history from that of Poland, where recurrent worker and student unrest was neither inspired nor manipulated from the top, and from the rest of Eastern Europe, where for thirty years after the mid-1950s, large-scale protest was extremely rare. In the Hundred Flowers period, the Cultural Revolution, the 1974–1975 protests (in Guangzhou, Hangzhou, and elsewhere), and the Democracy Wall movement of 1978–1979, elite factions at either the local or national level directly instigated and manipulated or gave tacit encouragement and support to protests. China, in other words, has been both a tightly regimented and a turbulent society for decades, in large part because mass protest has been an important resource for elite factions in their contests for power and influence.

Yet another paradox presents itself now, as a new pattern of popular protest has emerged. The 1980s have been the most prosperous period in China's postrevolutionary history. For most of the decade, China far outpaced its Eastern European counterparts in economic reform and income growth. China has not suffered from the severe stagnation and decline that characterized the 1980s in Eastern Europe and eventually contributed to the great political unraveling now under way. It has been among the most economically dynamic nations in the world. Yet serious challenges from below have shown increasing independence and persistence throughout the decade. For the first time in PRC history, China's aging leadership felt impelled in 1989 to resort to brutal military force to quell popular protest in its capital. In so doing, they narrowly averted the fate of their counterparts throughout Eastern Europe. If the nation was in the midst of a period of dynamic economic growth and prosperity, why has the leadership, and perhaps even the political system itself, been shaken to its very foundations?

This second paradox is not dispelled by the resolution I offered for the first. China in the 1980s has not been the same strictly regimented society of the 1950s, 1960s, and 1970s. Political relaxation and economic reforms greatly weakened the institutions of control used so effectively in past decades. And although the protests of 1989 received significant support and encouragement from some members of the leadership and key organs of the state apparatus, they were neither inspired nor manipulated by elites. Involving millions of people in over eighty cities and towns, the protests of 1989—and the student protests of 1986 that preceded them—were something new on the Chinese political scene: massive, independent, popular protests. The old mold of regimentation and elite-sponsored turbulence has been broken, and Chinese politics appears to have entered a new era. Why?

In this chapter, I discuss one of the more obscure aspects of this question: the causes and meaning of the sudden mobilization of ordinary workers into protest activities in mid-1989. First, I consider the evidence about wages and inflation in the 1980s: How well, or how poorly, did

TABLE 5.1 Official Cost-of-Living Index for Urban Employees, 1978-1988

Year	Annual Increase (%)	Cumulative Index (1978=100)
1978	0.7	100.0
1979	1.9	101.9
1980	7.5	109.5
1981	2.5	112.3
1982	2.0	114.6
1983	2.0	116.9
1984	2.7	120.0
1985	11.9	134.3
1986	7.0	143.7
1987	8.8	156.4
1988	20.7	185.7

Source: *Zhongguo tongji nianjian 1989* [Chinese Statistical Yearbook, 1989] pp. 687-688.

urban workers fare in the past decade? Second, I characterize what is known about the evolution of intrafactory authority and conflict since the Mao era: What changes in factory life during the era of reform might have served to make workers more contentious? And, finally, I offer some preliminary observations about the characteristic style of collective worker action in May 1989 and speculate about its implications for the future.

Macroeconomics: Wages, Inflation, and Living Standards

The 1980s were an era of rapid income growth and rising standards of living in Chinese cities. Average nominal wages almost tripled, and the ownership of many consumer items barely available ten years earlier became widespread. Yet as virtually every commentator on the 1989 protests has observed, the late 1980s also saw China's highest rates of price inflation since the last years of Nationalist rule after World War II. To what extent has inflation eaten into the striking gains of past years, and how might it have affected workers' politics?

We have little alternative than to work with official price indexes, which many economists argue systematically underestimate true rates of inflation. We should therefore view any analysis based on them as defining a conservative lower boundary. According to these official figures, inflation has been a fact of life for most of the reform era, but it has become a more serious and sustained problem since 1985 (see Table 5.1). From 1978 to 1984, inflation averaged only 2.8 percent a year. From 1985 to 1988, however, the average rate jumped to 12

TABLE 5.2 Wage Indexes for Urban Employees, 1978-1988

	Average Annual Wage			
Years	State Sector (Nominal)	State Sector (1978 yuan)	Collective Sector (Nominal)	Collective Sector (1978 yuan)
1978	644	644	506	506
1979	705	692	542	532
1980	803	733	623	569
1981	812	723	642	572
1982	836	729	671	586
1983	865	740	698	597
1984	1,034	862	811	676
1985	1,213	903	967	720
1986	1,414	984	1,092	760
1987	1,546	988	1,207	772
1988	1,853	982	1,426	756

Source: *Zhongguo tongji nianjian 1989* [Chinese Statistical Yearbook, 1989] p. 138.

percent.[1] Officially, consumer prices for urban employees increased by around 90 percent in the decade, most of this coming in the last few years.

These price rises have greatly moderated the spiraling average incomes of the urban worker (see Table 5.2). Instead of almost tripling, as they did in nominal terms for both state- and collective-sector employees, in real terms average incomes rose only some 50 percent in both sectors. Note, further, that all of this increase occurred before 1986. In both state and collective sectors, average wages stopped growing in that year. By the beginning of 1989, in other words, worker incomes had not grown in real terms for three years, according to official figures. If we assume that official figures understate inflation, these years clearly were ones of declining real income.

In addition to possibly understating inflation, aggregate wage statistics of the variety we have just employed may also be a flawed indicator of incomes as individual workers experience them. Aggregate wages reflect large-scale retirements from and entries into the labor force and the creation of new enterprises in rapidly developing regions of the country, and they may merge wide regional and sectoral wage disparities. It would be more relevant to the questions before us to trace a representative sample of individuals through time and measure changes in their incomes, adjusted for inflation.

We do have such data for a random sample of 740 employees in the nine urban districts of Tianjin (see Table 5.3). This is a local sample, by no means representative of urban China as a whole, but it is perhaps

TABLE 5.3 Wage Trends, 1976-1986: Sample of Tianjin Wage Earners

	Average Monthly Wage		
	1976	1986 (1976 yuan)	Percent Change
Blue-Collar Manual Workers (N=381)			
Salary	46.62	40.32	-13.5
Bonus	4.68	13.39	+186.1
Total Income	52.42	55.82	+6.5
Entire Sample (N=740)			
Salary	48.29	42.10	-12.8
Bonus	4.49	13.22	+ 194.4
Total Income	53.86	57.47	+6.7

Source: Survey of 1,011 urban households conducted in cooperation with the Institute of Sociology, Tianjin Academy of Social Sciences. See Andrew G. Walder, et al., "The 1986 Survey of Work and Social Life in Tianjin, China: Aims, Methods, and Documentation." Working Paper No. 25, Center for Research on Politics and Social Organization, Harvard University Department of Sociology, 1989.

indicative of the experience of workers in some of China's larger industrial cities.[2] These data offer us a significantly different perspective on wage trends. When viewed in this way, nominal wage increases are still large, but they barely outpace the rate of inflation for the entire decade after 1976—and this survey took place before the inflation became most serious. The experience of blue-collar workers is virtually the same as that of all urban employees: Instead of a 50 percent increase, real incomes rose by only 6 to 7 percent, less than 1 percent a year.

Whether we are speaking of aggregate official data or local sample surveys, we have so far only talked about average real wages. Average figures, however, may lead us to forget that there are wide variations around the mean. If, as both the Tianjin and national data suggest, there is at best a small and gradual increase in average real wages before the big inflation of 1985–1988, then it is likely that the wages of a large minority of urban workers were already falling behind the (official) rate of inflation by 1985. (Of our 1986 Tianjin respondents, 40.4 percent had lower real wages than in 1976.) These people would have suffered very serious declines in their purchasing power after 1986.

To understand the impact of inflation upon Chinese families and upon worker mentality, we need to recall that even after a decade of reform, some 59 percent of the average family budget is used to purchase food alone (52 percent in our Tianjin survey).[3] The urban worker therefore perceives inflation as a threat to subsistence, not simply as a reason for postponing the purchase of consumer durables. Diets in urban China have improved considerably since the 1970s. Families consume much more chicken, fish, eggs, and a variety of other nonstaple foods that were extremely scarce and rationed before the reforms. But these are precisely the foodstuffs whose prices have increased most rapidly, especially on the free markets, which have become an important source of supply. When the majority of family expenditures are for food, severe inflation immediately makes it much more difficult to buy the kinds of foods to which urban citizens became accustomed in the 1980s, and this can lead readily to a feeling that living standards are falling.

One area in which there has been striking and irreversible improvement in living standards, however, is in the quality and quantity of consumer items in urban households. In the late 1970s, the Chinese worker aspired to own a wristwatch, a foot-powered sewing machine, a name-brand bicycle, and a transistor radio. By the mid-1980s, such items were commonplace, and the consumer could realistically hope to own a color television (perhaps even an imported or foreign coproduced one), a washing machine, a refrigerator, or a tape recorder or stereo with AM, FM, and shortwave reception. In 1987 as compared to 1978, twelve times as many people owned electric fans, thirty-eight times as many had television sets, 131 times as many had refrigerators, and the number of washing machines skyrocketed from around 1,000 to 5.7 million.[4] Urban workers thus had good reason for their rising consumer aspirations. This heightened expectation, however, was frustrated in the latter 1980s for those families suffering the worst effects of inflation.

There were many indications of widespread anxiety and discontent over living standards in the years preceding the 1989 upheaval. A long series of public opinion polls indicated very clearly that disaffection over price rises had come to dominate the public consciousness. A national sample in 1986, for example, found that inflation was second only to official corruption as the matter about which citizens were most dissatisfied (and it finished well ahead of the third).[5] An internal Tianjin government survey in fall 1987 found that 98 percent of the households were worried about inflation more than any other issue and that almost 80 percent of the respondents considered their income unsatisfactory (26 percent) or barely adequate (52 percent).[6] Similarly, a large 1988 survey by the Sociology Institute of the Chinese Academy of Social Sciences (CASS) and the State Statistical Bureau found inflation to be by far the most serious problem in people's social lives, with 94 percent of respondents mentioning it.[7] Against this backdrop, rumors about impending price reforms led to runs on banks and panic purchasing of consumer items in many cities during the latter half of 1988.

Purchasing power and commodity ownership are important features of the reform era in the minds of workers, but housing conditions continue to be a source of frustration for urban families. Even though as much new housing was built in the 1980s as in the previous three decades of the People's Republic, urban families in 1988 occupied a national average of only 8.8 square meters per person—well above the 4.2 meters of 1978 but still very crowded and difficult to obtain.[8] Overcrowding is most serious in the large industrial cities. In Tianjin in 1986, respondents' families lived in an average of only 5.4 square meters, 2.4 persons per room. Only 15 percent were satisfied with their current housing, and 52 percent were dissatisfied (the rest were in-between); 35 percent said that they had no hope of getting a larger apartment. Although this situation has not worsened because of inflation, it certainly is a source of chronic disaffection.

These macroeconomic data suggest that a large number of urban workers had ample reason to judge the fruits of reform with a critical eye. The material lives of urban wage earners have improved strikingly in the 1980s, but the real incomes of a large minority of the population began to suffer serious declines in the last half of the decade, and inflation became a major source of concern for all. Housing remained a source of dissatisfaction. Although it is true, as many Chinese and foreign observers have noted, that the aspirations of ordinary citizens raced far ahead of their realization, we should by no means underestimate the limits of progress in the 1980s or the serious impact of inflation.

Macroeconomic indicators, however, do not tell us the whole story. And "dissatisfaction" in the abstract cannot really account for the response of workers to the student movement, support of which was the focal point for worker political activity. The apparent post-1985 declines in real income in China, after all, were not nearly as severe or prolonged as those experienced in Poland and Hungary over the past decade. And if the rising intensity of dissatisfaction and frustration is thought to be responsible for worker activism, it is curious that before June 3 they engaged in so little violence. Apparently only in Xi'an, Changsha, and Chengdu did rioting accompany political protest, and looting of shops was not a common objective of participants. Especially in Beijing and Shanghai, the two cases documented most extensively in the media, workers acted primarily to protect student protesters from the police or joined in peaceful marches for greater "democracy" themselves. How, then, do macroeconomic conditions affect workers' political perceptions, and, in particular, how do they relate to a demand for "democracy"? Some would prefer to point to frustrated expectations as a direct cause of worker protest; I believe, however, that qualitative changes in workers' lives and in their political perceptions went hand in hand with these macroeconomic conditions to bring about the political response of 1989.

Microsociology: Life in the Factory

The 1980s have not brought dramatic changes in factory life or labor relations in state and large collective enterprises. Workplaces still provide a wide array of benefits for their employees, and in fact many enterprises are probably more active now in giving employees benefits than they were before the reforms. Despite efforts to make it easier for managers to fire workers and despite the opening of alternative careers in the small but thriving urban private sector, permanent employment is still an entrenched reality, and the urban labor market long urged by some reformers has so far not come to pass. Even with the relaxation of political indoctrination and coercion, there have emerged no institutional means to represent workers' interests within the firm, and all indications are that the workers' congresses revived in the early 1980s are just as ineffective and ritualistic as they were before the Cultural Revolution.

Yet factory life and labor relations have by no means remained the same. There have been no decisive changes in the employment relationship or in institutions of governance, but it appears that subtle yet important changes have taken place within the old frameworks. We know far too little about these changes, and we would need to complete sustained field or interview research to begin fully to understand them. We may nonetheless speculate, largely on a view from the outside, about the ways these changes have served to alter workers' mentalities and helped drive them into the streets in support of student protestors.

The first such change is greatly increased managerial responsibility for the income and welfare of employees, as symbolized by the drastically altered composition of the wage bill. Table 5.3 shows the greatly increased proportion of the wage bill composed of bonuses—from virtual nonexistence to some 23 percent of the 1986 Tianjin sample, and Table 5.4 indicates some 29 percent in official national figures for 1988. As the basic salary has shrunk in real terms, bonuses have loomed very large as a determinant of individual welfare in an inflationary era. These bonuses, and to a considerable extent the basic salary (which now often floats above state scales in more profitable firms), are determined by the prosperity of the enterprise and by the willingness of managers to commit retained funds to worker income. The reforms, in other words, have given managers the ability directly to affect the incomes and livelihoods of workers, whereas in the 1970s managers were largely passive implementers of rigid state wage policies.

TABLE 5.4 Composition of Wage Bill in State Sector, 1978 and 1988

	Percentage of National Wage Bill	
Type of Compensation	1978	1988
Base salary or hourly wage	85.0	49.0
Piece rate and quota bonus	0.9	11.7
Other bonuses	2.3	17.2
Subsidies	6.5	21.4
Overtime pay	2.0	1.9
Other	3.4	1.1

Source: *Zhongguo tongji nianjian 1989* [Chinese Statistical Yearbook, 1989] p. 133.

Because managers were given the ability to influence worker livelihood directly, and because such large bonus incomes have a big impact upon pay levels, one would have predicted greatly increased intrafactory conflict over wage matters. This in fact did occur in the immediate post-Mao period, as initial efforts to evaluate workers for wage raises and to differentiate bonuses between and within workshops were met with a paralyzing wave of discord and slowdowns.[9] Yet it now appears that this period of conflict led managers and workers to a provisional accommodation in which managers sought to preserve workshop harmony by reducing variation in bonuses between workers and from month to month and tried to motivate workers by ensuring a smooth and stable rise in income and benefits.[10] In this new factory paternalism, managers were held directly responsible for worker livelihood, and they perceived strong pressures, especially in this new inflationary, consumer-oriented era, to improve the livelihood of their employees.[11] We should not miss the important implication of this subtle change in factory life. In the Mao era, the key issue in labor relations was the implementation of, and compliance with, political campaigns and rigid wage policy imposed from above. In the Deng era, the key issue in labor relations has become income and benefits, and this in an era of inflation and greatly expanded consumer expectations.

A second important change has been the emergence of wide variations in income, not within factories but among factories and among different segments of the labor force. It is of course widely known that the incomes of workers in the urban private sector, and of suburban peasant entrepreneurs, are usually many times the average of the best-paid state-sector worker. Wages in foreign enterprises, joint ventures, and joint state-private enterprises are also markedly higher than in state and collective firms.[12] The average worker is acutely aware of these differences, especially because by the late 1980s most workers probably knew personally a former co-worker who had begun to reap an astounding income in the private sector. The wealth of the private entrepreneurs appears to be resented for a number of reasons, even if the vast majority of workers still appear unwilling to leave their secure state jobs, with their benefits and pensions.[13] State workers quite rightly hesitate to risk a private venture because they rarely have the skills, capital, or connections necessary to be successful. Industrial skills do not usually translate readily to entrepreneurial activity. Few workers have either enough personal savings to serve as start-up capital or the opportunity to borrow it. Few workers have kinship or other connections to officials in local government or enterprises that might afford them start-up capital, protection from licensing and taxation agencies, secure sources of supply, or other advantages that are often necessary. And few workers have the audacity to create such connections with a series of bribes. As a result, many workers now appear to feel that the reforms have provided highly unequal opportunities. While they are stuck in dead-end jobs and inflation-ravaged state salaries, those with connections and capital or those who are dishonest are the ones who reap the greatest wealth.[14]

A third important change has been the emergence of job tenure as an issue in factory life. Open labor markets are still tightly restricted to small sectors of the urban economy, and managers still find it difficult to routinely lay off or fire workers, yet enough flexibility and uncertainty have been introduced to make this a cause of anxiety and resentment among some workers. One new development has been the widespread creation of "service companies" or related organizations within state enterprises. These service companies—restaurants, guest houses, nanny referral services—were originally branches designed to provide employment for children of employees and to earn extra money for factories. In some places they have afforded managers a hidden form of firing or layoffs. Workers who become superfluous or who earn the ire of their supervisors may be transferred to these companies at full salary but without the bonus that normally composes up to 30 or 40 percent of total income. Some of these service companies are empowered to send workers home and pay only one-half or three-fourths of the basic salary if there is not enough work. There are also worries introduced by the formal right not to rehire those workers hired on contracts during the 1980s and the occasional outright layoffs of workers in local campaigns to reduce overstaffing. And this flexibility goes the other way: As some workers have become anxious about the possibility of losing their current jobs, others have become frustrated by their inability to take advantage of new opportunities outside the firm.

A fourth important change has been the decline of the party's claim to omnipotence and in its imposing role in factory politics. As the national party, along with its continually trumpeted ideological claims and campaigns, has withdrawn from factory life, factory leaders have lost the aura of intimidating rectitude they previously had as direct representatives of a virtuous and correct political line at the party center. Factory officials now represent themselves and their factories and to some extent are expected to guard the interests of their employees. Yet in this new situation many factory officials continue to arrogate privileges to themselves and their families. The preferential distribution of apartments to cadres and especially their relatives and friends has been a major source of discontent within factories, but there is also resentment over large "wage supplements" given openly to cadres, virtual "no-show" jobs at high pay given to spouses or other relatives, and other advantages. Although it is certainly true that factory officials enjoyed privileges in the Mao era, in the Deng era, with the desanctification of factory authority, such privileges are much more likely to appear illegitimate and provoke resentment. Cadres—at least the "bad" ones that unfortunately appear to exist in so many work units—are seen increasingly as corrupt and self-serving, ensuring that they benefit preferentially in the reforms, whereas workers struggle with the effects of inflation and overcrowded housing.

A final important factor is a change that has not occurred. All of the changes I have just described—increasing responsibility of managers for employee welfare and rising pressures for improvements, increased gaps between labor-force segments that create frictions among permanent state and collective workers, greater salience of job tenure as an issue of contention and concern, and the decline of ideologically sanctioned authority along with continued cadre privilege and corruption—all point to a crying need for new institutionalized means of negotiation, interest representation, and dispute resolution. Yet the Deng reforms have failed utterly to institute new formal means of negotiation. As a result, individual workers who challenge official malfeasance are highly vulnerable to retaliation by the named officials—no new housing or a shift to low-paid work in a "service company." Collective pressures are still brought to bear with the old tools of the late Mao era: soldiering, deliberate breaking or loss of machines and tools, grumbling, gossip, cursing. There is no reliable recourse for workers angered by the award of a coveted apartment to the son of a party secretary, even though that anger may slow production down for over a week. The resentments stay hidden and fester, the workers still locked in the factory, unable to affect their own lives and, for the most part, unable to leave.

This is the grassroots setting that helps us understand how inflation for the first time helped stimulate worker participation in prodemocracy protests. Inflation did not simply lead to widespread dissatisfaction, which in turn translated directly into sympathy for student demonstrators. It was experienced within workplaces, into which new demands and sources of contention were injected as the old means of intimidating workers and sanctifying cadre actions eroded. Yet no new means of interest representation or negotiation arose. Chinese factories are still places where dissatisfaction is expressed indirectly, where individual workers are vulnerable to victimization by cadres with ill will, and where there is continual factional competition between cadres the workers consider "good" and those they consider "bad." Against the backdrop of falling real wages, resentment of the illegitimate advantages of cadres, and political helplessness within the firm, student calls for democracy spoke directly to workers' immediate situation.

Workers' Collective Action in 1989

Workers did not participate in the 1989 demonstrations in a highly organized or particularly class-conscious way. Especially in the city of Beijing, they took part largely as citizens who had chosen to involve themselves in the national political drama unfolding in Tiananmen Square. Although this activity did not come close to realizing the leadership nightmare of the Deng era—a Chinese Solidarity movement—it certainly raised the specter of one, had an enormous impact upon the democracy movement itself, and will have reverberations in Chinese politics into the twenty-first century, even if such activism does not recur.

Workers participated in the Beijing protests in three distinct ways. Each represented a significant departure from past patterns of worker collective action. In the least organized means of participation—the street pattern—workers bolstered the student protests as bystanders and spontaneous participants. In the second, more organized form—the work-unit pattern—delegations of workers and sometimes cadres from named state enterprises marched in street demonstrations in support of the students. And in the third—the insurgent pattern—an autonomous workers' organization declared its existence at the very outset of the student movement, issued proclamations and handbills, and established an important presence in the square for over two weeks.

The Street Pattern

At the outset of and throughout the student movement, workers, along with other ordinary citizens, played an important role in the streets as sympathetic bystanders, appreciative audiences, and protective shields. There was no apparent coordination of their activities, but throngs of citizens readily identifiable as blue-collar workers lined the streets during the crucial demonstrations of April 27 and May 4, cheering on the student marchers, offering money and refreshments, and, most significantly, pushing aside police and army barriers, allowing the protesters to march back and forth across the city and into the square. Later, these throngs of workers would join alongside the student marchers or trail behind them. As the square became occupied continuously in mid-May, workers on their way to or from their jobs formed appreciative audiences for speeches. After the declaration of martial law, they played a key role in blocking military vehicles. And of course after the massacre began in the evening of June 3, workers took part in the violent resistance to the military in Beijing and elsewhere.

In none of this activity were blue-collar workers clearly distinguishable from other urban citizens, nor did they organize themselves to represent their special interests. Nonetheless, their evident support for the protesters in the streets represents a new departure for post-1949 Chinese politics. Workers were amply represented in Tiananmen Square in April 1976, but that was a smaller and more short-lived affair. Workers participated individually in the Democracy Wall movement of 1978–1979, but these were a small and rather special collection of individuals who had critical political views and sought to circulate them. Worker support for similar student processions throughout the country at the very end of 1986 certainly never reached the scope it did in 1989. The sheer numbers that turned out on the streets, perhaps especially because they were unorganized, have undoubtedly left an indelible mark upon the consciousness of all Chinese leaders, no matter their faction.

The Work-Unit Pattern

A second pattern of participation was centered on state-owned factories. This pattern, however, was short-lived: It began with the even-handed reporting of student protest in early May, rose to a climax as several national newspapers and the central television station sought to mobilize pressure for open negotiations with the student associations, and ended with the declaration of martial law.[15]

As student demands received increasing national and local publicity, many workers, often joined by factory cadres, began to discuss the student protests openly and sympathetically. This was commonly followed by an effort to collect donations for the students and then by the organization of a delegation to march to the square, present the donations, and express the workers' sympathy and support. Workers used factory materials to make posters and banners and drove their delegations to the city center in factory trucks. Photographs of the huge street processions of mid-May show that large numbers of work units sent delegations who openly proclaimed their identity.

This pattern apparently depended both on the perception communicated by the mass media that at least a part of the national leadership encouraged support for the students and on a corresponding sympathy, or caution, on the part of factory cadres. There are known instances in which factory cadres encouraged or personally led large delegations to the square. The most common response, however, appears to have been a cautious noncommittal attitude on the part of factory officials, whether they sympathized with or opposed the democracy protests. Unsure in mid-May which leadership faction would ultimately win and long schooled in the art of political survival, factory cadres knew that to encourage delegations openly might cause trouble for them if the movement were ultimately suppressed and branded counterrevolutionary. By the same token, if they suppressed worker sympathy and victimized politically active workers, they might be called to account later for putting down a genuine people's movement. The cadres' noncommittal response allowed large numbers of delegations to march to the square; as soon as the imposition of martial law made it clear which way factory cadres were to lean, these organized processions stopped.

What is so striking about this pattern of protest is that it is precisely the work unit that the Chinese polity has heretofore relied upon to exercise political control. Yet now we find that work units make up organizing points for protest and resistance. A distinctive Chinese work-unit pattern of protest has come to mirror the distinctive Chinese pattern of work-unit control. This experience is not likely to be forgotten quickly by urban workers, and Chinese work-unit organization appears to facilitate it. All that is apparently required to give it free rein is a situation of political uncertainty at the center that disorients local cadres, coupled with a public protest or political event to stimulate worker activity. It is not difficult to imagine these conditions being repeated in the coming final transition from gerontocratic rule.

The Insurgent Pattern

The 1989 protests in Beijing, and reportedly in some other cities, saw what is apparently the first public attempts since the 1950s to organize an independent association of industrial workers. The Beijing Autonomous Workers' Association, known commonly as Gongzilian,[16] sought to represent workers' specific interests, in addition to expressing support for the democracy movement. Among their demands were higher wages, control of inflation, the right freely to choose places of work, and the right to be represented by genuine union organizations. One very important aspect of this group's outlook is that it recognized the dangers of being played off by one leadership faction against another. Gongzilian's leaders were from the outset critical of the party leadership as a whole, reformers and conservatives alike. Zhao Ziyang, the bourgeois golf enthusiast with corrupt sons, was treated no more sympathetically in their literature than Deng Xiaoping, the doddering elder, or Li Peng, the incompetent toady. Their statements reflected an understanding that neither reformers nor prodemocracy students would in the end speak for workers' interests—workers would finally have to take up the task of speaking for themselves. This distinctively anti-elitist, trade union orientation is significant not only because it is new but because it is a clear challenge to both the conservative party elders as well as the reformers who engineered the economic changes of the 1980s. Perhaps most significant is that Gongzilian became most active in the period after the declaration of martial law.

One could easily imagine that such a message, and the promise of formal factory representation and negotiation, would have broad appeal among state- and collective-sector workers. Although Gongzilian members claim to have signed up around 20,000 new recruits in the square during the last days of May, the group never attempted to organize places of work. The group had a continuous presence on the square from mid-May on. It had a broadcasting station, a small headquarters, organized security teams, a logistics department, and rudimentary printing operations. Its leaders made impassioned speeches in the square, and it posted proclamations, distributed handbills, and broadcast news and statements provided by ordinary citizens in the square from midmorning until evening. In an action that finally earned it widespread publicity abroad, when some of its leaders were arrested near the end of May, Gongzilian mobilized for a large protest rally outside the city government offices and the public security bureau and eventually secured the release of its members. But it had no grassroots organizations inside factories, and its calls for a general strike after the military began shooting civilians on June 3 went unheeded. We can only speculate how far the organization would have developed had it not been crushed by armed force. Its mentality and activities, no doubt extremely alarming to party leaders—and not only the original hard-liners—may well have been a factor in the decision to exterminate public opposition by any means.

The Future

Despite the bloody suppression of the movement, workers' active involvement in the democracy protests of 1989 will reverberate through the Chinese political system for some time to come. However unorganized and dependent upon openings created by elite dissensus and government paralysis, workers for the first time played a major role in independent street protests. More ominously, some workers for the first time made highly visible steps toward the creation of a workers' insurgency that spoke not for or against elite factions but on behalf of workers as a class. The workers' evidently widespread dissatisfaction with the recent leadership of the Communist party and the strong streak of anti-elitism displayed by many may serve to paralyze future party leaders of whatever faction, when and if future economic reforms are contemplated.

If economic reform is some day to continue, the currently massive subsidies of urban food consumption and housing will need to be phased out, a labor market capable of transferring labor to the most dynamic sectors of the economy will have to be created, and unprofitable firms will begin to close or cut back their work forces at a pace far greater than we have seen so far. All of these changes, of course, will also entail more serious threats to worker job security and living standards. Yet the reservoir of support that reformers had hoped would be created by rising living standards in the 1980s clearly was not there even before June 4. After witnessing worker activism in spring 1989, even the most ardent future reformer will be very hesitant to introduce more far-reaching economic changes. Elite memories of 1989—on both sides of the political divide—will likely induce policy paralysis in this area for years to come.

Observers often ask whether industrial workers in Communist regimes are proreform or are more conservative in their political orientations. In China the Deng era showed the potential of economic reform and international openness for speeding economic growth and living standards, but inflation served to take away many of these gains, and future reforms promised to threaten workers' vested interests. Workers' mass reaction to the student democracy movement, however, suggests a new way of posing the question. For in all three of their patterns of activity, workers were neither proreform nor antireform. They exhibited a clear frustration that the opportunities for decisive advancement were available only to other segments of Chinese society, and they exhibited a clear anger toward party officialdom from top to bottom for arrogating so many of the opportunities for advancement for themselves, their families, and friends. But it is evident that workers fully appreciate the opportunities for greatly enhanced living standards that only a policy of reform and openness can promise. Workers, in other words, are very much for the opportunities promised by reform but are very much against the institutional conditions that illegitimately, in their view, give those opportunities almost exclusively to other groups and leave workers unprotected against the ravages of inflation.

Perhaps more than the participation of any other group, the workers' responses to the democracy movement underscore the political limits of the Deng reforms. Baldly put, the leadership of the Communist party no longer enjoys the popular trust and support among workers necessary to continue economic reform or survive a genuine opening up of the Chinese political process. This problem is by no means limited to the post-Tiananmen leadership: The protests of April to June 1989 did not make careful distinctions among party leaders. The "lesson" of 1989 may well enhance the attractiveness of an authoritarian solution among reform-minded leaders and many of their intellectual advisers, at least with regard to blue-collar workers. But it is hard to imagine that China can extract itself from its current impasse without decisive changes in its institutions of grassroots rule. For these institutions, which provide a framework for corruption and privilege and which deny open negotiation of workers' claims, have derailed the economic reforms and have deeply eroded popular acceptance of Communist party rule.

Notes

1. Nicholas Lardy, "Consumption and Living Standards in China, 1978–83," *China Quarterly* 100 (December 1984):849–865.

2. Of a total sample of 1,011 urban workers, 740 had jobs in 1976 and were not retired in 1986. We gathered information about current incomes and those in 1976, the last year of the long wage freeze of the Mao era. We adjusted reported 1986 incomes by official national price indexes in order to obtain the real incomes reported in Table 5.3. Note that price inflation in Tianjin may have varied from the national average.

3. Guojia tongji ju, *Zhongguo tongji nianjian 1989* (Chinese statistical yearbook, 1989) (Beijing: Zhongguo Tongji Chubanshe, 1989), 727.

4. Guojia tongji ju, *Zhongguo tongji nianjian 1988* (Chinese statistical yearbook, 1988) (Beijing: Zhongguo Tongji Chubanshe, 1988), 804.

5. "Gaige de shehui huanjing: bianqian yu xuanze" (The social environment of reform: changes and choices), *Jingji Yanjiu* 12 (1987):56–62, at p. 57, which reports the results of a large study by the Social Research Office of the Institute for the Reform of the Economic Structure.

6. Wang Hui, "Municipal Administration in China and Sociological Studies" (unpublished; courtesy of the author, who is president of the Tianjin Academy of Social Sciences).

7. Zhu Qingfang, "Yi jiu ba ba nian dalu chengshi zhigong xintai lu" (The state of mind of mainland urban workers in 1988), *Liaowang* (Outlook, overseas edition) 2 (1989):7–8, at p. 7.

8. *Zhongguo tongji nianjian 1989,* 719.

9. Susan L. Shirk, "Recent Chinese Labour Policies and the Transformation of Industrial Organization in China," *China Quarterly* 88 (December 1981):575–593; and Andrew G. Walder, "Wage Reform and the Web of Factory Interests," *China Quarterly* 109 (March 1987):22–41.

10. Walder, "Wage Reform and the Web of Factory Interests."

11. Andrew G. Walder, "Factory and Manager in an Era of Reform," *China Quarterly* 118 (June 1989):242–264.

12. For example, in 1988 the average annual wage in ownership forms other than the state and collective sectors (excluding private entrepreneurs) was 2,382 yuan, and in joint state-private enterprises 3,229 yuan, compared to a national average of 1,747 yuan. *Zhongguo tongji nianjian 1989,* 139, 143, 146, and 149.

13. "Gaige de shehui huanjing," 61, reports that 83 percent of the respondents desired work in the state sector.

14. Ibid., 60–62, documents the dissatisfactions traceable to inequality of opportunity.

15. Andrew G. Walder, "The Political Sociology of the Beijing Upheaval of 1989," *Problems of Communism* 38:5 (September-October 1989):30–40.

16. The group underwent a couple of name changes from April through early June. It was originally called Beijing Gongren Lianhe Hui, then Beijing Gongren Zizhi Hui, and finally, in late May 1989, Shoudu Gongren Zizhi Lianhe Hui.

6

Urban Entrepreneurs and the State: The Merger of State and Society

Dorothy J. Solinger

Decomposition of the Elite Mobility Channel and Interpenetration of Bureaucrat and Merchant

Urban economic reform in China has not yet led to the emergence of what is popularly labeled "civil society"[1] among the business class. Nor has it hewed out any sharp and novel borderline between the state and a distinctive sphere of society among its subjects in this particular realm. No "repluralization"[2] can be said to have issued from some genuine formation of a private realm truly separate from the still enveloping public one for those who make their lives in the marketplace. Instead, the essential economic monolith of the old party-state now shapes official and merchant alike; both have become dependent, mutually interpenetrated semiclasses, even as both share a new kind of dependence on the state. As a Chinese commentator described the situation:

> China's private economy has developed . . . during the transformation from a product economy of unitary composition into a planned commodity economy of coexisting multiple economic sectors. . . . Because the strong socialist public sector occupies the dominant place in the national economy, the private sector developing in this situation cannot but be related to, as well as influenced and restricted by, the public sector. . . . Hence it must be dependent on the socialist public economy and at the same time supplement it.[3]

Thus it is yet difficult to speak of any real "autonomy" of social forces from the state in China, in contrast to Eastern Europe,[4] at least where what might be called the bourgeoisie is concerned.[5]

This joint dependence—on the state and on each other—fosters collaboration in some instances but also intense competition in many others, as merchant and bureaucrat both battle over but at times jointly participate in the expansion of a single pot of state resources, state-owned supply channels, and state-dominated sales outlets.[6] The complexity of the concept of entrepreneur and its applicability to a range of actors within what is typically termed the public sector as well as within the new, so-called private sphere in the cities exemplify this pattern.

Because there are no clear indications of where this historical formation is heading in the short run, any assumption that we are witnessing an ultimately predictable transition from a planned to a market economy may skew the analysis away from considering this particular period as sui generis and as potentially quite protracted. It is neither plan nor market, although it partakes of both. Consequently, agents of the plan and practitioners in the market are, respectively, no longer fully bureaucrats nor yet true merchants operating autonomously.

The most dominant and determining characteristic of this stage is what may by this point be termed a prolonged decomposition of the hereditary monolithic elite mobility channel once constructed by the party-state at its peak. Within that totalistic channel, all commercial and industrial social forces were steered toward and caught within the all-encompassing net of orthodox associations. This envelopment was first accomplished for the business class through the socialist transformation of the mid-1950s, and soon thereafter reaffirmed by the assimilation of that class into such institutions as the *danwei* and the trade union federation (for the lesser fry) and the Chinese People's Political Consultative Congress and its associated All-China Federation of Industry and Commerce and "democratic parties" (for the bigger fish). Positioned atop the rigid hierarchy and holding it firmly together was the mighty *nomenklatura.*

Ironically, however, the party-state's imposition of an organizational and leadership framework that obliterated the operational and political autonomy of once private social formations actually *emphasized* rather than erased or made more porous the boundary[7] between what may be called state and society in the urban business world. In fact, despite the single route to power, influence, and status for the elite under the socialist system, and regardless of the absorption of the business sector into elite-contoured and -commanded collectivities, there was a *sharper* demarcation between state and urban society (understood as what is commonly called the private sector, the capitalist class) in the prereform era than has developed since the reforms began.

That is, there was in those times an absolute bar against entering the preferred state sectoral jobs and obtaining their perquisites plus an impenetrable restriction against party membership for formerly "bourgeois" social forces, who were, in essence, ascriptively excluded from these privileges.[8] Thus one might speak of a society of former business forces that was at once detached, even barred, from the state yet was locked up within the bonds of that state's very institutions.

The onset of reform has begun to erode this singularity of the path to power, just as it has seemingly freed nonstate actors, by opening opportunities for new occupational alternatives for the members of the long-isolated society. Nonetheless, the differentiation of social forces that is accompanying the reform is quite a partial one, so that categories that were previously discrete and unrelated have instead become in some senses symbiotic. The result is a continuation (if in quite altered form) of the state's social hegemony, under which a business sector that is still largely incorporated and captured has appeared. The presence of this new sector has recast officialdom as well. Thus as the monolith of the party-state's elite stratum breaks apart, freeing both official and merchant from the fixity of the former party-controlled frame, the pieces chipping off it are all different amalgams of that monolith. It is as if forces that were once incapable of combination have merged, even if often in complicated, uncongenial, and competitive fashion.

Most importantly, except in the southeast coastal region, where overseas remittances and joint ventures with Hong Kong partners provide a foundation for a capital formation that is truly separate from the state, there is as yet no true autonomy of economic power for a private sector, nor any genuine division of labor between economic and political power in the cities. For the Chinese urban entrepreneur who operates on a scale of some size, the state and its institutions remain the principal source of start-up capital; in addition, entrée to the state's means of production and guidance through its regulatory and informational labyrinth has been the sine qua non for business activity. All of these constraints keep the new merchant force dependent. The new "bourgeoisie," such as it is, then, is one whose members usually lack their own means of production, independent capital, material supplies, and modes of operation.

Simultaneously, party cadres, state bureaucrats, and state enterprise managers have engaged in exchanges with the incipient merchant force and constantly essayed to collude with it and incorporate it or simply squeeze its profits, skills, connections, and time. These actions have rendered officialdom dependent not just on the state, as before, but sometimes on the new "private" sector as well. The outcome to date has been a stratum of people exclusively pursuing business who are inextricably entangled with cadredom and an official class increasingly corroded by commercialism. Both are "entrepreneurs."

Given this overlap of social forces, concretized in a sometimes intentional, sometimes constrained collaboration among mutually dependent semiclasses, the bribery, extortion, corruption, and bargains that have frequently been the object of at least rhetorical opprobrium do not, at the analytical level, really occur between two distinct groups. One could rather claim that because doing business often involves the participation of both formations, such exchanges in fact take place within a single, blended class.

This complex class, much like the bureaucratic capitalists at the apex of the imperial order in late dynastic times or the gentry-merchants who inhabited its base in the localities,[9] is the paradoxical product of a splitting off of new, officially sanctioned professions from the formerly monolithic elite mobility channel. In the late Qing as in the recent PRC, diversification of the economy (in both cases initiated at the peak of the polity) and a crisis in the orthodox ideology together brought into being new occupations or helped to legitimize trades disparaged when the regime was stronger and more authoritative, the economy less elaborate.

What appears as a liberation of society has actually at both times (though more so today) been an incorporation of society, albeit under grossly altered terms. As John King Fairbank expressed this situation in writing of the late Qing, "The line between landlord-gentry and merchant was blurred; merchant-gentry now acquired degree status, just as the roles of official and merchant became homogenized in bureaucratic entrepreneurs."[10]

Taking a long view, we can see the present moment as one in which a familiar historical cycling has so far repeated itself. In a kind of dialectical interaction, state and business class recurrently merge and come apart. The start of the Communist party regime in the early 1950s, as with the period of consolidation of Kuomintang (KMT) power in the late 1920s, saw the state gathering its power and mustering all available social capital as it placed itself in blatant opposition to the business class.[11] Both new regimes treated this class as a force first to be preyed upon but ultimately conquered. The outcome was to create from separate and potentially competing classes a monolithic order in which the bourgeoisie, having lost its ability to defend its political and economic interests, was emasculated.

In a structural sense, a second stage in this dynamic matches the long years of essentially unbroken party economic power in the People's Republic after 1956, on the one hand, to the heyday of dynasties, on the other. During such eras, because the state's power, confidence, and hegemony were at their heights, it was able to impose upon society a monolithic mobility channel, sometimes excluding and at other times subsuming, capturing, co-opting, and incorporating within itself alternate, unofficial, or unorthodox economic forces in society.

True, Communist party hegemony was far more encompassing and exclusive than anything attempted or even intended by the Qing. In its most benign guise, as in the high Qing tax farming to the merchants described by Susan Mann[12] or the self-managing guilds depicted by Gary Hamilton,[13] this merging admitted a certain autonomy and entailed in some spheres a form of official-societal collaboration sanctioned by the state. But the primary impulse of all money-holding families in this era was to prepare the conditions for at least one of their offspring to enter the elite stratum, and the dominance of just one channel of real prestige sustained the hegemony of the state.

The third and final phase of this process is the one in which the PRC finds itself today: This is a time of partial state withdrawal, of state admission that society has become too large and too unmanageable and that the state's tasks have turned too complex and massive for the more or less totalistic controls—or the attempt at them—of the past. In such periods the state begins to shuffle off its multitude of responsibilities. New channels of mobility open, enabling alternate professions to emerge. This is the overwhelmed state, the state in decline or collapse. The emergence of merchants after 1980 bears a vague resemblance to the appearance of urban activists in late nineteenth-century Zhejiang as delineated by Mary Rankin[14] and to the guild federations that arose to manage social life in William Rowe's Wuhan in this period.[15] The era of the most pronounced flourishing of a separate bourgeoisie, from the mid-1910s until the consolidation of power by the KMT in 1927, however, was exceedingly brief, only possible in a period when there was no national government at all.[16]

The merchants of the 1980s were certainly an altogether far more dependent class than those of earlier eras, issuing as they did from a vastly more hegemonic central power that, even as it falters, continues through the ownership structure to command a weighty proportion of the national material resource and capital base. Still, similarities in the shifts in balance between state and societal business forces in China provide insights into the relation of the one to the other.

In order to underline these historical parallels in social structure, I adopt the labels "bureaucrat" and "merchant" in referring to the members of what are conventionally termed public and private sectors (or state and society), respectively. For the Chinese urban entrepreneur of today is neither wholly a private operator nor a member of the state; to be financially successful in the cities, the entrepreneur must become involved in both of these spheres. This perspective provides a way of understanding those cadre "obstructions" of the private sector that have been impossible to wipe away despite a decade of nearly continuous regime injunctions against them; the ambiguity in the application of the incentives offered to the merchant sector; the merchants' preference for registering their ventures as "collective" rather than "private" or "individual"; and the inconclusiveness and ambivalence in the political elite's debates over the role of the private sector in the reform era.

The durability and indeed so far the stasis of this historical juncture is buttressed by the interpenetration and interdependence of elites. Witnessing the cracking apart of the monolithic mobility channel, this period has been marked by the development of a set of institutions new to the socialist political economy of the People's Republic. These are institutions that have issued from the reforms and that aim either explicitly or implicitly at co-opting the bureaucrats or the merchants into the process of "reform." A number of them generate that blur between social forces described above.

In short, the erosion of the single-stranded elite mobility pathway under conditions of continuing state ownership of the overwhelming bulk of national resources has not clarified but rather has blurred the borderline between state bureaucrat and private merchant. This decline of central power—over resources and in overall capacity and, attendant upon that, over mobility channels open to aspiring elites—is a recurring theme. The merger, interpenetration, and sometimes dependence of occupational strata that ensue may take the form of collaboration or, alternatively, may find expression in open competition.

In the following sections, I use this perspective to explain some features of the ambiguity in the relationship between bureaucrat and merchant and to show how the institutions of the reform period have so far served to perpetuate the stasis of that relationship. I conclude with some speculations about the prospects for abandoning this pattern. The framework laid out above can help to elucidate the seemingly endless and ultimately inconclusive disagreements among political elites over the extent of economic reform.

Ambiguities and Mutual Dependency in the Bureaucrat-Merchant Relationship

The most common themes in discussions of the interaction of the bureaucratic and merchant strata can be analyzed in light of the argument above. Probably the most prominent of these themes concerns the hindrances that some bureaucrats have been posing to private business.[17] Paradoxically, these efforts at obstruction—which it seems would eliminate the practitioners of market activity—are accompanied by bribery, corruption, and extortion forced on the merchants,[18] activities that apparently imply that bureaucrats value merchants for their ability to generate capital. Other areas that have received attention are the contradiction between the appeal that private-sector jobs have for those in state jobs since about 1984 or 1985[19] and the periodic decline in numbers of operators and firms over the same years.[20]

In the late 1980s there were also increasing reports of subterfuge. First the individual firms (those allegedly employing no more than seven workers in addition to the owner) and later the newly authorized private enterprises (those officially permitted after July 1988 to hire eight or more workers) registered themselves as "collective" or even state-related firms instead of as private.[21] In all of these activities we may find evidence of new forms of dependence and symbiosis between bureaucrat and merchant.

Actions against private-sector activity have taken place since its appearance in the cities after 1980. Indeed, such obstruction reflects long-standing ambivalence toward private enterprise present in China after the birth of the PRC. As ever, it has been fueled by a mix of rivalry between state-sector and private-sector practitioners and by ideological scruples among the cadres.[22] Stories aimed at giving this interference bad press in order to discredit it told of cadres' wrecking the little shops' equipment, stealing their tools, ransacking their premises, ruining their materials, and delivering to them only leftover, spoiled products to sell. Licenses, difficult to obtain in the first place, were later confiscated and customers threatened; merchants themselves were barred from operating in certain sections of town.[23]

Alongside this apparent urge to abolish competitors in the marketplace, another sort of cadre behavior appeared: collusion between the two strata that is by no means, however, always witting on the part of both sides. This collusion involves the bribery into which merchants are coerced by extortionate cadres; the not uncommon requirement that merchants offer a bribe simply to obtain a business license or a loan;[24] the higher prices (often retail prices for wholesale quantities) they must pay to procure scarce state-owned and state-managed materials and supplies;[25] the higher tax rates;[26] and the myriad of fees and assessments (in addition to the basic assessments, called "management fees") levied at will, often in transgression of central governmental policy, by local departments in charge of sanitation, urban construction, public security, transportation, and weights and measures.[27] As one informant put it, not just the major private entrepreneurs but the *getihu* as well "need to lubricate all the joints from the police station to the tax offices to the market control commissions to the neighborhood committees. . . .

All those working in the hierarchical levels of the bureaucracy must be bribed."[28]

Though these practices may fleece the merchants, bureaucrats who manage such squeeze, who connive for a share of the profits,[29] or who in effect pull the private traders into "protection rackets"[30] have become to some extent dependent on the private sector, as they plainly benefit from its continued existence. There are cases where local governments "have found it more profitable to coordinate with private traders than to rely on state markets";[31] in other instances local governments encourage the expansion of private economic activity in the interest of fostering local industrialization, expanding the tax take, and solving problems of local unemployment.[32]

On a grander scale, the central government published in early 1986 its intention to incorporate collective and individual investments into the overall state plan for fixed-assets investment. The opportunism in this project is apparent in the announcement's calculation that, over the previous four years, these investments had accounted for almost one-third of the total social investment in fixed assets nationwide, terming it "an important means for expanding reproduction in society."[33]

For these reasons, it is inadequate to picture local bureaucrats as simply *opposing* privatization as a threat to their power and privilege or as a betrayal of socialist values,[34] though certainly such attitudes do exist. The simultaneous presence for cadres of new chances for gain (whether for themselves personally or for their cities—there is no way to measure or weigh the proportions) underlines the symbiotic connection into which reform policies have thrust cadre and merchant, with both groups dependent on some of the same inputs but both also to some degree dependent on each other.[35] If some merchants lose from harassment and squeeze, surely others have thrived on collusion.[36]

A second contradiction lies in the appeal of the private sector even for people with secure jobs and the generous state-conferred benefits that go with them. Coupled with this is the periodic decision of some merchants to relinquish business licenses already acquired and the opting by others to hide their firms under more orthodox registration as collectives, a phenomenon dubbed "wearing a red hat."[37]

The proposition of symbiosis illuminates this paradox as well. Even with its risks, the private sector has attractions for those seeking a chance to develop their talents and a freer environment in which to work. Personal growth is not the only motive for breaking one's tie with a state-run unit, however. Some do so in response to the state's use of material incentives. These incentives include special loan funds allocated by the Industrial and Commercial Bank, higher interest rates on business deposits, tax holidays, and the right to inherit private property (written into the 1982 state constitution).[38] It is clear that the state at the policymaking stratum has nurtured private business, thereby acknowledging its dependence on the tax revenues private ventures can yield.[39]

This contradiction illustrates not just the state's new willingness to draw upon privately garnered profits but also the merchants' ultimate dependency on the state. For those who give up their right to work as traders on their own often find that the political climate and the economic environment in which they must operate is hostile. Problems of discrimination, low status, difficulties in securing supplies from the bureaucracy, and general harassment plague private-sector entrepreneurs who lack an entrée into the bureaucrats' world.[40] The weakness of these individuals who try to move without the crutch connections provide offers glaring proof of their reliance on officialdom.

The estimated nearly 50 percent of private firms that register as affiliated with collective or state-owned enterprises or as collectively owned do so for reasons that, again, illustrate the symbiotic relationship that exists for many successful merchants.[41] Through such arrangements, the private enterprises can obtain preferential tax rates and cheaper raw materials, receive political protection, and generally find it easier to conduct business. The existence of these deals, however, shows that it is not just the merchant firms that need the public ones. A mutually beneficial exchange is struck, as merchants present a portion of their profits as "management fees" to their state-sector partners.

These various contradictions are rooted in competition between bureaucrats and merchants as rivals in a market where state resources and those able to command them still hold dominion. But they are also based in a set of mutually dependent ties between the two. This paradox explains as well the difficulty of pinning down the respective stances of "conservatives" versus "reformers" on the issues of political and economic reform.

Those most firmly ensconced within the party hierarchy—those with the richest network of cronies—should be best placed to take advantage of the opportunities today's distorted market can offer. Self-interest may dictate that they attempt to throttle challenges to the power structure but not that they eliminate a market that so clearly can be made to work on their own behalf.

By a similar logic, many merchants ideally would like to cut the tie between old political and new economic power that remains so firmly in place. But it is that very bond that has generated this class in the first place and that sustains it economically, as the supports offered by the old framework continue to help many opting for the private sector to get their start and go on to prop up their daily dealings. Thus cadres of all cuts have been the beneficiaries of economic reform, just as large numbers of merchants are the beneficiaries of the bureaucracy.

A return to a regime based purely on planning would undermine newfound opportunities now enjoyed by cadres, whereas a leap to fully open and unobstructed markets would deprive the most successful merchants of their special inside channels. As a result, there is an implicit pact to preserve the monolith and a stasis in the symbiotic tie between bureaucrat and merchant.[42]

The Institutions of the Reform and Their Role in Prolonging the Transition

As noted above, in the 1980s new institutions emerged that co-opt either the bureaucrats or the merchants into dependent relationships. Their combined effect has been to prolong the decomposition of the monolithic position of the state and to foster a symbiosis between the two groups. These institutions are of several types. One category contains institutions established by the state bureaucracy to incorporate the private sector. Second are those formed by the merchants themselves, albeit with assistance from the state or its assets. And a third variety includes institutions that are generated directly by the reforms. All three facilitate deals across the now more than ever blurred boundaries between sectors. They do so in a way that serves to freeze the transition to a market economy so that this amalgam of classes persists.

Institutions to Control the Merchants

In this category we find such institutions as the associations of private entrepreneurs formed at the urban level and the new business guilds brought together under official aegis. In the past decade there has also been an effort to encourage merchants to join the Communist party and to make models of them by nominating them to serve on local boards and even in the National People's Congress.

Individual workers' associations first arose locally in 1980, under the party's auspices; in 1986 they were united into a national body. The state bureaucracy's Industrial and Commercial Administrative and Management Bureau monitors these groups, and its cadres serve among their board members, ensuring that the merchants imbibe pertinent state and party policies and the political ideology of the moment.[43] There is nothing secret about the state's concern to keep these organs under its mantle: In late 1989 Wang Zhongming, the secretary general of the National Association of Individual Laborers of China, was announced as the director of the Individual and Private Economy Department of the State Administration for Industry and Commerce.[44]

The associations are charged with mobilizing the merchants to pay their taxes and with helping them to maintain the quality of their service and sanitary conditions.[45] They are also supposed to provide assistance to the members; to the extent that the associations meet this obligation, merchants no doubt find themselves becoming dependent on these bureaucratic bodies. Among their other responsibilities is to foster mutual aid among the merchants, to protect their legal rights and represent their opinions and demands, to help them solve problems in their operations, and to offer technical training, legal advice, and information.[46] But the dependence, it turns out, is on both sides: Criticism has held that the offices meant to assist the associations often treat them as the commercial and industrial departments' own appendages, in effect turning them into their own little branches.[47]

Other, related types of co-optation also provide for mutual penetration and control. The first provincial congress of private entrepreneurs held in Guangdong, for example, met in late 1989. In attendance were the vice-chairman of the standing committee of the provincial People's Congress, the provincial vice-governor, and the director of the department in charge of individual and private economic affairs under the State Administration for Industry and Commerce. The congress had the ambitious goal of absorbing into the state's networks all the private entrepreneurs in the province, as it planned to send out an appeal to them all to become members of a provincial association of private entrepreneurs then in the midst of formation.[48]

Not only were the merchants permitted and even encouraged to join the Communist party after 1982[49]—one source claims that as of late 1988, 15 percent of the owners of private enterprises were party members[50]—and to become representatives of both local and national bodies. Going further, in 1989 the first party branch within a private enterprise was created in a Shenyang factory in the food industry. Of the eighty-two people in the factory, a full nine of them were party members.[51]

At the end of 1989 the All-China Federation of Industry and Commerce announced its revival of 150 business guilds operating as "non-official bodies." These associations were obviously designed to be far more closely linked to the bureaucracy than those that Rowe and Mann studied from the nineteenth century: "The Federation pledges to give full support to the development of guilds . . . [which are] to bridge businesses with the government and provide services," read the notice.[52]

All of these new corporations link merchant with state, in part to limit the competitive threat merchants pose as they draw largely upon the same capital, equipment, and supplies that the state and its bureaucrats use. These associations' presence also embodies the state's effort to bind the merchants into a dependency upon its offices; in the process these corporate agencies bolster the bureaucracy's ability to play out its own dependence by helping them more readily to tap the skills and profits of the merchants.

Dependent Institutions Formed by Merchants

In this category are technology development centers and corporations, the most notorious of which is the Stone Group; joint ventures that merge merchant skills and needs with bureaucratic connections and supplies; small-scale collective firms that are tied to the state's neighborhood committees; and moonlighting practices that involve the use of state-owned facilities, equipment, and assets.

The Stone Corporation is China's leading high-technology firm. It was brought into being in 1984 by the famous entrepreneur Wan Runnan, who is now one of the four top democracy leaders abroad. The advantages that undoubtedly launched Wan on his successful career exemplify once again the centrality of ties between bureaucrat and merchant.[53]

Wan had been exiled to the countryside with other Cultural Revolution victims, in part for his audacity—perhaps even perceived in that era as his criminality—in marrying the daughter of Liu Shaoqi in 1970. He made his comeback into Beijing in the late 1970s through his choice for his second wife, the daughter of Li Chang (at the time Li was party secretary of the Chinese Academy of Sciences). Once in the capital, Wan quickly became a software engineer in the computer center under CAS (one suspects with help from his father-in-law), where he studied diligently. By the early 1980s, Wan had been named director of that center. Soon he was helping to run training classes for IBM, invited into China by the top political elite to train ministry-level personnel.

The economic reforms' encouragement of a commercial spirit elicited a boom in company formation by government offices of all sorts. Wan grabbed the chance to put into practice a pet idea of his, to join laboratory research with moneymaking ventures. Borrowing 20,000 yuan from the Agricultural Bank of China, he set up a joint venture with a township government in the Haidian district of Beijing and began to adapt a U.S.-made printer to Chinese market requirements, with the help of the Mitsui Corporation. Wan went on to manufacture custom-made typewriters and printers, including electronic typewriters capable of printing in both Chinese and English. By the time Wan left China in 1989, the Stone Corporation had cornered 80 percent of the domestic market, managing some 600 stores, 40 wholesale centers, and 100 maintenance and training centers, and ran joint ventures with Japanese and Hong Kong companies.

Wan's corporation is representative of the thousands (no one knows how many) of hi-tech collective enterprises known as *minban* companies across the country, of which there are three main types: those (like the Stone Group) supposedly owned and managed by "people" (*minyou-minban*); those owned by the state but managed by "people" (*guanyou-minban*); and those jointly operated and owned by the state and "people" (*guanmingongyou*). Wan's type is in the minority. Indeed, of the top ten computer companies in China in terms of 1987 sales, only Stone was *minyou-minban;* all of the others were offshoots of the Ministry of Electronics, either wholly so or through joint ventures with "people," even though they all are classified as *minban.*

Nonetheless, despite his company's alleged "collective" status and the supposed absence of state capital in its portfolio, Wan was forbidden to claim any of the property as his—or his employees'—own. In fact, any attempt to withdraw funds from the venture would have brought on the criminal charge of *sifen jiti caichan* (privately dividing up collective property). For this reason, before the Tiananmen massacre, Wan had essayed to set up a share system and to sell his stock, chiefly in order to clarify the ownership rights of the firm. Zhao Ziyang's backing for this scheme was its death knell after June 1989.

In doing business, Stone, just as any other company interested in importing, needed more than funds to do so. In addition and perhaps even harder for nonstate firms to come by is the precious importing license. Because only governmental ministries legally have this privilege, connections with bureaucrats are essential for the undercover purchase that is the only way to obtain the license.

Stone's work was also greatly expedited by the attention the firm received at least indirectly from Zhao Ziyang in early 1988. For it was very probably Zhao who delegated Wen Jiabao (then director of the Central Work Office) and Rui Xingwen of the party Secretariat to investigate Stone and who later wrote out instructions for the creation in May 1988 of the Beijing New-Tech Industrial Development Experimental Zone. In this zone, where Stone was located, firms received a three-year tax exemption, another three years of tax reduction, and permission to retain a sizable percentage of the foreign currency they earned over a three-year period, plus promises of help in solving problems with visas, electricity supply, and the local bureaucracy. Similar parks for other such companies exist in Shenzhen and three other cities. Firms of this sort are sometimes distrusted, resented, and even harassed (Wan himself got into legal trouble on two occasions between 1985 and 1988). Some have found themselves entangled in more red tape than are ordinary state-owned firms despite promises that this will not be the case. But it is clear that those who succeed on a large scale must combine their skills with bureaucratic backing.

In addition to this very blatant and well-publicized kind of collaboration, there are other forms of combination that grow out of a merger of funds and thus an overlap of interest between merchant and bureaucrat. Many smaller individual firms got their start with loans or grants from their neighborhood resident committees, again making use of capital from the state. Ventures between private enterprises and state-run firms and between private and collective enterprises that began to appear in the late 1980s constitute another variation. Shareholding arrangements also bring together bureaucrat and merchant capital in mutually beneficial ways.[54]

And one more example is the moonlighting craze that has sprung up in Chinese cities as the monolithic mobility channel erodes.[55] A common pattern is for a person to labor in a state firm during working hours and in leisure time to perform the same services for other units introduced to him by friends. In large cities like Guangzhou, the state's estimate is that about 30 percent of workers and staff hold supplemental jobs. One survey showed that nearly half of those taking on extra employment were workers, teachers, doctors, and scientific and research personnel, with managers constituting the other half. It is likely that these people ply their second trades with either direct or indirect help from bureaucrats or with state assets. All of these opportunities for "private" achievement are only accessible to those able to anchor their activities with bureaucratic bargains and blessings. Thus, one could say, such moonlighting co-opts the new-style merchants into the state's own structure and thereby perpetuates its monopoly on economic power.

Reform-generated Institutions

This set of organizational forms and practices permits bureaucrats to utilize the resources of the state system—connections, information, credit, supplies—to amass market power. Probably most significant of these is the double-track price system, which makes specially advantaged insider salespeople out of any bureaucrats with control over or even access to valued supplies in demand. In this class I would also place the multifarious supply and trading "companies" set up by bureaucrats, their offices, and their offspring in recent years: share companies, materials exchange markets, wholesale trade centers, and newly forming enterprise groups forged among state firms.

The double-track price system was initiated in the mid-1980s. The idea was to allow the coexistence of market prices and administered prices in order to placate interests potentially threatened by further price reform yet to permit marketlike transactions to go forward. This obviously created an open field for arbitrage that bound bureaucrats to a state that guaranteed their privileged access to goods and information. Officials found that they could enjoy reform immensely so long as the system it introduced remained frozen. And any merchant who was not to be shut out of the market by this arrangement was forced to ally with these now doubly empowered bureaucrats.

On several occasions since 1985 there have been campaigns publicized to eliminate and cashier the uncountable hordes of "companies" that sprang into existence once the economic reform program legitimized making money.[56] Put together with the assets of state offices, these companies are backed up by networks of favors and mutually granted access to scarcities among bureaucrats. Movements to wipe them out have never succeeded, no doubt because both the numbers and clout of those who benefit from their existence far outweigh the numbers or the influence of those who might have an interest in their abolition.

Though officials in the materials supply bureaucracy have probably been the chief offenders, those in commercial wholesaling and foreign trade work have also benefited mightily from the establishment of such concerns; even the public security and judicial departments, and the army have formed their share. The tight linkage between the bureaus and their commercial activities is captured in the phrase, "one shop with two signboards," signifying that most of these companies are at once internally government institutions and externally business companies.[57]

Enterprise groups constructed to free up the movement of materials and commodities once entrapped within the constraints of the vertical bureaucracies that administered the state plan have spawned their own bureaucratic trappings. They do this by gathering under one much more massive unit far more assets than any one firm ever mustered in the old days. At their heads sit powerful officials well connected with local party and state bureaucrats.[58]

Similarly, share companies, markets for the means of production, and wholesale trade centers all heighten the sway of officials whose influence was already notable before the reforms. These bureaucrats now can make use of fractures in the planning system and imperfections in the market to capitalize on whatever assets and connections they command, earning extra commissions as they do—all to a degree unimaginable in days of tighter controls.[59]

To the extent that bureaucrats may have had misgivings about the reform program and its potential for undermining their own potency, institutions and measures such as these co-opt bureacrats into the transition but continue to tie them to the state at the same time. The economic reforms also encourage bureaucrats to join forces with merchants when to do so would enhance the capabilities of the ventures the bureaucrats manage.

All three of these kinds of institutions, then, draw either merchant or bureaucrat into the transition to the market economy and create vested interests that prolong that transition. Through this co-optation, these institutions also serve to bring the two forces into more explicit dealings and closer confrontations with each other—whether it be through competition or collusion—than they experienced in the time of the planned economy.

Conclusion: Prospects for Change?

I have reiterated the point that the arrangements of the reform era have merged, if under vastly shifted conditions, the entities we call state and society. The monolithic mobility channel has begun to disappear, but its dominance is far from totally gone. The result is the further solidification of the old bond that has always tied the bureaucrat to the perquisites offered by state employment. What is new is a bonding and incipient interdependence between the bureaucrat and the merchant, who compete with one another for state funds, supplies, and markets but who also bargain and collude together.

What prospects for change lie latent in the present scenario? There are two sources of change—interestingly, the same two that eventually and finally split apart the long-decaying imperial order. These are tied to the forces that pushed both that order and the present one on its downward spiral: the diversifying economy and the discredited belief system.

In the current era we see these forces at work in the pressures for political liberalization that merchants were backing even before the Tiananmen demonstrations, which they financed from behind the scenes (probably with tacit support and encouragement from Zhao Ziyang and his advisers, one may surmise, in light of the link that later became public between Yan Jiaqi and Wan Runnan).[60] Given what was explained above about the constraints on ownership under which the *minban* hi-tech firms must operate today, it is clear what the larger merchants have to gain from a freeing up of political structures. Similarly, in the decade before 1911, merchants—in those days merchants in the provinces—were also at the forefront of the demand for loosening the autocratism at the political center.

The other power potentially capable of smashing the monolith, then as now, lies in groups whose source of finances comes from outside the system. At the turn of the century there was Sun Yatsen with his overseas communities; today it is those living in the southeastern coastal provinces who have relatives abroad or who have managed to underwrite their new economic ventures with investment from those places and so have become released from the hegemonic dominion of the state economy. It is notable that in late 1988 a Chinese-sponsored analysis of the owners of private enterprises—who were labeled "a new social stratum"—spoke specifically of a federation of entrepreneurs in Fuzhou that publishes its own newsletter, lives by its own regulations, and conducts direct business negotiations with foreign merchants.[61]

It is hard to claim there are any immediate grounds for hope of change. In the aftermath of June 4, 1989, we find the chief merchant—and probably many of his lesser colleagues—resident abroad and the southeast coast mainly going its own way, cut off from the larger concerns of the country. Still, the existence of these two pockets of potentially vigorous protest and autonomy within the merchant stratum suggests the likely points at which the stasis that has been the dominant pattern to date will one day be altered. In the meantime, the cords that connect merchant to bureaucrat and both to the state continue to tighten.

Notes

1. Thomas B. Gold, "The Resurgence of Civil Society in China," *Journal of Democracy* 1, 1 (Winter 1990), 18–31.

2. See John P. Burns, "China's Governance: Political Reform in a Turbulent Environment," *China Quarterly* (hereafter *CQ*), No. 119 (September 1989), 481–518, for a statement of this claim.

3. *Beijing Review* (hereafter *BR*), May 8–14, 1989, 25.

4. See Ivan Szelenyi, "Eastern Europe in an Epoch of Transition: Toward a Socialist Mixed Economy?" in Victor Nee and David Stark, eds., *Remaking the Economic Institutions of Socialism: China and Eastern Europe* (Stanford: Stanford University Press, 1989), 222, 225.

5. Here I must emphasize that in this chapter I concentrate purely on the relationship between the state and the sector of society that deals in business. I would not venture to extend its conclusions to other classes or social groups.

6. Here I am speaking of the entrepreneurs managing sizable enterprises. But the *getihu,* even if they own their own assets, must still compete and collaborate with the state to survive.

7. David Stark and Victor Nee, "Toward an Institutional Analysis of State Socialism," in Nee and Stark, *Remaking Economic Institutions,* 1–13, speak of "reforms . . . [as] redrawing the boundaries between state and society and shaping new patterns of transaction, mediation, and bargaining across them" (p. 16), and of "porous state-society boundaries" during the Maoist era (p. 23). Now, they claim, we see "a system in which state and society are insulated from each other to a greater degree" (p. 23).

8. Though since about 1983 private entrepreneurs have been encouraged to join the party, and party officials have been enjoined to enlist them, this is a fragile arrangement. In autumn 1989 that trend was terminated, at least for the time being, when party chief Jiang Zemin spoke out against it. See U.S. *Foreign Broadcast Information Service* (hereafter *FBIS*), October 23, 1989, 19.

9. See Susan Mann, *Local Merchants and the Chinese Bureaucracy, 1750–1950* (Stanford: Stanford University Press, 1987), 21–23. See also Wang Jingyu, "The Birth of the Chinese Bourgeoisie," *Social Sciences in China* (hereafter *SSIC*) 3, 1 (March 1982), 220–240; and Editorial Board for Modern and Contemporary Chinese History, *Historical Research,* "Chinese Historical Studies on Early Modern China's Bourgeoisie," *SSIC* 5, 1 (March 1984), 9–31, for discussions on the complexity of the overlapping class formations in the late nineteenth century.

10. John King Fairbank, *The Great Chinese Revolution, 1800–1985* (New York: Harper & Row, 1986), 147.

11. For the study that sets out this thesis quite sharply for the KMT, see Parks M. Coble, Jr., *The Shanghai Capitalists and the Nationalist Government, 1927–1937* (Cambridge: Council on East Asian Studies, Harvard University, 1980).

12. Mann, *Local Merchants,* 21–23.

13. Gary G. Hamilton, "Why No Capitalism in China? Negative Questions in Historical Comparative Research," *Journal of Developing Societies* 1 (1985), 187–211.

14. Mary Backus Rankin, *Elite Activism and Political Transformation in China: Zhejiang Province, 1865–1911* (Stanford: Stanford University Press, 1986).

15. See William T. Rowe, *Hankow: Commerce and Society in a Chinese Society, 1796–1889* (Stanford: Stanford University Press, 1984).

16. See Parks M. Coble, Jr., "The Kuomintang Regime and the Shanghai Capitalists, 1927–1929," *CQ,* No. 77 (March 1979), 3; and Marie-Claire Bergère, *The Golden Age of the Chinese Bourgeoisie* (New York: Cambridge University Press, 1989).

17. Two examples of work emphasizing obstructions are Linda Hershkovitz, "The Fruits of Ambivalence: China's Urban Individual Economy," *Pacific Affairs* 58, 3 (Fall 1985), 427–450, and Dorothy J. Solinger, "The Petty Private Sector and the Three Lines in the Early 1980s," in Dorothy J. Solinger, ed., *Three Visions of Chinese Socialism* (Boulder: Westview Press, 1984), 73–111. Thomas B. Gold, "Urban Private Business in China," *Studies in Comparative Communism* (hereafter *SCC*) 22, 2-3 (Summer-Autumn 1989), 187–201, refers to this problem on p. 187.

18. The following articles deal specifically with corruption: Alan P. L. Liu, "The Politics of Corruption in the People's Republic of China," *American Political Science Review* 77, 3 (1983), 602–623; Connie Squire Meaney, "Market Reform in a Leninist System: Some Trends in the Distribution of Power, Strategy and Money in Urban China," *SCC* 22, 2-3 (Summer-Autumn 1989), 203–220; Athar Hussain, "Chinese Economic Reforms, Irregularities and Crimes," paper prepared for Conference on Social Consequences of the Chinese Economic Reforms, Fairbank Center, Harvard University, May 13–15, 1988; and James T. Myers, "Modernization and 'Unhealthy Tendencies': Toward a Definition of the Problem," paper presented at 1985 Sino-American Annual Conference on Mainland China, Columbus, Ohio, 1985.

19. Thomas B. Gold, "China's Private Entrepreneurs," *China Business Review*, November-December 1985, 46–50, makes this point.

20. In both 1986 and 1989 the numbers of private firms dropped. See *Renmin Ribao* (People's daily; hereafter *RMRB*), overseas edition, November 25, 1986. This article states that in the first half of 1986 the numbers of private firms fell for the first time in the previous several years. Compared with the end of 1985, there were 360,000 fewer (registered) private firms and 470,000 fewer private entrepreneurs. *BR*, November 6–12, 1989, 11, states that the 23.049 million individuals working in private business as of the end of 1988 had dropped to 19.43 million by the end of the first half of 1989. The specific cause for these declines in a long-term rising trend were not given in the data. However, we must assume that because the appeal of the private sector has by and large been a secular trend over the decade, it has generally been unaffected by periodic attempts to intimidate or tax its practitioners or by times in which credit has been scarce, causing some merchants to be at least temporarily forced out of business.

21. Ma Jisen, "A General Survey of the Resurgence of the Private Sector of China's Economy," *SSIC* 9, 3 (September 1988), 78–92, claims that only 115,000 of the 225,000 private enterprises in China have properly registered themselves as private.

22. I elaborate on this in Dorothy J. Solinger, *Chinese Business Under Socialism* (Berkeley: University of California Press, 1984), especially in Ch. 4.

23. Ibid., 201–202. See also Gold, "Urban Private Business," 197.

24. Hussain, "Reforms, Irregularities and Crimes," 9; Jisen, "Survey of Resurgence," 89.

25. Ibid.

26. Before 1986 the private sector was only made to pay a business tax. Regulations in force as of 1981 left it to urban regulatory agencies to work out procedures for taxing. In 1986, a ten-grade, progressive income-tax scale was promulgated for the private sector, whose rates were pegged much higher than those for state-sector business. The highest taxes reached a rate of 84 percent. See Hershkovitz, "Fruits of Ambivalence," 444; *China Daily* (Beijing) (hereafter *CD*), January 27, 1986, 3; and Jisen, "Survey of Resurgence," 89.

27. Hershkovitz, "Fruits of Ambivalence," 447.

28. Interview, February 2, 1990.

29. Hussain, "Reforms, Irregularities and Crimes," 9.

30. Meaney, "Market Reform in a Leninist System," 210–211, came up with this helpful characterization.

31. *FBIS,* July 22, 1988, 49.

32. Some of this is suggested in the early research of Jian Yuan, as stated in her dissertation proposal to the Department of Political Science at Yale University, "Private Property and the Socialist Economy," December 1989.

33. *BR,* March 31, 1986, 26.

34. For this argument, see Thomas B. Gold, "Stimulating Initiative in Urban China's Private Sector," paper prepared for the annual meeting of the Association for Asian Studies, San Francisco, March 25–27, 1988.

35. This perspective resolves what otherwise would appear to be two mutually contradictory statements in Meaney, "Market Reform in a Leninist System," 203–204: "Market reform threatens the party's organizational base by creating spaces for actors . . . outside the purview of the *nomenklatura* system"; and "Market reform in Leninist states creates new opportunities to make money, but access to these opportunities tends to favor party cadres and their networks of connections." This is an excellent article, but it does not explicitly come to grips with this internal contradiction.

36. Here again we find an instructive historical parallel. See Rowe, "Hankow: Commerce and Society," 177–181, for a thoughtful and thorough analysis of four different, not altogether mutually incompatible approaches that scholars have taken in assessing the stance of the traditional Chinese state toward commerce: what he calls the "repression," "neglect," "collusion," and "stimulation" theses. As Rowe admits in settling for the stimulation thesis (the idea that the state primarily encouraged commerce in order to increase state revenues and to benefit the populace) to describe the situation in nineteenth-century Hankow, "the other [theses also] have some validity as the Qing administration's role in commerce was complex and at times contradictory" (p. 180).

37. Jisen, "Survey of Resurgence," 87–88, and *CD,* June 25, 1988, 4.

38. Gold, "Urban Private Business," 194, 199, and Gold, "China's Private Entrepreneurs," 47. In the early 1980s, there were also selective incentives for specific sectors, such as the waiving of commercial taxes for two or three years in the service and repair trades and a two-year period of income tax exemptions for unemployed young people who opened individual enterprises. This is recounted in Charlotte Hart, "Urban Private Businesses in China, 1978–1984," Asian Studies Program, Dartmouth College, May 6, 1985.

39. Gold, "China's Private Entrepreneurs," 47.

40. Gold, "Urban Private Business," 197.

41. See *CD,* November 7, 1989, 1, and June 25, 1988, 4, and Jisen, "Survey of Resurgence," for discussion of this issue.

42. See the conclusion to this chapter for a qualification of this claim.

43. Gold, "Urban Private Business," 199.

44. *CD,* November 7, 1989, 1.

45. Hu Guohua, Liu Jinghuai, and Chen Minzhu, *Duosediao di zhongguo geti jingyingzhe* (Many-hued Chinese individual operators) (Beijing: Economic Academy Publishing, 1988), 195–196.

46. Wang Hui and Guan Mi, eds., *Geti jingying yishu* (The art of individual management) (Tianjin: Tianjin Social Science Academy Publishing, 1989), 216.

47. Hu Guohua et al., *Duosediao di zhongguo geti jingyingzhe,* 197.

48. *FBIS,* December 26, 1989, 38.

49. See note 8 above. In 1989 this effort was terminated.

50. *FBIS,* December 7, 1988, 36 (a translation of an article from *Jingji Cankao* [Economic reference], November 14, 1988, 4).

51. *RMRB,* January 6, 1989, 4.

52. *FBIS,* December 7, 1989, 32–33.

53. The material that follows comes from an interview with an insider who worked with one of the hi-tech companies for some years and from Marc Abramson, "*Minban* Science Firms in China," *China Exchange News* (hereafter *CEN*) 17, 4 (December 1989), 12–17; Richard P. Suttmeier, "Chinese Scientific and Technology Reforms: Toward a Post-Socialist Knowledge System," *CEN* 16, 4 (December 1988), 7–13; Adi Ignatius, "Fast-Growing Chinese Electronics Firm Emulates IBM," *Wall Street Journal,* June 3, 1988, 16; "Zhongguancun: A Look at Five Companies," *Asian Venture Capital Journal,* July 1988; Tai Ming Cheung, "Stone Keeps on Rolling," *Far East Economic Review,* October 13, 1988; Seth Faison, "Stone Group Could Set Trend of Share Ownership in China," *South China Morning Post,* October 27, 1988; and Dori Jones Yang, "Can Chinese Computers Survive in the Wild West?" *Business Week,* December 26, 1988.

54. Jisen, "Survey of Resurgence," 90.

55. *BR,* November 6–12, 1989, 25.

56. For two examples among dozens of such announcements, see *RMRB,* November 8 and 9, 1989, both on p. 1.

57. *BR,* November 13–19, 1989, 18–23.

58. An example of such an official entrepreneur is Yu Zhi'an of Wuhan, who stood at the core of several such enterprise groups in mid-1987, managing vast holdings of raw materials, energy sources, and commodities.

59. I have written of these various "reforms" in Dorothy J. Solinger, "Capitalist Measures with Chinese Characteristics," *Problems of Communism* 38 (January-February 1989), 19–33.

60. Meaney, "Market Reform in a Leninist System," 216.

61. Ibid., 216–219, and *FBIS,* December 7, 1988, 32–36 (a translation of an article from *Jingji Cankao* [Economic reference], November 14, 1988, 4).

7

Ideology and Rural Reform: The Paradox of Contingent Stability

Thomas P. Bernstein

The reshaping of agricultural institutions and policies that began in 1978 and culminated in the virtually universal adoption of household contracting by 1983 was among the most spectacular of China's post-Mao reforms. The dismantling of the commune system, the repudiation of radical leftist practices such as egalitarianism, and the new reliance on family incentives and family initiative altered the relation between the party-state and society. Peasants gained substantial autonomy from cadres. They could organize the family's labor, search for new sources of income, and enter the proliferating markets. Rural reforms allowed large numbers of peasants to engage partially or fully in nonagricultural pursuits, whether as "specialized households" contracting to operate collectively owned undertakings, small individual entrepreneurs (*getihu*), larger private entrepreneurs who employed eight or more workers, or migrants working on urban construction projects. The abolition of the multifunctional people's communes formally separated political from economic power, thereby at least in principle enlarging the space for popular initiative. The disappearance of the lowest tier of the three-level commune, the production team, increased the distance between cadres and peasants, although in some areas a version of the team continued to exist under the label *group* (*zu*).

These reforms seemed to presage further changes in which the scope of markets would increase and the controls of the plan be reduced, thereby limiting even further the party-state's role in rural society and the rural economy. However, the evolving realities of the relations between the party-state and the peasants in the 1980s did not bear out this optimistic prognosis of increasing peasant autonomy. The autonomous sphere of the peasants was not institutionalized, and the party-state continued to claim the right to intervene extensively in peasant life. The party-state's goals in the village did not simply consist of the maintenance of law and order, nor did they consist only of the pursuit of development and modernization. The party-state still pursued ideological goals, including preservation of certain socialist values and practices, which influenced the way in which the other goals were carried out. Thus law and order were defined in terms of the goal of promoting "socialist spiritual civilization," which meant attempting to wipe out peasant popular religion because it was regarded as "feudal superstition." As before, the party-state's economic interest in agriculture was in significant respects that of a traditional Marxist-Leninist state: Planning continued, including the assignment to peasants of acreage and grain procurement quotas, despite the 1985 substitution of contracts for compulsory state purchase assignments. And the party-state affected peasant lives because of its intense interest in family planning.

Implementing policies was not a simple task, if only because of the changes brought about during the reforms, which affected how peasants, local cadres and officials, and the larger party-state interacted. Informal relations played a major role, and there was no simple one-way street from Beijing to the villages. There was much variation in the capacity of the party-state to implement its goals in the villages, depending on such factors as geographical remoteness, the extent of development of markets, and the role played by local officials. But on the whole, though I may risk overstatement, the underlying reality seems to have been that the party-state continued to reach deeply into rural life.[1] In comparison with the endless transformative campaigns of the Maoist era, the "reach of the state" had declined and peasant autonomy had increased, but the state's impact was as substantial as ever.[2]

In this chapter I examine one aspect of the party-state's relations with the peasants, namely, the impact on peasants of ideologically based assumptions and definitions and of policies about household contracting and associated reforms. These assumptions communicated themselves to the peasants via local officials, the media—peasants had increasing access not only to radio broadcasts but also to television and newspapers—growing peasant contact with the urban sector (which was also a major change of the era of the 1980s), and in the form of policies and practices of the party-state or its agents. It need not be assumed that peasants had an understanding of "ideology" in its conceptual or philosophical sense, but they did know whether policy was moving away from the reforms or toward more reform. Peasants, in other words, had long experience with leftist and rightist policies that contracted and expanded the private sector.

"Will Policy Change?"

The issue of ideology can be approached from the peasants' point of view by examining evidence of peasant anxieties and fears about the durability of household contracting and individual enterprise. Insecurity about this issue was an important fact of peasant life. Household contractors yearned for stability but feared not only change in the particulars of government policies but a change in line, that is, abrogation of the reforms and a return to collectivism. Peasants voiced fears of recollectivization during the transition period to household contracting, when uncertainty was rooted in fresh memories of the frequent policy reversals of the Maoist period. But worries persisted throughout the reform period. In 1983 some peasants were reported as saying: "Now the state has a policy for cherishing the people. . . . We are living and working in peace and contentment. We are determined to get well off through hard work but fear that the policy might change and the good times will not last long."[3] In the same year, rumors swept through villages in Heilongjiang that mutual-aid teams and cooperatives would be set up and an old-style production campaign launched, precipitated by an impending readjustment of family contract holdings.[4] When the spiritual pollution campaign was briefly promoted in rural China, peasants asked, "Is the party's policy going to be changed?"[5] In 1986 similar rumors were reported from Shaanxi Province and elsewhere. "Many peasants" asked whether policies were being changed.[6] A year later, peasants were quoted as saying: "Fear neither waterlogging nor drought but change in the party's policies."[7]

A 1988 survey of 10,938 households conducted by the Rural Survey Office of the Central Committee's Rural Policy Research Center showed widespread fear of policy change. To a question about confidence in the staying power of the party's rural policy, 42.2 percent said they did have such confidence, 9.8 percent said they were "not very convinced," and 48 percent said they were "not sure." "These responses indicate that most peasants have doubts about the continuity of the party's rural economic policies."[8] Smaller surveys replicated versions of this finding. The responses of 100 households in four provinces and two cities showed that 80 percent worried about whether "the party's policy that enables people to become rich will change." A newly prosperous sixty-year-old Jiangsu peasant remarked: "What I am in fear of is that there will be a change of policy. I have just had a few days of comfortable life and do not want to see a good policy cancelled."[9] A poll of 500 households in Jiangxi showed little confidence in the stability of the party's present rural economic policy. In response to the question, "Do you believe the party's rural economic policy will change?" 63.4 percent said it was "hard to say"; 7.2 percent said they "did not believe" that it would not be changed.[10]

In 1989, during the reassertion of Marxist-Leninist orthodoxy after Tiananmen, rumors circulated in Jiangsu that household contracting would be abolished. In Ningxia "some peasants" had written to the newspaper reporting on hearsay that the party would recollectivize in 1990. Peasants consequently "stopped spreading manure and applying fertilizer," sold sheep, and felled trees, causing "heavy losses to our country's agricultural production." In Henan similar rumors caused peasants in some places to "chop down trees, sell animals, and destroy cultivated land."[11]

As these quotes indicate, peasant fears were not trivial. They caused destruction of property and were one source of peasant reluctance to invest in land, which was widely reported throughout the 1980s. This was a reason for major concern on the part of reformers, as household investment in land was supposed to be the primary way in which land quality was to be maintained. Peasants did not invest because they feared that the resources so used would be lost to the family were the land recollectivized.[12] Instead, they invested in housing. An immense housing boom swept through rural China in the 1980s, caused at least in part by these fears. As one editorial pointed out, peasant houses had not been confiscated since land reform. "Those who build houses own them," in contrast to other investments.[13] Peasant attitudes to the land were those of risk-taking entrepreneurs. Without proper guarantees that the fruit of the investment would go to them, peasants sought alternative uses for their money, including housing but also business opportunities with short profit horizons.

Moreover, peasant insecurity exacted a cost in arousing opposition to such measures as consolidation of land, which was on the agenda because the division of land among families had led to much fragmentation of holdings. Peasants viewed attempts to alter the status quo as a threat to household contracting rather than as an adaptive policy measure of potential assistance to them. The same point applied to party-state efforts to promote nonproducers' cooperatives, which were designed to provide needed services to peasant households, for example, acquisition of inputs and market outlets as well as assistance during the process of production—collective goods that households could not easily provide on their own. But peasants distrusted the nonproducers' cooperatives because of their association with collectivization. Fear that establishment of cooperatives signified abolition of household contracting led in "some places" to sale of draft animals and tools and to cessation of family management.[14]

The concerns of peasants who engaged in individual or private enterprise paralleled those of ordinary household contractors. During the 1983 campaign against spiritual pollution, party members and branches were accused of failing to combat "decadent capitalist ideas" of "putting money first." Fear of running political risks caused some entrepreneurs to cut back on investment, for "we do not want to become landlords." "Some wealthy households" were "on tenterhooks, apprehensive and uneasy."[15] In 1985 a *People's Daily* reporter visiting some villages was asked: "There is little news about specialized households in our newspapers now; does this mean that we no longer encourage their development?"[16] In 1986 some entrepreneurs feared that their property would be taken away and class labels pinned on them, from which "generations of their descendants would suffer." In Jiangsu, six specialized households substituted short-term workers for long-term ones, the latter having been the CCP's land reform criterion for defining who is and who is not an exploiter.[17] A spate of similar articles in spring 1986 claimed that specialized households were "oppressed by doubts and misgivings." Henan's governor, He Zhukang, described them as "under great pressure."[18]

In 1987 "certain comrades" sought to use the campaign against bourgeois liberalization to oppose rural reforms. Prosperous peasants reportedly reacted with fear to these political signals: "Why don't the cadres come to visit us? Why won't the banks lend us money?" In some instances, peasants got rid of their assets, "distributed their shares," or relabeled their enterprises as ideologically safer "cooperatives." And they did not "dare . . . invest in expanded reproduction." Ordinary peasants felt freer to extort money from specialized households. Entrepreneurs considered themselves to be in an unstable policy environment in which "some localities" supported them one day but not the next, causing "doubts and worries" about the party's policies.[19] In 1988, despite the positive signals from the Thirteenth Congress, "well-to-do individuals in urban and rural areas are now afraid of change in the party's policies and reclassification of their social status."[20] And in late 1989, rural entrepreneurs wrote the *People's Daily* asking whether the line had changed and whether the authorities were planning "a big accounting." They reported that some enterprises had been dissolved.[21] In sum, both ordinary peasants and entrepreneurs harbored fears about the stability of policy, not simply during the early years but throughout the 1980s.

Political insecurity and lack of confidence in a stable and predictable future did not prevent the development of rural individual or private enterprise, though this factor may have affected the rate of development, especially the speed, scope, and staying power of such enterprises. As the examples quoted above indicate, political insecurity prompted some to get out of business, others to curtail operations, and still others to adopt short-term rather than long-term investment strategies. Most important, political insecurity prompted peasant entrepreneurs to adopt protective strategies to reduce political risk and vulnerability to harassment by local cadres and officials. These tactics included the display of "good conduct," as in making local contributions or in acquiring "good conduct" certificates (often prominently displayed in peasant homes) for having prospered through hard work (*chinlao zhifu*).[22] The strategies also included formation of alliances with local cadres and joining the party. The need for protection against political risk stemming from the socialist environment was one of the sources of the symbiotic relationship between local bureaucrats and entrepreneurs and was one reason why many of the latter were themselves of cadre background. But political risk was not by any means the only source of such behavior. Other important factors that came into play included the access that local party and government cadres had to scarce goods and also the entrepreneurs' need for protection from arbitrary or rapidly changing administrative policies and regulations.

Role of Ideology

The party-state's ideological commitments were an important source of peasant insecurity. First and foremost, ideology shaped the establishment of household contracting, blocking full privatization of the land and thereby setting a decisive limitation to reform. Household contracting meant that peasants contracted land from the collective for a limited period of time, the land continuing to belong to the collective. As policymakers emphasized, household contracting was a change in management, not a change in ownership. The period of the land contracts was extended to fifteen years in 1984, and peasants were given the right to transfer them with some compensation. There was talk of extending the contract period to fifty years, permitting inheritance, and the sale of land contracts, thereby presaging the transition to de facto ownership. So far, however, the central leaders have not allowed either. Thus an issue fundamental to the peasants, ownership, was not resolved in the peasants' favor.

It need not be assumed that the ideological commitment of party-state leaders to collective ownership was the sole cause of this crucial limitation on the reform. Even in the absence of ideological preferences, management of China's arable, a shrinking and extremely precious resource for which both agricultural and nonagricultural users compete, would be a difficult task, and a case can perhaps be made for relying on administrative mechanisms rather than the market to manage the land. Reportedly the failure to extend land contracts to fifty years was motivated not so much by ideological concerns with ownership as by unwillingness to freeze for decades the currently fragmented patterns of land use.[23] But at least for the more conservative leaders, judging by vehement denunciations of privatization in the post-Tiananmen period, privatization was a central issue determining the ideological direction of the country.

Second, and following from the preceding, ideology made the commitment to household contracting and individual and private enterprise contingent, not absolute, thereby keeping open the possibility of a rollback. Paradoxically, major attempts at recollectivization or at outright abolition of individual and private enterprise were not actually made in the 1980s, but there was uncertainty as to the party-state's ultimate intentions. As long as there was a socialist commitment, why could it not include recollectivization? And third, ideology influenced the process of reform because it endowed certain practices, such as the hiring of labor, with an aura of illegitimacy, even when officially sanctioned and legalized. The same point applied to certain outcomes, as when entrepreneurs reaped "staggering profits" or when inequality became more marked.

The assertion that ideology had an important impact on the peasants ran counter to the widespread belief among observers of China that a decline in ideology has taken place since 1978. This view is not inaccurate. How otherwise can the willingness of Chinese leaders to decollectivize by restoring household-based farming be explained? Decollectivization was surely evidence for the proposition that pragmatism had triumphed in China. Pragmatism was a principle enunciated by Deng Xiaoping himself in his famous quip that it didn't matter whether a cat was black or white as long as it caught mice and in the slogans of "Truth through facts" and "Practice is the sole criterion of truth," which suggested willingness to discard ideological dogma that stood in the way of innovation. Reformers seemed willing to make policy based on the criterion of efficacy or, as the Thirteenth Congress put it: "All things advantageous to the development of the productive forces serve the people's interests and are also a demand of socialism or allowed by socialism."[24] Reformers seemed willing to adopt a practical, problem-solving approach and to experiment freely with various solutions. All policy options seemed to be open. The "Four Principles" proclaimed by Deng in 1979 seemed to be a mere fig leaf for bolder and bolder reforms. As the reforms gained momentum, outside observers could only gasp, wondering what Chinese leaders would do next as reform policy entered one "forbidden zone" after another, and as more and more practices, such as hiring labor or experimenting with stock markets, were borrowed from the capitalist world.

Chinese pragmatism included not only rejection of Maoist leftism but also explicit questioning of Marxism-Leninism and explicit redefinitions to suit China's new needs. Hu Qili, a rising young leader until his purge after Tiananmen, said in 1986 that "while we must uphold the basic Marxist tenets under new historical conditions, we must have the courage to break through the few conclusions that experience has already proven to be outmoded or not entirely correct."[25] In 1987 General Secretary Zhao Ziyang redefined the nature of China's socialism in order to find a legitimate place for the private sector, telling the party that China was only at an "initial stage of socialism," characterized by a mixed economy of public ownership together with a supplementary but "necessary" individual and private economy. Zhao asserted that this stage would last 100 years. Some proposed that even after a century a mixed economy would still exist.[26] And the regime sought to legitimate private enterprise by promulgating a constitutional amendment to this effect.[27]

Willingness of leaders to question ideological dogma and to reformulate precepts in order to rationalize reforms reflected the battering that ideological beliefs had taken during the years of leftist excess. It also reflected the declining intensity and salience of belief that is characteristic of Marxist-Leninist systems in their later, postmobilization stages. Ideological legitimation seemed less essential to the party-state in the 1980s. National greatness, the Four Modernizations, and prosperity were invoked as substitutes. In society at large, the counterpart to the decline in the official insistence on ideological purity was indifference to ideology, noticeable particularly among young people, especially students. Marxist-Leninist-Maoist beliefs seemed to be increasingly irrelevant to China in the 1980s. Even the intense effort to revitalize ideology in the wake of the Tiananmen massacre of 1989 had an artificial and sterile flavor.

At the same time, however, dismissing ideology as simply a declining fringe phenomenon also distorts reality. Disillusionment among the populace and especially among elites such as students or intellectuals did not mean that ideology no longer played a role in party-state policies and practices. Ideology persisted in that even market-oriented economic reforms were presented within a framework of socialist goals and principles, which were articulated in public discourse, as in policy statements, speeches by leaders, and editorials in the press. They included the Four Principles, the notion of "socialism with Chinese characteristics," and the goal of fostering "socialist spiritual civilization." Socialist values were publicly extolled, including those of public ownership, the primacy of planning over the market, the continuing commitment to equality (that is, the goal of common prosperity even as some could legitimately get rich ahead of others), and a moral order that continued to rank the interests of the state first, then those of the collective, the individual coming last. According to this morality, market values were essentially viewed as instrumental to the ultimate attainment of socialist and Communist goals but not as good in their own right. In other words, the market was acceptable to the extent that it promoted the growth of the "productive forces."

In agriculture this meant that when output of major commodities such as grain stagnated in the second half of the 1980s, "certain comrades" called for recollectivization on the grounds that household contracting had outlived its usefulness because it could no longer promote the growth of the productive forces. As the *Farm Daily* put it in 1988, "nine years after its birth on the vast land of China the contract responsibility system with payment linked to output is actually facing a new test."[28] Opponents of these "comrades" argued strenuously that the household contract system could not develop because in the second half of the 1980s peasants had to cope with state's highly unfavorable price scissors and rampant inflation, which were robbing them of incentives to produce. More marketizing reform had to be instituted in order to make the new system work. The regime sided with those who viewed household contracting as still generally viable, but the commitment was a contingent one—that is, household contracting was acceptable because it still had potential.

Retention of Marxist-Leninist values even while market values were also espoused meant that reform policies were necessarily based on contradictory premises.[29] Socialist values of community, collectivism, and equality were in conflict with market values of the pursuit of individual profit. The former is premised on the legitimate primacy of the collective interest. Individuals are evaluated according to the extent to which they are willing to subordinate their interests to those of the collective. Conversely, the dominant value of a market system was that the individual pursuit of self-interest led to the common good.

In the agricultural reforms, this conflict between two different value systems expressed itself in the regime's offering the peasants a stream of reassurances that policies were stable even as it tried to keep open the possibility of future change. Throughout the 1980s, the party-state's commitment to the rural reforms were reaffirmed in major policy statements, including the annual Document No. 1 issued until 1984 by the Central Committee and since then jointly with the State Council, speeches by the leaders, editorials, and authoritative comments in the "Observer" feature of the *People's Daily* and the *Farm Daily*. The underlying reason for maintenance of rural reform was the same as that which had prompted reform in the first place, namely, necessity. The reforms had been adopted because peasants responded to the new incentives, resulting in increased productivity, output, and incomes. Abrogation of the reforms would lower the "enthusiasm for production" of the peasants and hence exact costs to China's development. Fear that this might happen and that one of the great successes of the Deng era would therefore be jeopardized led to these reassurances. The regime recognized the need to strengthen peasant interest in production and to allay peasant anxieties.[30]

Conversely, however, when Chinese leaders and officials talked about the stability of the reform, they chose language that undermined the very assurances the regime provided. Examination of the earnest affirmations that reform policy was stable shows that such avowals actually had ambiguous meanings and avoided making the kind of binding commitment the peasants wanted and needed. A frequently used formula was that policy "will not change for a long time" (*changqi bu bian*), which obviously left open the possibility of future change.[31] In Henan in 1987 "a rumor ran around some villages to the effect that the collective would recover all the contracted fields," resulting in lowered willingness to invest in land. Henan's party secretary, Yang Xizong, "explicitly announced to the cadres and masses that the contract responsibility system with payment linked to output, based on the household, will be kept unchanged for a long time."[32] Or peasants were told that household contracting was a basic party policy that "will certainly not be lightly changed."[33] Or a high official might tell peasants that "this year's central documents clearly stipulated that the policies on the individual economy and private enterprises will also remain unchanged," making listeners wonder about next year's central documents.[34] In some formulations, peasant preferences were mentioned, as by Hu Yaobang at the Twelfth Party Congress in 1982: "Family contracting is the party's long-term policy. It will certainly not be changed arbitrarily against the peasants wishes."[35]

Sometimes, authoritative comment flatly stated that policy on household contracting "will not change" (*bu hui bian*).[36] But this didn't mean abandonment of qualifications. In October 1989, the "Observer" of the *People's Daily* proclaimed that household contracting would definitely be maintained (*jianchi bu bian*). But the text, quoting Jiang Zemin, opened a loophole in stipulating that in advanced areas with "appropriate conditions"—that is, where peasants had alternative employment opportunities, where the level of mechanization was high, and where the masses agreed—"an appropriate scale of management can safely (*wen tuo*) be promoted." This meant farming on a larger scale than that of the individual household. In most places, household contracting was necessary "at present" but in a few places change could be introduced.[37] This formulation, it is worth noting, was the obverse of the loophole opened for decollectivization in 1979–1980, when household contracting was permitted in very poor areas, thereby legitimating local initiatives that in time led to the spread of household contracting to wealthier areas and ultimately to the entire country. As of 1991, it was not clear whether this new approach was having a significant impact in the rural areas.

The point is that ambiguous formulas had a long history in rural China. In the early 1950s, for instance, commitments to private property were made, especially to the preservation of the rich peasant economy, "not as a temporary policy," as Liu Shaoqi put it, "but as long-term policy."[38] It lasted for barely five years. Unwillingness to make binding commitments for the future is a central characteristic of the Marxist-Leninist orientation.[39] It was a sign that socialist aims had not disappeared. The reform program was thus presented to the country in uneasy coexistence with continued affirmation of Marxist-Leninist ideology and goals. It was intended to be lasting, but the dual goals of stabilization without sacrifice of the socialist future in effect caused peasants to view the program as unstable.

How to reconcile Marxist-Leninist and market values and how much importance to attach to each was a major problem for policymakers. It was a problem that would exist even if Chinese leaders were united on just where the balance should be struck, which of course they have not been. A united leadership had to deal with the management of the contradictory values of the market and socialism. As long as there was a stated commitment both to socialism and to reform, and as long as there was political pressure to behave as if ideology mattered and as if it were an operative and governing part of the system, conflicting objectives and values arose. If one assumes that China's paramount leader, Deng Xiaoping, made all the decisions, one can discern a fluctuating course in which Deng attempted to reconcile competing goals. Deng fought a two-front war, deciding when reform had gone too far and had to be reined in and when it should be further unleashed, giving rise to a pattern of letting go (*fang*) and reining in (*shou*).

Deng pursued reform even while decreeing adherence to the Four Principles in spring 1979. In 1983, reportedly incensed by erosion of socialist values, he launched the campaign against spiritual pollution. After a *People's Daily* editorial charged that "some peasants had become receptive to rotten capitalist ideology and remnant feudal thoughts," some readers assumed that the campaign should be extended into the countryside.[40] But only a month later, when the deleterious impact on peasants of antipollution activities had communicated itself to the central authorities, an urgent edict specifically exempted the peasants from the campaign. Activities of specialized households were not to be considered polluting and peasants were to be assured that reform policy had not changed.[41] Although Deng sought to insulate the economic reform program from the effects of this campaign, especially in the countryside, he was not fully successful.

In 1986–1987, when student disturbances led to the purge of party General Secretary Hu Yaobang, Deng initiated a campaign against bourgeois liberalization but took steps to insulate the rural sector from its impact. Almost as soon as the struggle against bourgeois liberalization began, Central Committee Document No. 4 declared the countryside off-limits and assured peasants "the policy for developing the individual economy" would not be changed.[42] The *People's Daily* "Observer" noted that if the campaign did penetrate to the villages, instability would result. People would panic and property would be destroyed. If production were to fall and living standards failed to rise, peasants would lose interest in socialism, and this would provide soil for the growth of bourgeois liberalization.[43]

In the aftermath of Tiananmen, Deng called for struggle against counterrevolution and bourgeois liberalization, even while sticking to reform and the open door. With the purge of General Secretary Zhao Ziyang, conservative leaders known for distrust of private enterprise and for preferring a planned economy to a market economy gained ascendancy, and urban and rural reforms came under more sustained challenge. A crackdown on tax evasion and other offenses allegedly perpetrated by private entrepreneurs seemed to be directed not simply against delinquents among them but against private enterprise as such. Policy statements were harsh, and a number of enterprises were closed down.[44] With regard to household contracting, strong voices were heard favoring some kind of recollectivization, on grounds that efficiency required a larger scale of operations.[45] By October 1989, however, General Secretary Jiang Zemin and Prime Minister Li Peng came out strongly in support of household contracting, at least as far as most of the rural sector was concerned. In late fall 1989, support for private enterprise was also reaffirmed, including explicit denials that the crackdown on tax evaders was meant to do away with the private sector altogether.[46]

The record suggests that under Deng's leadership the balance of political forces generally ended up on the side of reaffirming and continuing rural reform. However, peasant responses cited above suggest that the effort to insulate the countryside was not fully successful, as the campaigns did play a role in keeping alive peasant worries. One reason for their ongoing worries was that peasants could not be sure whether the current repudiation of attacks on the reforms would in fact last or whether leaders ill-disposed toward private activity might not prevail in future campaigns. Lingering skepticism is well illustrated by a case from Fujian. In February 1987, when the Fujian provincial secretary visited Fuqing County, he met with nine specialized households, all of which reported that "the recent student unrest and personnel changes made by the central authorities had caused them to worry about possible policy changes." The dissemination of central documents calling for further reform had calmed them down somewhat; "nevertheless, they were still not completely reassured." The party secretary thereupon led them in study of Zhao Ziyang's Spring Festival speech, which had stipulated that five reform policies would be changed. Using everyday language, the party secretary then told them that socialism "aimed at making the country powerful and the people rich. . . . Combatting bourgeois liberalization will be carried out only in the political and ideological realm and within the party." He told them that as long as they followed party policy and acted in accord with the law and "in a civilized manner," they were free to promote their businesses. "Everyone was pleased to hear this."[47]

Deng's two-front war was not the only source of peasant insecurity. The 1980s were characterized by deep leadership cleavages over fundamental questions of how far the reforms should go and where the balance among different values, approaches, and policies should be struck. Different leaders attached different levels of importance to the preservation of socialist values. The reasons for this varied. Some leaders no doubt defined their interests in the struggle for power as requiring a stricter ideological stance; others adhered to orthodox beliefs; still others believed that socialist solutions worked better or were more appropriate to China's situation than those associated with the market. An impressionistic canvass of public discussion on individual and private enterprise in major policy statements, press articles, and academic journals shows three opinion currents.[48] One was unambiguously favorable to enterprise, the second was unambiguously opposed, and the third was conditionally supportive. Probably because individual and private enterprise has been supported by the country's dominant leaders, opponents remained anonymous. At the same time, opinion that favored private entrepreneurship without qualification was also fairly rare. The bulk of comment fell into the broad range of contingent views.

Supportive and Opposing Comment

The strongly supportive attitude believed that what really mattered was to transform rural China's "self-sufficient, natural" economy by developing the productive forces and the commodity economy. Whatever policies promoted such forces would help socialism. This view saw in specialized households "fine qualities of commodity producers under the socialist system."[49] Entrepreneurs were progressive because they represented the advanced productive forces. As producers for the market, they were pioneers in the advancement of the commodity economy, and their responsiveness to the market differentiated that market from the Stalinist "product economy" based on rigid control. In the forefront of modernization, entrepreneurs promoted diversification, scientific farming, a more complex division of labor, competition, and the absorption of surplus rural labor. They invested, introduced advanced technology, and had essential managerial skills; they played a key role in drawing smallholders into socialized production, thus promoting exchange, cooperation, and interdependence. Strongly supportive writings not only claimed a highly positive economic role for them but also a positive social role: Entrepreneurs helped in overcoming egalitarianism, developing linkages to the urban sector and thereby "naturally spreading the advanced ideology of the working class" to the villages. They actually promoted socialist goals, including the elimination of the differences between town and country and the consolidation of the worker-peasant alliance. In short, "specialized households represent the hope for future change in the countryside."[50]

Document No. 1 of 1984 endorsed the supportive view, stating that "we should treasure, cherish, and actively support" specialized households.[51] In that same year, when the media reported extensively on harassment of entrepreneurs, the Central Committee made advocacy of entrepreneurs into a test that determined whether localities were "in line politically with the CPC Central Committee." An implementing directive in Anhui Province defined the backing of specialized households as a yardstick for measuring a cadre's political orthodoxy: "The broad masses of cadres must realize that going against the households engaged in specialized production is tantamount to going against commodity production and the four modernizations."[52]

Documents No. 1 of 1985 and 1986 took a more guardedly supportive view of rural entrepreneurs, but a good deal of journalistic and academic comment continued to be highly favorable to them. A major example was the publicity extended to Wenzhou Municipality, Zhejiang, a case of urban-rural enterprise that demonstrated the developmental potential of private, family-based industrial manufacturing integrated into extensive commercial networks, including markets for labor, money, and means of production. Wenzhou became a celebrated model of "universal significance" for rural development.[53]

After the June 4, 1989, crackdown, the purged General Secretary Zhao Ziyang and the intellectual circles around him were accused of having advocated wholesale privatization, which suggests that some currents of opinion had gone beyond the relatively cautious formula adopted at the Thirteenth Party Congress, according to which private enterprise would play a necessary but only "supplementary" role. *Shijie Jingji Daobao,* (World economic report) a liberal Shanghai newspaper, reportedly wrote in January 1989 that household contracting had been the first step in reform and that "developing the private economy must be regarded as a task of top priority in China and the second step of reform. In the vast rural areas of China, the private economy should become the main force to develop the productive forces." Zhao Ziyang had allegedly failed to "take effective measures to criticize and stop such sinister propaganda which violated the Constitution." Zhao was quoted as having said in 1987 that no one could define the socialist road, encouraging his "think tanks and elitists" directly to attack public ownership. Even though Zhao had publicly affirmed the predominance of public ownership, he had connived "at the blind development of the private economy."[54] These charges, if true, suggest that some leaders may have been willing to allow greater scope for private enterprise.

Those who unambiguously opposed rural private enterprise were quoted as "some comrades" or "some people":

> Some people look at the rapid development of the rural private economy, worry that it is causing the disintegration and displacement of the cooperative economy, that a fundamental change in the rural socialist economy is taking place. They therefore regard the private economy as a "foreign body" that must be restricted, attacked, and weakened.[55]

"Some comrades" adhered to the leftist view that progress is measured by the degree of public ownership of the means of production rather than the growth of the productive forces. They saw activities such as private trade as a form of retrogression and compromise with capitalism.[56] Wan Li, the reformist vice-premier, charged that their view of commerce and profit was feudal, reminiscent of the traditional saying that "the gentleman seeks righteousness; the small man seeks profit," assumptions perpetuated by the Marxist thesis that commerce does not create social wealth.[57] "Some comrades" saw the "inflationary growth" of petit bourgeois ideology in the countryside as posing a stark choice: "In doing ideological and political work in the future, which banner should be upheld, the banner of wholeheartedly serving the people or that of trying to build up family fortunes?"[58] They saw the policy of letting some get rich first as leading to polarization and hiring of labor as exploitation. Although only a few comrades held such views, according to the press, their influence impeded reform, because their views communicated themselves to the lower levels, down to the village, causing doubt and confusion among cadres. Thus when village cadres were told to implement a new policy that ran counter to Maoist views of socialism, and when they heard that "some people" at the higher levels regarded the new policy as an unorthodox deviation, the village cadres would hesitate to act, fearing criticism, wavering at the first sign of "opposition and grumbling."[59]

Contingent Support

A wide range of politicians, from those with conservative viewpoints to those of liberal persuasion, gave conditional support to individual and private enterprise. Conditionality had several components. First, with regard to duration, the initial stage of socialism implied that nonsocialist enterprise would exist for a long time but not permanently. As the theorist Yu Guanyuan put it:

> When speaking of the development of non-public ownership economy, we have never forgotten to add such phrases as "appropriate" and "to a certain extent," proving that we have attached great importance to the adhering to the socialist orientation of the entire national economy. With this in mind, we will make the capitalist factor in the initial stage of socialism play a role favorable to the development of the socialist economy.[60]

The treatment of the nonsocialist sector would differ from the 1950s, when the goal was to eliminate it. It would exist during the entire historical period of the initial stage of socialism. But "long-term existence," Yu emphasized, was not equivalent to permanence: "Naturally, these nonsocialist economic sectors will not exist in the distant future. They belong only to China's initial stage of socialism. They will not live forever [*wan sui*]. . . . The nonsocialist economy will naturally change into the socialist economy."[61] The rub in this projection was that the Communist party could of course alter these time frames at any instance, as it had done before.

Second, the contingent approach evaluated entrepreneurs according to their moral conduct. Because of their goal of making a profit, they were regarded with suspicion. Their "lawful," "legitimate," and "proper" activities were supported, thereby drawing attention to unlawful, illegitimate, and improper activities. High praise combined with denunciations of a "small number" or a "very small number" of entrepreneurs who "reaped staggering profits" using improper, illegal, and "disgusting" methods.[62] At the 1985 Rural Work Conference, Du Runsheng, head of the two Rural Research Centers of the Secretariat and the State Council and a leader in rural reform, demanded that specialized households be protected, encouraged, and supported. But he also demanded improvements in the regulatory and legal systems, so that those seeking "exorbitant profits" by taking advantage of loopholes and who aroused "strong indignation in society" could be curbed and brought to justice.[63]

The conservative politician Deng Liqun employed the same contingent formula, praising specialized households for making "enormous contributions" to the state but accusing some of not being "civilized" in that they advanced their interests by fraud and speculation. Deng Liqun suggested that local party leaders check on such people, thereby combining the development of specialized households with the building of socialist spiritual civilization.[64] Hu Qiaomu, a well-known conservative, also endorsed the goal of becoming wealthy through hard work, provided the methods used were legitimate and the individual in question made contributions to society. "We should overcome the unhealthy tendency among some people of putting money above all or even judging a person's social status by his income."[65] But the liberal reform leader Wan Li, when offering a spirited defense of the desirability and legitimacy of seeking after profit, added that the socialist commodity economy required that profit be sought for the state and the collective, and that its goal was to pull everyone along to common prosperity. In this way, righteousness would be united with profit. Wan Li also did not recognize profit making as an inherently beneficial activity.[66]

Third, nonsocialist enterprise received support only as long as it was a supplement to the socialist sector, constrained by linkages to the socialist economy as well as any limits on size. Zhao Ziyang, when meeting with village entrepreneurs from the collective and individual private sectors, emphasized that businesses in the latter category were linked in multitudinous ways to the "powerful socialist economy." They could play a "certain role" in the development of the socialist commodity economy.[67] The implication was that because of these linkages, individual and private enterprise was not a threat. As for size, the question was how large private enterprise could become before the predominance of the socialist sector was threatened. Some academics envisaged very significant expansion, as did, for instance, the Beijing economist Li Yining, who suggested that the private sector should be kept below one-third of output value. Given the small size of the individual and private enterprise, this actually meant a tremendous expansion. Li also proposed that the one-third limit could be exceeded "in some departments and areas."[68] This latter point was important because of the territorially uneven growth of private enterprise. Did predominance have to apply to every village or town? A case in point was Wenzhou, Zhejiang, where, as of 1988, the individual private sector accounted for 83 percent of agricultural and industrial output value.[69] Wenzhou, as noted, was a much-praised example of development based on private entrepreneurship. But "some comrades" asked whether the dominance of the private sector in Wenzhou did not violate the principle of the predominance of the socialist sector, thereby requiring curbs. "Predominance" was reportedly a concept that would be applied to the country as a whole, not to specific places.

The question of when nonsocialist enterprise might constitute a risk also arose with regard to large specialized households, that is, large family enterprise. The rise of several "dozen large households" in Wenzhou, each with an output value in the hundreds of thousands or even in the millions of yuan, was praised because these households made a major contribution to investment at a time when state funds were scarce. But this developmental contribution was not adequate to qualify these households for approval. Instead, the risks of letting private enterprise expand had to be appraised: "The development of these private undertakings has arisen under our country's socialist, political, and macroeconomic control"; because the state-run economy was still dominant, "allowing them to exist and grow will not involve any risks."[70] But speaking about specialized households more generally, Document No. 1 of 1986 noted that "although we must encourage the various specialized households to become well off by hard work, we will not tolerate their 'becoming rich and influential families.'"[71]

Conclusion

The rural reforms have enjoyed a substantial degree of stability, certainly when compared with the endless policy reversals of the Mao era. Rural reforms began in 1978 and were essentially maintained. As of 1991, household contracting was still in place. Corollary reforms, such as individual and private enterprise, which also began in the late 1970s and early 1980s, have been continued as well, at least in broad outline.

Yet at the same time, much evidence exists of peasant insecurity about the permanence of the reforms. The root of this worry lies in the mixed nature of the reforms: They were attempts to combine socialist features and predominance with nonsocialist features. The leaders allowed peasant families to contract for land, but they did not allow them to own the land. They allowed private enterprise to do business, provided it didn't threaten the socialist essence in doing so. Peasants' fears exacted costs in that they adversely affected peasant investment choices. The unwillingness or inability to let go of fundamental ideological premises, that is, of the claim to be leading the country to socialism and ultimately to communism, was thus the reason peasants perceived the reforms as unstable.

What, for example, could cause a change to prompt the party-state to allow private ownership of land? In 1978 the Deng group launched reform because they believed that an economic emergency existed in which agricultural production had stagnated because the collective system had robbed peasants of the incentives to produce. In order to pave the way for change, the Deng group broke with the radical Maoist ideology. One result was household contracting. If in the 1990s a similar economic emergency were to arise, it is not inconceivable that a further, even more drastic break with principles could be made, such as one that would make the land into a marketable commodity and permit free ownership. Measures along such lines might well allay peasant insecurity and add incentives to invest, for example. It is of course unlikely that the current conservative leadership would adopt such a course. The deaths of party elders who rule behind the scenes would probably be required, as their commitment to socialist doctrine appears still to be very solid. At the same time, the passing from the scene of a senior leader with the immense authority of a Deng Xiaoping might also make it less likely that a momentous decision such as the privatization of land could be taken. Most likely, future regimes may be too weak to be able to take such a step. Unless the Chinese Communist system itself is abolished altogether, as happened in Eastern Europe in 1989–1990, chances are that the country will continue to muddle along, unable to do without the reforms but also unable fully to endorse them.

Notes

1. Some of these issues are examined in my forthcoming book, Thomas Bernstein, *The Political Challenge of China's Rural Reforms* (Armonk, N.Y.: M. E. Sharpe, forthcoming).

2. Cf. Vivienne Shue, *The Reach of the State* (Stanford: Stanford University Press, 1988). Shue suggests that in the reform era the reach of the state might actually expand rather than contract because the reforms broke up the protective web that local cadres had woven around their peasant charges during the Mao era. See p. 148.

3. *Renmin Ribao* (People's daily, hereafter *RMRB*), November 18, 1983, *Foreign Broadcast Information Service, People's Republic of China* (hereafter *FBIS-Chi*) 226, November 22, 1983, K16.

4. Radio Harbin, October 30, 1983, *FBIS-Chi* 211, October 31, 1983, Sl.

5. Xinhua News Agency, Beijing, December 8, 1983, *FBIS-Chi* 239, December 12, 1983, K6.

6. Radio Xian, February 26, 1986, *FBIS-Chi* 42, March 3, 1986, T3; *RMRB,* April 19, 1986, *FBIS-Chi* 79, April 24, 1986, K27.

7. *Nongmin Ribao* (Farm daily, hereafter *NMRB*), May 20, 1987, *FBIS-Chi* 109, June 8, 1987, K16–K17.

8. *Nongye Jingji Wenti* (Economic issues in agriculture), No. 8, August 23, 1988, 44–51, in Joint Publications Research Service—China Area Reports (hereafter JPRS-CAR) 88-078, December 8, 1988, 66.

9. Xinhua News Agency, Beijing, November 2, 1988, JPRS-CAR-88-081, December 22, 1988, 43–44.

10. *Jiangxi Ribao* (Jiangxi daily), June 1, 1988, JPRS-CAR-88-057, September 20, 1988, 44–46.

11. "Observer," *RMRB,* October 22, 1989, and *Ningxia Ribao,* November 14, 1989, *FBIS-Chi* 239, December 12, 1989, 41–43; Radio Zhengzhou, December 25, 1989, *FBIS-Chi* 3, January 4, 1990, 48.

12. Radio Xian, July 16, 1986, *FBIS-Chi* 139, July 21, 1986, T7.

13. *NMRB* editorial, March 28, 1987, *FBIS-Chi* 73, April 16, 1987, 19–20. See also Nicholas Lardy, *Agriculture in China's Modern Economic Development* (New York: Cambridge University Press, 1983).

14. Lu Wen, "Wo guo nongcun jingji de liang zhong fazhan qushi" (Two trends in the development of the agricultural economy), *Nongye Jingji Wenti,* No. 6, 1986, 16.

15. *RMRB* editorial, November 8, 1983, and Xinhua News Agency, Beijing, March 30, 1984, *FBIS-Chi* 65, April 3, 1984, K10ff.; *RMRB,* August 3, 1984, *FBIS-Chi* 65, April 3, 1984, K1–K14.

16. *RMRB,* November 14, 1985, *FBIS-Chi* 228, November 26, 1985, K21.

17. *NMRB,* June 4, 1986, *FBIS-Chi* 125, June 30, 1986, 23–25.

18. *Ban Yue Tan* (Bimonthly digest), 10, May 26, 1986, *FBIS-Chi* 116, June 17, 1986, P1.

19. "Observer," *NMRB,* August 5, 1987, *FBIS-Chi* 154, August 11, 1987, K20–K21; and Radio Shenyang, July 28, 1986, *FBIS-Chi* 146, July 30, 1986, S4–S5.

20. *Shijie Jingji Daobao* (World economic report), February 29, 1988, *FBIS-Chi* 51, March 16, 1988, 28–29. In this case, a Hebei party secretary explicitly reassured the entrepreneurs that class labels would not be pinned on them.

21. *RMRB,* December 6, 1989.

22. On *biaoxian,* or conduct, see Andrew Walder, *Communist Neo-Traditionalism: Work and Authority in Chinese Industry* (Berkeley: University of California Press, 1986), 132ff.

23. Information supplied by Chinese scholars, Beijing, December 1989.

24. Zhao Ziyang, "Advance Along the Road of Socialism with Chinese Characteristics," Radio Beijing, October 25, 1987, *FBIS-Chi* 206-Supplement, October 25, 1987, 33.

25. Xinhua News Agency, Beijing, April 30, 1986, *FBIS-Chi* 85, May 2, 1986, K4. In 1984 *Renmin Ribao* had declared that it would be "naive and stupid" to adhere rigidly to old-fashioned Marxist principles and that one could not expect the works of Marx and Lenin written in their time to solve today's problems. But three days later, the paper admitted error. The key sentence should have read "could not solve all of today's problems." Cf. *RMRB,* December 7 and 10, 1984.

26. *Guangming Ribao* (Guangming daily, hereafter *GMRB*), June 29, 1987, *FBIS-Chi* 136, July 16, 1987, K6–K10.

27. See, for instance, Radio Zhengzhou, October 28, 1987, *FBIS-Chi* 209, October 29, 1987, 17–18.

28. "Observer," *NMRB,* February 9, 1988, *FBIS-Chi* 32, February 18, 1988, 15–16.

29. Cf. David Apter, *The Politics of Modernization* (Chicago: University of Chicago Press, 1965), especially Ch. 1.

30. *NMRB* editorial, March 28, 1987, *FBIS-Chi* 73, April 16, 1987, K19–K20.

31. For examples, see *RMRB,* March 25, 1985, Document No. 1; Du Runsheng, interview, August 2, 1985; *RMRB,* March 24 and April 17, 1985; and *Ban Yue Tan* 7, April 10, 1986; *FBIS-Chi* 82, April 29, 1986, K21.

32. Radio Zhengzhou, January 31, 1987, *FBIS-Chi* 27, February 10, 1987, 34.

33. "Observer," *RMRB,* June 2, 1987, *FBIS-Chi* 120, June 23, 1987, K23–K24.

34. Xinhua News Agency, Beijing, March 16, 1987, *FBIS-Chi* 53, March 19, 1987, O1. Anhui's governor offered this assurance.

35. Hu Yaobang in *Hongqi,* No. 18, 1982, 13.

36. "Observer," *RMRB,* overseas edition, June 2, 1987.

37. "Observer," *RMRB,* October 1989 and November 27, 1989.

38. *Liu Shaoqi Wenxuan* (Selected works of Liu Shaoqi), Vol. 2 (Beijing: Renmin Chubanshe, 1985), 40.

39. Cf. Kenneth Jowitt, *Revolutionary Breakthrough and National Development,* (Berkeley: University of California Press, 1971).

40. *RMRB* editorial, November 8, 1983.

41. Xinhua News Agency, "Commentator" ("for special dissemination") Beijing, December 8, 1983, *FBIS-Chi* 239, December 12, 1983, K5.

42. *NMRB* editorial, January 27, 1987, *FBIS-Chi* 20, January 30, 1987, K31.

43. "Observer," *RMRB,* June 5, 1987, *FBIS-Chi* 109, June 8, 1987, K12–K14.

44. *RMRB,* August 2, 1989; "China in Crackdown Orders Many Companies to Close," *New York Times,* August 29, 1989, p. D1; and *Far Eastern Economic Review,* August 24, 1989, 51–52. One reason for the harshness was that private entrepreneurs in Beijing had reportedly given financial support to the democracy movement of May 1989.

45. *South China Morning Post,* September 7, 1989. See also Bernstein, *Political Challenge,* Ch. 2.

46. "Observer," *RMRB* October 22, 1989; *RMRB* December 6, 1989.

47. *Fujian Ribao* (Fujian daily), February 22, 1987, *FBIS-Chi* 45, March 9, 1987, O3–O4.

48. Cf. Dorothy J. Solinger, "Commerce: The Petty Private Sector and the Three Lines in the Early 1980s," in D. Solinger, ed., *Three Visions of Chinese Socialism,* (Boulder: Westview Press, 1984), 73–111.

49. *RMRB,* June 3, 1984, *FBIS-Chi* 111, June 7, 1984, K1–K3.

50. *RMRB,* July 16, 1984, *FBIS-Chi* 145, July 26, 1984, K15–K18; *RMRB,* February 10, 1987, *FBIS-Chi* 40, February 13, 1987, 26–27.

51. "The CPC Central Committee's Circular on Rural Work in 1984," Xinhua News Agency, Beijing, June 11, 1984, *FBIS-Chi* 115, June 13, 1984, K3.

52. Xinhua News Agency, Beijing, June 11, 1984, *FBIS-Chi* 116, June 14, 1984, K1–K2; "Observer," *Anhui Ribao* (Anhui daily), transcript of a Radio Hefei broadcast, October 6, 1984, *FBIS-Chi* 196, October 9, 1984, 0–1.

53. "Observer," *Jingji Ribao* (Jingji daily), July 31, 1986, *FBIS-Chi* 152, August 7, 1986, K11–K12. For a comprehensive description, see *NMRB,* October 11, 1986, *FBIS-Chi* 213, November 4, 1986, K9–K22.

54. See *RMRB,* September 4, 1989, *FBIS-Chi* 183, September 22, 1989, 31–35; *Wen Hui Bao* (Wen Hui report) (Shanghai), December 2, 1989, *FBIS-Chi* 237, December 12, 1989, 18–23; *GMRB,* July 22, 1989, *FBIS-Chi* 151, August 8, 1989, 30–33; *Jingji Ribao,* September 8, 1989, *FBIS-Chi* 183, September 22, 1989, 35–37.

55. Lu Wen, "Wo guo nongcun jingji de liang zhong fazhan qushi," 15.

56. "Observer," *NMRB,* May 10, 1986, *FBIS-Chi* 96, May 19, 1986, K14; *Hubei Ribao* (Hubei daily), April 14, 1987, *FBIS-Chi* 81, April 28, 1987, 2–4.

57. *RMRB,* November 27, 1986; for the point on commerce, see Radio Nanning, January 12, 1981, *FBIS-Chi* 8, January 13, 1981, 1–2.

58. *Yangcheng Wanbao* (Canton evening news) (Guangzhou) July 13, 1983, also *RMRB,* September 25, 1984, *FBIS-Chi* 188, September 26, 1984, K10–K12.

59. "Observer," *NMRB,* June 2, 1987, *FBIS-Chi* 113, June 12, 1987, K22–K23.

60. Yu Guangyuan, "Shehui Zhuyi Chuji Jieduan de Jingji" (The economy of the initial stage of socialism), *Zhongguo Shehui Kexue* (Chinese social science), No. 3, May 10, 1987, 81.

61. Ibid., 82.

62. *RMRB,* April 19, 1986, *FBIS-Chi* 79, April 24, 1986, K27–K28; *Liaowang* (Observer) (Beijing), February 10, 1986, *FBIS-Chi* 44, March 6, 1986, K13. "Disgusting" refers to the sale of fake medicines.

63. Xinhua News Agency, Beijing, January 26, 1986, *FBIS-Chi* 29, February 12, 1986, K6 and K8.

64. Xinhua News Agency, Beijing, September 6, 1984, *FBIS-Chi* 176, September 10, 1984, K6–K7; October 10, 1984; and 201, October 16, 1984, K1–K2.

65. *Fujian Ribao,* February 7, 1985, *FBIS-Chi* 38, February 26, 1985, K3–K4; *Fujian Ribao,* February 25, 1985, *FBIS-Chi* 49, March 13, 1985, 6–7.

66. *RMRB,* November 27, 1986.

67. *RMRB,* overseas edition, September 7, 1987.

68. *Jingji Cankao* (Economic reference), October 21, 1988, *FBIS-Chi* 212, November 2, 1988, 33.

69. *Liaowang,* No. 4, January 25, 1988, 7–9.

70. *NMRB,* October 11, 1986, *FBIS-Chi* 213, November 4, 1986, 19.

71. "Plan of the CPC Central Committee and State Council for Rural Work in 1986," Xinhua News Agency, Beijing, February 22, 1986, *FBIS* 36, February 24, 1986, K7.

8

Students and the State in China: The Crisis in Ideology and Organization

Stanley Rosen

In their postmortem analyses of the spring 1989 "turmoil," the more perceptive Chinese authorities were compelled to acknowledge that a significant number of students had become highly skeptical of some of the regime's core ideological, organizational, and economic values. Many students refused to accept uncritically that Marxism-Leninism–Mao Zedong Thought should be adopted as their governing belief system. More and more students questioned whether the Communist party's dictatorship was the most appropriate party-state form to lead the country to modernization. There were widespread doubts—even before the cataclysmic events that began to unfold in Eastern Europe and the Soviet Union—that socialism was superior to capitalism. In short, with regard to the sacrosanct Four Cardinal Principles, students had turned agnostic. This loss of faith inevitably affected the party's "transmission belts" to youth. The Communist Youth League had atrophied to the point that many students found it irrelevant to their concerns. In the absence of a viable belief system, students turned, almost reflexively, to any new thought trend that was introduced into China, pausing only briefly before moving on to some newer, usually foreign, hot topic to fill what had become an ideological vacuum. Bypassing the CYL and officially sanctioned student unions, they organized their own societies and special interest groups on campus, less fettered by the myriad constraints that had limited the appeal of the official organizations.

Although the developments described above were gradually unfolding throughout the reform period of the 1980s, the extent of student estrangement from the regime was perhaps not fully appreciated by the authorities until the dramatic events of April–June 1989. Far from seriously addressing the concerns that contributed to the students' loss of faith—which would have required, at a minimum, a wide-ranging public dialogue over the nature and direction of the Chinese Revolution at the current stage—Chinese authorities have responded to the authority crisis dividing state and society with policies primarily aimed at controlling any independent student behavior, only halfheartedly seeking to shepherd the wayward back into the flock. In their appeals to the glories of the pre-1949 Communist Revolution and their revival of the campaigns to study the selfless revolutionary heroes of pre–Cultural Revolution China, they have conceptualized a society that no longer exists, raising issues far removed from the concerns of Chinese students in the 1990s. Having "lost" the current generation of university students, the regime has focused on future generations, introducing extensive military and ideological training for new students in an effort to counter the influence of their more jaded peers on the university campuses. In this chapter I attempt to document the extent of the students' ideological and organizational estrangement from the regime and the response of the authorities.[1]

Chinese Student Attitudes by the Late 1980s

During the course of the reform decade, the relationship between Chinese students and the state underwent a number of important changes. Put most simply, at the start of the reform period, in 1978, Chinese youth faced highly indefinite prospects, relying on the state to expand educational opportunities, provide jobs, and integrate them into a very uncertain post–Cultural Revolution society. China was still relatively isolated from the outside world. By the late 1980s, the CCP had been so successful in meeting these most basic demands that youth expectations had changed dramatically. Market reforms and the opening to the outside world had altered and expanded the structure of opportunity for youth beyond the abilities and inclinations of the CCP to meet them.[2] By the end of the decade, many youth had rejected the regime's core values and were actively searching for a new belief system; enthusiasm for studies had seriously declined; the regime's transmission belts to youth had atrophied; and students openly and expectantly looked West, both as a source for new beliefs and as a potential escape from a China still under the control of an aging leadership clinging to power.

TABLE 8.1 The Belief Systems of Secondary School Students (in percentages)

N=1,079

	Junior High Students	Senior High Students
No belief system or do not know	44.7	41.9
Marxism-Leninism-Mao Zedong Thought and the Communist party	30.0	30.4
Truth	7.4	5.4
Both Marxism-Leninism and Buddhism	2.1	2.5
God and Jesus Christ	2.6	3.1
Reality	3.0	5.4
Freedom	7.0	8.8
Fate	3.3	2.5

Source: Wang Shuzhi, "Zhongxueshengde zhengzhi xinyang yu Malie zhuyi jiaoyu" [Secondary school students' beliefs and Marxist-Leninist education] (Liaoning), *Xiandai zhongxiaoxue jiaoyu* [Modern primary and secondary education] No. 2, 1990, p. 24.

The Search for a Viable Belief System

Although they differ among themselves on the causes for the phenomenon and the solutions necessary to reverse the trend, Chinese authorities have acknowledged that student belief in the regime's core values has seriously eroded, particularly in comparison to the pre–Cultural Revolution period. Recent survey data show the extent of the problem from the junior high through the university levels. For example, a survey of 2,000 university students in Hangzhou found that 76 percent agreed that ideals are necessary. When asked their own ideals, however, 66 percent said they did not know what they were; another 20 percent answered that it was impossible to formulate such ideals; and only 14 percent responded that they actually had ideals.[3]

The regime sees the spread of this phenomenon to secondary school students as particularly worrisome. Table 8.1 reports the results of a study of 1,079 junior and senior high school students from rural and urban schools around Jinzhou, Liaoning Province. More than 40 percent of the students either had no belief system or did not know what they believed; only 30 percent gave the "correct" answer of Marxism-Leninism–Mao Zedong Thought and the Communist party.[4] A survey of the value system of 569 third-year junior and third-year senior high school students in four Shanghai districts offered a limited number of specific choices, pitting the regime's rather abstract core political values

TABLE 8.2 What Kind of Person Should One Become?

Choices	N=569 %
One who is honest, has integrity	56
One who observes discipline and obeys the law	22
One who is patriotic	20
One who persists in the Four Basic Principles	3

Source: Investigation Group of the Educational Information Research Office of the Educational Research Institute of Shanghai Municipality, "Shanghai bufen zhongxuesheng jiazhi quxiang diaocha" [An investigation of the values of some secondary school students in Shanghai], *Shanghai jiaoyu keyan* [Education research on Shanghai] No. 6, November 1989, p. 36.

TABLE 8.3 Ideals Chosen by Secondary School Students in Shanghai

Ideals	N=569 %
To have freedom of choice	59
To realize the Four Modernizations	18
To find a satisfying profession	16
Communism	6
To establish a comfortable family	2

Source: Investigation Group of the Educational Information Research Office of the Educational Research Institute of Shanghai Municipality, "Shanghai bufen zhongxuesheng jiazhi quxiang diaocha" [An investigation of the values of some secondary school students in Shanghai], *Shanghai jiaoyu keyan* [Education research on Shanghai] No. 6, November 1989, p. 36.

against concrete values of more immediate relevance to the students. Tables 8.2 and 8.3 present some data from that survey.

Although it is perhaps not surprising that respondents saw honesty as a higher value than "persisting in the Four Basic Principles," or that control over one's life was more salient to the students than the realization of communism, the overwhelming percentage difference between these choices was disturbing to the authorities. Of particular concern was that CYL members were more likely to choose "honesty"

(64 percent) over the Four Principles (2 percent) than those outside the league. In like manner, only 4 percent of league members and third-year senior high students opted for communism as their value choice.[5]

In recent years, inspired by Chinese translations of such classics of the U.S. behavioral literature as Gabriel Almond and Sidney Verba's *Civic Culture,* Chinese researchers have begun to examine their own country's political culture through sample surveys. The most ambitious study used a national sample and published results that disaggregated the findings by occupation, age, educational level, location of residence, and political status, but most such studies are more limited in scope.[6]

Nevertheless, even local studies can at times provide revealing insights into the political culture of Chinese youth. For example, a study of over 1,500 youth in Guangzhou concluded that the most prominent characteristic of these youth was their "concern with concrete matters relating to their work" (*wushi*).[7] Both direct and indirect questions were used to elicit youth attitudes toward government and politics in China. The researchers were pleased that 70 percent of the youth acknowledged—in answer to a direct question—that the Four Cardinal Principles were the foundation of the state and used this finding to explain why Guangzhou youth maintained order during the "fifty days of turmoil." But a far more interesting question asked the youth to rank the criteria that make a country successful. As Table 8.4 shows, "widespread acceptance of a common belief system" was seen as least important to a country's success. Collectivist values generally—such as "a small gap between rich and poor" and "a highly developed system of public social welfare"—found little support. Most highly rated was "a high standard of living," whereas students demonstrated their patriotic/nationalistic beliefs by also ranking "power" and "high international status" as key criteria for a country's success. This was consistent with another finding from this survey, that 81 percent viewed the victory of Chinese athletes in an international competition as a "national victory" (*minzu de shengli*) that would make them proud. The government, of course, sought to use China's success in the 1990 Asian Games to convert these nationalistic sentiments into increased support for the regime.

Although surveys have shown that youth desire to live in a powerful, internationally respected China, the regime has been disturbed by studies that have revealed that many youth do not necessarily equate a strong China with a socialist China, and by a lack of knowledge of some of the symbols and core beliefs of the revolution. Published in 1990, a study of the effects of moral and political education on more than 1,000 secondary school students from ten high schools in a city in Henan Province provides some evidence that this concern is justified.

TABLE 8.4 Criteria That Make a Country Successful

Rank	Criteria	N=1,508 Point Total
1	High standard of living	88.7
2	Social stability	66.7
3	Power	42.0
4	High international status	38.5
5	Fully guaranteed individual rights and freedoms	34.8
6	Highly developed system of public social welfare	18.3
7	Small gap between rich and poor	5.5
8	Widespread acceptance of a common belief system	2.2

Source: Wang Zhixiong, Liang Feng, Wu Xiaoping, and Zhang Bin, "Guangzhou qingnian zhengzhi wenhua tedian tantao" [An inquiry into the special characteristics of the political culture of Guangzhou youth], *Qingnian tansuo* [Inquiries into youth] No. 6, 1989, p. 16.

Excluding those who did not answer, the study found that 45 percent of the students could not sing the national anthem; 21.8 percent did not know that 1989 was the fortieth anniversary of the PRC; 54.9 percent did not know that the final goal of the CCP was the realization of communism (some thought it was the realization of capitalism); and 26.1 percent thought capitalism was superior to socialism.[8]

The Influence of the West

In their search for a viable belief system, Chinese youth have been strongly influenced by concepts imported from the West and, in their suspicion of some of the core collectivist values of the regime, appear to have become much more individualistic in their thinking. This change in thinking has been accompanied by the growth of a moral viewpoint that stresses concern primarily with one's own behavior and the avoidance of moral judgments about others. Surveys have shown, for example, that even though students were not supportive of cheating on examinations or living together before marriage, they were also unwilling to criticize others for doing so, considering such behavior a private matter.[9]

TABLE 8.5 Comparison of Secondary School Students' Views on the 1987 and 1989 Demonstrations

Question: If you were a university student during the recent disturbance, what would you have done?

	N=100	
	1987 Sample	1989 Sample
Participated	9	12
Not participated	43	35
Watched the excitement	34	38
Not participated and also dissuaded others from participating	14	15

Source: Song Xinmin, "Zhongxuesheng dui Tiananmen fengbode kanfa" [The views of secondary school students on the Tiananmen turmoil], *Qingnian yanjiu* [Youth research] No. 2, February 1990, p. 28.

This "decollectivization of morality" clearly has important political implications. Before the Cultural Revolution, the link between students and the state was strong in part because of the fierce competition among upwardly mobile student activists who monitored their classmates to prevent any deviation from the regime's core values. With the students no longer "true believers" and a reward structure no longer so fully under the control of the state, political activism in support of regime values is now rare. Nor do university authorities really expect it. Table 8.5 shows the results of a survey of high-achieving, future university students from the attached secondary school of Wuhan University after the 1986 and 1989 demonstrations. The students were asked whether they would have taken part. Significantly, though at least 50 percent in both years said they would not have participated, only 14–15 percent would also have made an attempt to dissuade others from participating. Moreover, the surveyors made little distinction between the nonparticipants and the more activist elements (those younger students who answered either that they would or would not have taken part), affirming both as backbone elements of the state.

Conservatives, however, treat this decline in collectivist concerns much more seriously. There had, in fact, been a lively debate on whether these trends were necessarily negative before June 4, 1989. In the aftermath of the military crackdown, however, the concern with individual success and the Western ideas that have contributed to the introduction of these values into China have been severely criticized. Indeed, in the wake of the June events, an abundant supply of survey

TABLE 8.6 Should We Allow Western Thought to Have an Impact on China Now? (in percentages)

	Yes	No	Sample
Total Sample	75.49	9.26	1,365
Occupation			
Worker	73.49	15.26	246
Self-employed	62.81	10.74	122
Intellectual	85.52	3.42	361
Cadre	86.74	3.94	290
Peasant	58.80	15.95	317
Age			
25 and below	74.09	10.12	494
26-35	79.33	5.67	353
36-45	76.29	11.64	232
46-55	70.71	11.62	198
56-65	66.67	15.28	62
66 and above	50.00	18.25	16
Education			
Illiterate	47.72	27.27	44
Primary school	43.51	18.32	131
Junior high	72.50	13.33	460
Senior high or secondary technical	77.17	9.45	381
College and above	86.86	2.35	426
Political Status			
Communist party member	80.26	9.21	380
Communist Youth League member	89.02	6.27	383
Democratic party member	70.29	14.71	34
Influential figure	33.33	25.00	12
Ordinary citizen	68.17	10.94	512
Residence			
Large city	82.09	6.54	413
District central city	84.49	6.53	245
Suburban	79.31	7.76	116
County town	72.85	10.34	232
Village	61.11	13.19	288
Border and poor areas	47.05	31.37	51

Source: Min Qi, *Zhongguo zhengzhi wenhua: minzhu zhengzhi nanchande shehui xinli yinsu* [Chinese political culture: The social psychological elements that make it difficult to produce democratic politics] (Kunming: Yunnan renmin chubanshe, 1989), pp. 128-129.

results has been released, revealing just how far Chinese students and other youth have strayed from officially sanctioned values. Yet if a persuasive argument could be made that the widespread publication—albeit largely in internal journals—of the failures of political socialization were at least in part politically motivated thrusts by conservative officials, there is more than enough documentation prior to June 4 that suggests the disaffection of students and other youth was real and that Western values had made major inroads into Chinese belief systems. In the next few paragraphs I therefore use survey data published both before and after June 4.

The first point worth noting is that the interest in Western ideas is not limited to Chinese youth. A broad spectrum of the population seemed to agree that Western thought could be beneficial to China. Table 8.6 is from a national survey of Chinese political culture conducted in 1987 by an independent group of young and middle-aged Beijing political scientists who were dissatisfied with the philosophically oriented discussion of political questions and turned to behavioral and post-behavioral" methods.[10] It is not surprising to find support for Western ideas strong among the highly educated and urbanized segment of the population or among those forty-five years old and younger. What is striking, however, is the overwhelming support by party and CYL members, as well as cadres in general. But there is no suggestion in this very interesting survey that Chinese political culture approximates its Western counterpart. For example, in one of their tests of political tolerance, the surveyors asked respondents whether they supported the following expression: "I firmly disagree with your viewpoint, but I will defend to the death your right to express it." The majority of the respondents—including youth—could not understand what this meant.[11]

Yet some surveys clearly suggest that Western concepts of tolerance have been used to evaluate Chinese policies. A large-scale survey of 3,697 students (4,874 questionnaires were issued) at nine universities in Guangdong, which claimed to use stratified and other systematic sampling techniques, was published in early 1988. When asked about their understanding of the well-known Chinese policy to "let a hundred flowers bloom, let a hundred schools of thought contend," only a minority "correctly" identified the party line on this slogan. As Table 8.7 shows, over 50 percent understood the expression as permitting unrestricted speech in a wide variety of contexts rather than as a cultural policy intended only for artists and writers. Such results dismayed the surveyors, who saw in such responses "the influence of Western bourgeois ideology."

After June 4, 1989, a wide variety of survey data was published revealing student admiration for Western democracy, even praise for capitalism, in the period leading up to the "turmoil." Because of the limitation of space, only a sampling can be presented here. Parallel surveys were done in Xian (at four colleges), at Nankai University in Tianjin, and at the Chinese University of Mines in Jiangsu. When asked if the Western political system was real democracy, 62 percent in Xian, 66 percent in Tianjin, and 53.5 percent in Jiangsu either agreed or totally agreed. When asked if everyone was equal before the law in Western countries, 46 percent in Xian, 49 percent in Tianjin, and 35.4 percent in Jiangsu either agreed or totally agreed.[12] In a 1988 survey at the Chinese University of Science and Technology, about 50 percent of the students felt that "it doesn't matter what the 'ism' is, so long as it can make the country rich and powerful." Even after the "turmoil" had ended, 72.87 percent of the students still either basically

TABLE 8.7 What Is Your Understanding of the "Double Hundred" Policy?

N=3,697

Responses	Number	Percentage
You can say and do what you want without fear of suppression	505	13.7
It should bring about a flourishing situation in culture, while discovering our cultural heritage	1,261	34.1
It should permit those with different political and ideological opinions the right to speak out	1,376	37.2
I cannot understand it	405	11.0
Other	105	4.1

Source: Zhi Ming and Lian Xuehua, "Daxueshengde jiben zhengzhi guandian," [The basic political views of university students], *Nanfang qingshaonian yanjiu* [Studies on teenagers in the south] No. 1, 1988, p. 42.

or fully agreed that "democracy must be fought for from the bottom up, not bestowed from the top down."[13]

Surveys of universities in Beijing done by political work cadres before the 1989 spring demonstrations reportedly found, inter alia, that 45 percent of the students either rejected or were skeptical of Marxism; 53 percent of the students supported "bourgeois democracy," including a multiparty system and the separation of powers; 79.2 percent were uncertain about the future of the Chinese reforms and were indifferent to whether China followed a socialist or a capitalist path; and only 20.1 percent had a basic trust in the government. Moreover, 50 percent of the students listened to the Voice of America or other foreign broadcasts, with the number rising to more than 80 percent when there were important domestic or foreign events.[14]

This seeming orientation toward Western liberal democratic values—combined with pessimism over the future of Chinese reforms and frustration with the low standard of living of Chinese intellectuals—has begun to have a major impact on China's educational system. It has become almost a cliché to say that everyone wants to leave China to study abroad. Though clearly an exaggeration, there is ample evidence to document the dissatisfaction with opportunities in China and the desire to leave, at least until such time as conditions in China improve.[15]

Surveys published before and after June 4, 1989, asked university students in various large Chinese cities to rank twelve "professions" by social and economic status and then to rank in order their actual choice of profession. In each of the surveys, "student studying overseas" ranked first in actual choice, despite lower rankings in terms of economic and social status. Other professions ranked near the top were closely tied to China's foreign economic policy. It is notable that being a graduate student or a university teacher within China was ranked both low in status and actual choice in the two surveys.[16]

Interest in going abroad can also be seen from the increase in those sitting for the test of English as a foreign language (TOEFL, the standardized international exam for foreign applicants to U.S. universities) given in Beijing each year. In 1981, the first year it was offered, 285 people took the exam; by 1988 the exam had to be offered three times and there were more than 26,000 examinees.[17] Moreover, the desire to study abroad appears to be widespread at all educational levels. For example, according to official sources with restricted circulation, at Shanghai's prestigious Jiaotong University, 30–40 percent of the young teachers have already left, and the number of those who desire to leave is at least 80 percent.[18] Among the more than 5,300 master's degree students at the Chinese Academy of Sciences, 65 percent have already made contact with overseas institutions.[19] At several Shanghai secondary schools, 600 students were asked in a sample survey whether they were thinking of studying abroad. Over 83 percent said they were. One can easily see the impetus behind the recent regulations to stem the flow of students leaving China.

Such attitudes are clearly linked to the higher expectations generated by the reform program and the resulting dissatisfaction and impatience when those expectations are unmet. For example, in a study of young intellectuals in Shanghai, 88 percent said their talents were not being effectively utilized, even when their job assignment matched what they had studied; this was seen as a key reason why they wanted to go abroad.[20] However, the problem goes even deeper. Students appear at times even to reject the right of the state to regulate their behavior. Authorities in Shanghai were dismayed when 81 percent of the 2,000 university students surveyed felt that whether they attended class was their own business and that the school did not have the right to monitor their behavior.[21]

The Rejection of Officially Sanctioned Organizations

If the regime's ideology has lost a great deal of its appeal to youth, a similar argument could be made for its key political organization, the Communist Youth League. Membership within the CYL has become virtually universal among college students. Unlike the pre–Cultural

Revolution period, when students eagerly competed for entrance to prove their revolutionary credentials and when membership would enhance one's chances for future success in the wider society, today's CYL offers neither glory nor obvious benefits. Membership therein is merely pro forma. Indeed, the regime has ample evidence of the league's decline.

Prior to June 1989, a national survey of 9,018 undergraduate and graduate students at forty-seven universities was conducted. At some schools, virtually every student had become a CYL member by the junior or senior year. Thus, of the total sample, 7,880 (87 percent) were league members. Another 7 percent were party members, leaving only about 6 percent (517 students) politically unaffiliated. The researchers sought to discover the CYL's role in student life. Table 8.8 provides some answers. Several points are worth noting. First, the majority of students were dissatisfied with the league (over 65 percent), doubted its effectiveness in carrying out political and ideological work (over 60 percent), did not find its organizational life "rich and varied" (74 percent), and so forth. Second, the percentages of those who fully agreed that the CYL has "great prestige," "is the organization youths cherish and trust the most," has "a rich and varied organizational life," "can reflect the hopes and demands of youth," and "can effectively carry out ideological and political work" ranged from 3.68 to 7.09 percent. Perhaps most damning, over 42 percent either basically or fully agreed that the league existed in name only. Not surprisingly, the survey showed that the students' assessment of the league's prestige declined as they ascended the educational ladder; thus 38.55 percent of first-year college students basically agreed that the league had great prestige, dropping steadily to 10.53 percent of Ph.D. students.

Other responses documented the estrangement (*shuyuan*) of students from the CYL, a point repeatedly emphasized by the researchers. For example, one question asked: "To reveal your true feelings, or when you have a vexing problem, to whom would you most want to speak?" The largest number—59.5 percent—would seek out close friends; another 27.42 percent would bury their feelings inside and not reveal them to anyone; 5.16 percent would choose a teacher; only 2.08 percent—221 students of the 7,880 queried—chose the party or the youth league.[22]

These results are broadly consistent with other surveys that reveal the importance of friends and classmates over that of teachers and political counselors in shaping the activities and decisions of college students. Table 8.9 presents the results of a random sample survey of 364 students from three different years at Zhongshan University in Guangzhou.

TABLE 8.8 University Students' Assessment of the Communist Youth League

	N = 7,880 CYL Members							
	Fully agree		Basically agree		Basically disagree		Completely disagree	
	number	%	number	%	number	%	number	%
1. I feel that the CYL has great prestige	559	7.09	2,601	33.01	3,017	38.29	1,152	14.62
2. I am very dissatisfied with the existing state of affairs in the CYL	1,840	23.35	3,296	41.83	1,758	22.31	459	5.82
3. The CYL still can serve as a direct bridge between the Communist party and China's youth	984	12.49	3,227	40.95	2,400	30.46	688	8.73
4. The CYL is the organization youths cherish and trust the most	425	5.39	2,263	28.71	3,227	40.95	1,380	17.51
5. I find the CYL's organizational life rich and varied	290	3.68	1,187	15.06	3,244	41.17	2,586	32.82
6. The CYL now exists in name only	1,054	13.38	2,282	28.96	2,668	33.86	1,328	16.85
7. The CYL can represent and reflect the hopes and demands of youth	381	4.84	2,468	31.32	3,396	43.10	1,042	13.22
8. The CYL can effectively carry out ideological and political work	396	5.03	2,123	26.94	3,481	44.18	1,276	16.19

Source: Yuan Zeqing, "Gaoxiao gongqingtuan gongzuo gaige chuyi" [My humble opinion on the reform of the work of the Communist Youth League in universities], *Jiaoyu yu xiandaihua* [Education and modernization] Nos. 1-2, May 1989, p. 73.

A provincewide random sample survey of 2,658 students from twenty-nine universities and colleges in Jiangxi Province likewise documented serious weaknesses in the functioning of officially sanctioned organizations like the CYL and the student unions. For example, only 27.3 percent considered the league to be effective; 44.1 percent thought it ineffective. Although 43.3 percent had confidence in the league branch, 39.9 percent did not. Only 36.2 percent saw the student union functioning as it should, whereas 50 percent did not.[23]

Concurrent with these developments was the growth of new organizations, often initiated by the students themselves. Political work cadres generally saw these new student associations (*shetuan*) in a positive light, yet they also recognized the potential threat to state

TABLE 8.9 Whom Would You Contact? (in percentages)

N=364

	Parents	Friends Outside of School	Course Teachers	Political Counselors	Schoolmates	Other
To discuss study problems	1.5	4.0	36.7	1.2	54.5	1.1
For entertainment activities	2.3	26.0	1.3	3.4	65.9	2.1
To discuss social problems	12.5	23.1	0.1	7.3	52.0	1.0
When there are difficulties in your life	61.0	8.9	0.0	6.3	18.3	0.0
To discuss questions relating to your own love and romance	22.9	25.1	0.0	1.7	31.6	17.0
To discuss your future plans	27.9	25.9	2.0	4.0	33.4	6.8

Source: Li Ping, Ou Xiaowei, and Hou Hong, "Daxuesheng qunti chutan" [A preliminary exploration of university student groups], *Nanfang qingshaonian yanjiu* [Studies on teenagers in the south] No. 2, 1987, p. 39.

control in such relatively autonomous groups. Indeed, some reports explicitly noted that the rapid growth of these organizations stemmed from the failures of the officially sanctioned CYL and student unions to meet the needs of the students.[24] Party and league authorities sought to monitor the activities of the larger and more influential groups, in part by providing money, personnel, and campus space to the group leaders but also by regulating and periodically evaluating the group's activities.

A large-scale survey conducted in 1986 among Beijing's fifty universities found 500 such groups, with more than 40,000 students taking part in group activities, making up about one-third of the city's university students.[25] The survey suggested the steady growth of these organizations. For example, from the end of 1983 to the end of 1986, there was a 58 percent increase in the number of associations, and the number of those taking at least some part in group activities jumped from 13,000 to 40,000. Figures from other large cities suggest that the growth continued. For example, a 1989 Guangzhou study found more than seventy such associations at Zhongshan University, with 29.9

percent of the university's students joining in and another 11 percent ready to participate. In total, 30.2 percent of the students had already taken part in activities organized by these groups.[26] Table 8.10, from the Beijing survey, provides some indication of the general nature of these groups.

Based on geographical proximity (same home area, dormitory, or classroom), common interests, work relationships (particularly among student cadres), or other such factors, most of these groups appear to have been and continue to be rather innocuous. Often the core membership is small, with one account suggesting that they could contain as few as two to three members or as many as ten to twenty.[27] Nevertheless, their very prevalence—and acceptability—on virtually all university campuses at the same time that the influence of more official organizations was in decline posed a potential threat to the authorities.

But the league's inability to compete with these new associations in attracting youth had not gone unnoticed. Indeed, there was an internal debate over the most appropriate orientation of the CYL. The conflict can be seen by examining two articles published a month apart in a restricted-circulation youth journal just after the Tiananmen crackdown. In the first article, the authors began by noting the difficulties the league has had in meeting its "quotas"—40 percent membership in the cities and 20 percent in the countryside—comparing China's 17.9 percent age-cohort membership to the much higher figures in the Soviet Union and Eastern Europe.[28] Moreover, they sought to explain why neither youth nor the larger society held the league in high regard, and why the organization was not functioning well. The answer stemmed from a series of contradictions confronting the organization, centering on the need to be "advanced" yet still attract youth. As the article notes in summing up the past ten years, there has been an imbalance, marked by an overemphasis on being ideologically advanced, without considering what Chinese youth really want. The league has not been given enough independence from direct party control. The flavor of the critique is caught in the following passage: "At the basic levels one frequently hears the following reaction: The league organization is like a youth party, it's not dynamic, the political hue is too thick. League cadres are too 'serious,' they're only concerned with higher levels, not lower levels, they float on the surface, they don't go down to the bottom. It must be said that this is a mistake in our tactics!"[29]

A month later the league faced a critique from the opposite direction. But where the first article designated five errors, the second discovered ten.[30] Far from decrying the overemphasis on politics, the authors saw the imbalance on the other side: CYL cadres were neglecting the "advanced" character of the league by catering to the whims of the

TABLE 8.10 Student Associations on Beijing University Campuses, November 1986

	Academic Associations		Interest, Hobby Associations	Cultural Associations	News, Information, Media Associations	Service Associations	Totals
	by Specialization	by Research Interest					
Number of associations	115	53	227	54	27	23	499
Percentage of all associations	23.05	10.62	45.49	10.82	5.41	4.61	100

Source: Wang Ling et al., "Dai daxuesheng shetuan zhuangkuangde diaocha" [An investigation of university student associations] in Beijing Municipal Party Committee Research Office, ed., *Xinshiqi daxuesheng sixiang zhengzhi jiaoyu yanjiu* [Research on ideological and political education of university students in the new period] (Beijing: Beijing Normal University Press, 1988), p. 240.

less progressive youth. One survey of eighty-six cadres found that 73 percent of them saw youth work as only human relations (*renqing gongzuo*). Thus they won over their charges by being "good old boys," joining the youth in such activities as playing mah-jongg and accompanying them to bars, dance halls, and casinos. Nor did they take political education seriously; 43 percent did not bother to prepare for classes. This often meant that league cadres deviated from the intentions of the party committee, doing whatever satisfied the youth. Even when it seemed from the outside that the league branch was very active, such activity was unrelated to political education.

Ironically, in the aftermath of June 4, one can argue that the real threat to the authorities came not from CYL or student union cadres unconcerned with politics and merely joining with other students in various forms of entertainment but rather from more committed student cadres who found the officially sanctioned organizations irrelevant and therefore created new ones. For example, Shen Tong, who established the Dialogue Delegation that negotiated with government officials and ran the student news center at the time of the Tiananmen demonstrations, had become involved in Chinese student politics when he was seventeen. After arriving at Beijing University, he soon became an official in the school's Student Association. In early 1989, however, he established the Olympic Institute, an independent student organization that promoted discussion of new ideas about science, philosophy, and, eventually, politics.[31]

Conclusion

In this chapter I have documented the estrangement in significant numbers of a key segment of Chinese society, even before the events of spring and summer 1989. The data have pointed to a decline in the legitimacy and importance of the state-sponsored ideology in motivating student attitudes and behavior and a corresponding loss of organizational control through party-directed transmission belts, notably the CYL.

It would be a mistake, however, to assume that this merely reflects an "ideological gap" dividing wayward students from a unified party line. The decline of ideology, coupled with the search for a viable belief system and the tolerance for competing ideologies, is not only widespread among intellectuals but reaches into high levels of the party. A good indication of the legitimacy accorded this quest before June 4 is an article that appeared in the party's premier ideological journal, *Qiushi* (Seek Truth), on June 1, 1989.[32] The author begins by noting that there is no consensus on the meaning of ideology and that Lenin's views—that there can only be a bourgeois or socialist ideological system with no third choice—"can no longer reflect the actual situation in the world." Ranging widely over Western theories on "the end of ideology," the rise of "Euro-Communism," and the common concern for "global development," he argues that many interests and values, for example, those relating to man's existence and development, "are of a non-ideological nature," and quotes approvingly from Soviet and Eastern European leaders who have argued that socialist countries should not practice "ideological dictatorship" but rather should encourage "diversification."

The contentious intellectual debates of the late 1980s—such as the suitability of neo-authoritarianism in promoting economic modernization and political development or the role of traditional Chinese culture in aiding or hindering development—and the reluctance of the party leadership to intervene openly in such debates likewise revealed the decline of ideological rigidity.[33] The study groups and associations set up by leading intellectuals such as Jin Guantao of the Chinese Academy of Social Sciences and Chen Ziming of the private Beijing Institute for Social and Economic Research brought university students into these and other debates. At the same time, the interaction between members of these associations further promoted the diversification of views.

In the aftermath of June 4, this intellectual tolerance has been denounced by a conservative leadership with a tight control over China's media. The former trend toward ideological "pluralism" has been condemned in the country's leading newspapers and journals, with the primary villains now seen as the "turmoil elites," many of whom have fled China.[34] Lenin's dichotomy of ideological systems has been resurrected and, as a *Qiushi* article put it, "there is no exception whatever." Those viewing "science" and ideology as opposing forces are said to have fallen prey to a "liberalization" that serves the interests of the West, which has long advocated the "peaceful evolution" of China. According to this argument, Chinese students studying abroad are seen by Western leaders as a "strategic investment"; after imbibing Western ideology and culture, they will return home as a "force that will greatly exceed that of tens of thousands of troops."[35]

In their attack on pluralism, conservative Chinese theorists do see as an "objective fact" that "various social groups, strata, and individuals have their special interests." They use this fact, however, to justify the continuing need for CCP leadership. Because the overall goals of socialism are higher than any special interests, a political party and a government that represent the fundamental concerns of the entire people are needed to coordinate different interests and exercise leadership. Virtually all discussion of the growth of a Chinese middle class—a key theme in sociological writings before June 4—has been banished from the literature, particularly because some of the exiled "elites" attributed the outbreak of the demonstrations to the existence of such a class and blamed the movement's failures on the weakness of that class.[36] In short, the government has become extremely sensitive to any discussion about individual interests or autonomy of social groups and, by extension, to the possible emergence of a civil society outside the sphere of state control.[37]

Aside from a holding operation, however, the regime has been unable to arrest the movement of society away from the state. The events of April–June 1989 were merely the culmination of an estrangement evolving for at least the past decade, arguably since the Cultural Revolution. In response, party leaders have taken as their highest value the avoidance of trouble. Thus Li Zemin, party secretary of Zhejiang Province, began a 1990 speech on the subject by emphasizing that "on-campus stability is the most important task of the party in colleges."[38] Patriotism, considered "a historical phenomenon . . . with different meanings . . . under different historical conditions" is now equated with "loving socialist New China, which is under the leadership of the Communist Party."[39]

Recently decreed "General Supervisory Stipulations for Students in Higher Education"—the first comprehensive stipulations since 1949—explicitly ban illegal organizations and publications and require the schools to exercise stronger leadership and management over all student mass organizations.[40] New freshmen at Beijing University, after a year of military training, have been isolated from the rest of the student body, housed in separate dormitories, and enrolled in separate classes and a separate student union. They must get special permission if they want to participate in extracurricular activities outside the scope of their regular activity program.[41]

Some efforts appear to represent a desire to will a return to the past. For example, a recent front-page article in *Renmin Ribao* admonished Chinese citizens to eschew such bourgeois terms of address as "Miss," "Mister," and "Mrs." Instead, they were urged to revive the use of "Comrade."[42] But the tensions and contradictions marking the party's relationship with youth cannot be resolved through sheer exhortation. An authoritative article by CYL leader Song Defu made one of the contradictions explored above particularly explicit without really moving toward a solution. Song noted simply that the CYL is a mass organization of advanced youth. As he put it, it is not a club of people sharing the same interests and hobbies; rather, it is a school for teaching and upholding communism. It is not a loose mass organization; rather, it is a close-knit political organization supporting the CCP. At the same time, he continued, it is not an administrative department; rather, it is a youth organization that has close ties to the masses of young people and expresses and safeguards the concrete interests of youth.[43] The problem, however, is obvious. How can an organization that is struggling to increase membership among a youth disaffected by regime values appeal to these youth on the basis of those same values? In such circumstances, a "vanguard" organization cannot be a "mass" organization. Until China's leaders can square that circle, by offering something more than anachronistic ideological appeals—an outcome that will have to wait at least until the physical demise of the gerontocrats—the league's appeal to youth will go unheeded.

Notes

1. The data I present in this chapter derive from four major sources. First, academic/professional journals for those engaged in youth work are published by social science academies and CYL offices. These journals often report on social science research conducted throughout the country on youth attitudes and behavior. Second, the majority of Chinese universities produce a quarterly or semiannual journal devoted largely to educational and student-related issues specific to their campuses. Some provinces also publish a journal of higher education, in which the issues addressed go beyond the individual campuses. Third, provincial and municipal educational research institutes issue journals that report findings from behavioral and attitudinal studies of primary and secondary school students. All three of these sources, intended for professionals engaged in educational and youth work, tend to have restricted circulation. For example, the university journals are generally not sold but sent to educational research offices on other campuses on an "internal exchange" (*neibu jiaoliu*) basis. The fourth source is the more familiar, openly circulated official press, including specialized journals that have unrestricted circulation.

Much of my argument relies heavily on survey research conducted by Chinese social scientists, including those working directly for the party or government. I include surveys conducted before and after the June 4 crackdown. Indeed, some of the surveys were undertaken specifically to assess the effects of the party's propaganda campaign on students who had participated in the "turmoil." Elsewhere I have addressed the issue of the reliability of Chinese surveys—including problems of sampling, questionnaire design, data analysis, and so forth: See Stanley Rosen and David Chu, *Survey Research in the People's Republic of China* (Washington, D.C.: U.S. Information Agency, 1987), and Stanley Rosen, "Value Change Among Post-Mao Youth: The Evidence from Survey Data," in Perry Link, Richard Madsen, and Paul Pickowicz, *Unofficial China: Popular Culture and Thought in the People's Republic* (Boulder: Westview Press, 1989), 193–216.

I therefore would only note some specific problems of the surveys employed in this chapter.

First, most Chinese surveys tend to be snapshots taken at a given time rather than as part of an ongoing survey project. Thus we have little in the way of time-series data. Moreover, because survey research, as a by-product of the reform program itself, began to appear only in 1979, the quasi-time-series data that do exist cannot help us compare youth attitudes in the 1980s with those of their counterparts during the Maoist era. Chinese researchers, well aware of this problem, will sometimes suggest comparisons based on their knowledge of earlier generations of students. They will also relate results of recent surveys to similar studies conducted at different periods of the reform decade, even when the earlier data had not been published.

This suggests a second problem, however. Survey research in China, lacking a strong tradition of independent, nonstate polling organizations, often has an implied political agenda. This of course most obviously applies to surveys published in widely circulated party newspapers like *Renmin Ribao,* where publication is intended to educate more than merely to inform. But the problem is a broader one. In a real sense, surveys contain right and wrong answers. For example, when students who participated in the spring 1989 demonstrations are surveyed as to their current attitudes, they know the correct party line they should have absorbed. University officials conducting such surveys will be reluctant to publish results that demonstrate that their reeducation program has failed. Even unpublished surveys sent to higher levels that document such a failure could conceivably be damaging to the careers of university administrators.

For their part, the conservatives who gained control over the mass media after June 4 may have a vested interest in publishing surveys done prior to the demonstrations to reveal the extent of "bourgeois liberalization" rampant under the influence of Zhao Ziyang and his supporters, when political education was not given high priority. These results can then be used to press for increased attention to proper political socialization.

Students as well have been concerned that survey questionnaires may be attempts to elicit their true beliefs that, once discovered, could then be used to justify retaliatory action by the authorities. Although this had been openly raised as an issue even by Chinese researchers in the early 1980s, the problem appeared to have receded until June 4, 1989. However, a recent survey at the Chengdu Institute of Geology, which polled students of the classes of 1987 and 1988 who had been most deeply involved in the "political turmoil," showed the difficulties researchers had in discovering the views of such students (see Deng Liya, "An Investigation and Analysis of the Ideology of Contemporary University Students," *Qingnian yanjiu* (Youth research), No. 7, July 1990, 5–11). For example, "not a few" students believed the school could trace them through coded questionnaire forms or even fingerprint analysis. Moreover, the researchers discovered that questionnaire results frequently did not correlate with what the students were saying in discussion meetings. Students were most honest in one-on-one discussions. In addition, almost 25 percent of the returned questionnaires were internally inconsistent. On the front, students seemed to absorb fully the party line; on the back, they would write, "We've learned well how to lie." Finally, students would write as ambiguously as possible, making it difficult for researchers to determine their meaning.

Such problems, among others, are serious but not insurmountable. There are several ways to reduce the distortion factor. First, one can avoid surveys published in the open and widely circulated sources and concentrate on journals intended for academic researchers. Second, one can seek surveys with national, provincial, or municipal samples rather than very localized surveys with small samples. Surveys that provide detailed information on sampling techniques and that disaggregate the data by relevant sociological variables such as age, sex, education, and so forth are of course most preferable but quite rare.

Third, one can examine the analyses of the data provided by the Chinese researchers themselves. Analyses that overtly use the results to make a political point are likely more suspect than those which report the data dispassionately and academically. In addition, surveys that elicit responses to questions that are not overtly political, for example, ascertaining student role models, can provide valuable information. Fourth, one can compare the survey results to what is known from other sources. Highly counterintuitive results (e.g., "99 percent of the students surveyed support the military crackdown") should be examined with particular skepticism. In fact, as a reaction against the distortions of attitude studies in the official press, students at Beijing University have organized their own surveys and mailed the results to foreign scholars abroad. For example, a survey in May 1990 of 250 graduate students and 350 undergraduate students (453 valid questionnaires returned) was conducted by the Beijing University Graduate Student Association. The twenty questions covered current student attitudes on a variety of issues. See *Beijing daxue xuesheng sixiang diaocha baogao* (Report on investigation of the thought of Beijing university students) (mimeo). Fifth, one should approach surveys conducted after the military crackdown very cautiously. However, as will be shown below, even surveys that appear to have a political agenda may, albeit unintentionally, provide revealing insights about student attitudes that the Chinese researchers choose not to highlight.

2. On the changes from 1978 to 1989, see Stanley Rosen, "Youths and Social Change in the People's Republic of China," in Ramon Myers, ed., *Two Societies in Opposition: The Republic of China and the People's Republic of China After Forty Years* (Stanford: Hoover Institution Press, 1991), 288–315.

3. Ying Hang, "On the Establishment of Ideals by Contemporary University Students," *Zhejiang daxue jiaoyu yanjiu* (Educational research at Zhejiang University), No. 1, March 1990, 17–21.

4. Wang Shuzhi, "Secondary School Students' Beliefs and Marxist-Leninist Education," *Xiandai zhongxiaoxue jiaoyu* (Modern, middle, and primary education), No. 2, 1990, 24–25.

5. Investigation Group of the Educational Information Research Office of the Educational Research Institute of Shanghai Municipality, "An Investigation of the Values of Some Secondary School Students in Shanghai," *Shanghai jiaoyu keyan* (Education research on Shanghai), No. 6, November 1989, 36–38.

6. For the national survey, see Min Qi, *Zhongguo zhengzhi wenhua: minzhu zhengzhi nanchande shehui xinli yinsu* (Chinese political culture: The social psychological elements that make it difficult to produce democratic politics) (Kunming: Yunnan renmin chubanshe, 1989). For a brief description of a Beijing pilot study for a national sample survey of the political attitudes of Chinese citizens, which was conducted by Shi Tianjian, a graduate student at Columbia University, see Andrew J. Nathan, *China's Crisis: Dilemmas of Reform and Prospects for Democracy* (New York: Columbia University Press, 1990), 197–198.

7. Wang Zhixiong, Liang Feng, Wu Xiaoping, and Zhang Bin, "An Inquiry into the Special Characteristics of the Political Culture of Guangzhou Youth," *Qingnian tansuo* (Inquiries into youth), No. 6, December 1989, 12, 15–16.

8. Cheng Mingwu, "Survey Results That Cause Concern," *Qingshaonian tantao* (Inquiries about young people) (Guangxi) No. 2, 1990, 23, 42–44.

9. Stanley Rosen, "Political Education and Student Response: Some Background Factors Behind the 1989 Beijing Demonstrations," *Issues and Studies* Vol. 25, No. 10, October 1989, 12–39.

10. Min Qi, *Zhongguo zhengzhi wenhua.*

11. Ibid., 123.

12. Tan Shumin, "Looking at the Necessity to Oppose Bourgeois Liberalization from the Influence of Western Democratic Thought on Contemporary Chinese University Students," *Meitan gaodeng jiaoyu* (Higher education for coal mining), No. 3, September 1989, 26–29. This journal is published by the Chinese University of Mines.

13. Zhang Yibin, "The Infiltration of Western Ideology and Culture, and Our Countermeasures," *Jiaoyu xiandaihua* (Educational modernization), No. 4, December 1989, 8–13. This journal is published by the Chinese University of Science and Technology in Hefei.

14. Quan Jinglian, "An Investigation and Analysis of the Ideological and Political Education of University Students in Beijing," *Qingnian yanjiu* (Youth research), No. 3, March 1990, 15–18.

15. The data presented below are drawn in part from Stanley Rosen, "The Influence of the United States and the West on the Attitudes and Behavior of Chinese Youth," in William T. Tow, ed., *Building Sino-American Relations: An Analysis for the 1990s* (New York: Paragon House, 1991), 162–202.

16. Zhao Ying, "The Changes in Contemporary University Students' Views of Professions," *Gaodeng jiaoyu yanjiu* (Studies in higher education) (Xian) No. 2, December 1989, 93–96; Tang Yucheng and Yin Qing, "An Investigation of the Choices of Professions by University Students," *Shandong gongye daxue xuebao* (Journal of Shandong College of Industry), Vol. 3, No. 4, 1988, 54–58.

17. Xiao Qinfu, *Wuci langchao* (Five tides) (Beijing: Zhongguo renmin daxue chubanshe, 1989), 141.

18. Chen Hao, "'Hot Topics' Among Teachers and Students at Shanghai's Universities After the Start of Classes," *Gaojiao xinxi yu tansuo* (News and inquiries about higher education), No. 5, March 15, 1990, 1–2.

19. Xiao Qinfu, *Wuci langchao,* 146.

20. Ibid., 169–170.

21. Special Task Force on Improving School Discipline, Shanghai Higher Education Research Institute, "An Analysis of Some Problems in the Atmosphere on University Campuses at Present," *Sixiang lilun jiaoyu* (Teaching thought and theory), No. 1, January 1989, 40.

22. Yuan Zeqing, "My Humble Opinion on the Reform of the Work of the Communist Youth League in Universities," *Jiaoyu yu xiandaihua* (Education and modernization), Nos. 1-2, May 1989, 75.

23. Wen Zhizhou, "Summing Up the Feedback from an Investigation of Student Beliefs at 29 Universities," *Jiangxi gaoxiao yanjiu* (Research on higher education in Jiangxi), No. 1, March 1988, 28–30.

24. Jiang Ming and Zhang Xuehui, "On University Students' Small Groups," *Gaojiao lilun yu shijian* (Theory and practice of higher education), Nos. 1-2, June 30, 1990, 18–23.

25. For the Beijing study, see Wang Ling et al., "An Investigation of University Student Associations," in Beijing Municipal Party Committee Research Office, ed., *Xinshiqi Daxuesheng sixiang zhengzhi jiaoyu yanjiu* (Research on ideological and political education of university students in the new period) (Beijing: Beijing Normal University Press, 1988), 239–256.

26. Yi Zhifeng, Zhou Zheng, and Hu Xiaocheng, "An Inquiry and Analysis of Campus Culture in Guangzhou," *Nanfang qingshaonian yanjiu* (Studies on teenagers in the south), No. 2, 1990, 2–6.

27. Huang Anyong, "How Can We Guide the Organizations Set Up by University Students onto the Path of Collectivism?" *Gaojiao lilun yu shijian* (Wuhan Industrial University) No. 2, June 1990, 24–25.

28. Huang Zhenping and Zhang Qifen, "Five Errors in Youth League Work," *Qingnian yanjiu* No. 7, July 1989, 47–49. As the authors note, if CYL members actually followed the guidelines of the Twelfth League Congress and resigned at age twenty-five instead of age twenty-eight, the percentage of members would be even smaller.

29. Ibid., 47.

30. Wei Qinyun, "Ten Errors Influencing the Efficiency of Ideological Work Among Youth," *Qingnian yanjiu* No. 8, August 1989, 20–22. A somewhat shorter version, which does not identify the author as a member of the political department of the Jinan Military District Headquarters, appears in *Zhongguo qingnian* (Chinese youth), No. 8, August 1989, 27–28.

31. See Shen Tong and Marianne Yen, *Almost a Revolution* (Boston: Houghton Mifflin, 1990), as described in "A Dream of Democracy Follows the Nightmare," *Los Angeles Times,* November 19, 1990, E1.

32. Song Huichang, "The Basic Characteristics of the Evolution of Ideological Theories in the Contemporary World," *Qiushi,* June 1, 1989, translated in Joint Publications Research Service—China Area Reports (hereafter JPRS-CAR) 89-076, July 21, 1989, 20–24.

33. Perhaps the most telling example of the relative tolerance at that time was the almost comical efforts of conservative ideologue and Vice-President Wang Zhen to convince other party leaders to watch and then ban "River

Elegy," the 1988 television series that condemned traditional Chinese culture and openly advocated the view that China's development could only occur through a much greater orientation toward the West. For a translation of "River Elegy" and the debate, see Stanley Rosen and Gary Zou, *Chinese Sociology and Anthropology,* forthcoming (three issues). For the debate over the "new authoritarianism," see Stanley Rosen and Gary Zou, *Chinese Sociology and Anthropology,* 1990–1991 (four issues).

34. Chun Yang, "Commenting on Ideological 'Plurality' and Other Concepts," *Qiushi,* June 16, 1990, translated in JPRS-CAR-90-059, August 2, 1990, 23–37; Feng Yuzhang and Zhou Shi, "Comments and Analysis on 'Political Pluralization,'" *Renmin Ribao* (People's daily), July 13, 1990, translated in *Foreign Broadcast Information Service, People's Republic of China* (hereafter, *FBIS-Chi*) 90-138, June 18, 1990, 11–13.

35. The quotations are from Chun Yang, "Commenting on Ideological 'Plurality,'" 23–37.

36. Feng Yuzhang and Zhou Shi, "Political Pluralization."

37. On the development of a civil society in China, see Thomas B. Gold, "Party-State Versus Society in China," in Joyce K. Kallgren, ed., *Building a Nation-State: China After Forty Years* (Berkeley: Institute of East Asian Studies, 1990), 125–151. More generally, see John Keane, ed., *Civil Society and the State* (London: Verso, 1988).

38. *Zhejiang Ribao* (Zhejiang daily), July 24, 1990, translated in *FBIS-Chi* 90-156, August 13, 1990, 53–54.

39. Editorial in *Qiushi,* May 1, 1990, translated in JPRS-CAR-90-050, July 12, 1990, 1–3.

40. *Daxuesheng* (University students), No. 4, April 1990, translated in JPRS-CAR-90-055, July 26, 1990, 81–82.

41. "Students at Beijing U. Trying to 'De-Program' Freshmen Exposed to Year of Indoctrination," *Chronicle of Higher Education,* October 17, 1990, A45, A47.

42. "Tian An Men is Over But for Democracy's Lament," *Los Angeles Times,* December 16, 1990, M2.

43. Song Defu, "The League Must Properly Handle League Affairs and Unite the Youth," *Qiushi,* May 1, 1990, translated in JPRS-CAR-90-050, July 12, 1990, 3–8.

9

The Intellectuals in the Deng Xiaoping Era

Merle Goldman

Until the Tiananmen crackdown on June 4, 1989, the position of Chinese intellectuals had improved considerably since the Mao years. In China there are about 6 million high-level intellectuals, defined as those with university degrees or some university education. Although these intellectuals form a proportionately small group (about 0.6 percent of the population), the Deng regime regards them as the key to China's modernization. This view plus the fear of another Cultural Revolution not only enhanced their stature but also limited their political repression. They had more leeway and access to the outside world than at any other time since 1949, and they were reclassified as members of the working class rather than characterized as bourgeois or even reactionary. They enjoyed better working conditions, more responsibility, and opportunities to travel abroad. More significant, the party acknowledged that not only the anti-intellectual violence of the Cultural Revolution but the party's domination over intellectual life and the centralized economic and political structure had led to stagnation. Thus the party retreated somewhat from the intellectual realm and partially devolved authority to the intellectuals, technocrats, and managers in specialized fields. Consequently, intellectuals gained some degree of professional autonomy.

Diverse opinions on a wide range of issues were expressed in the daily media, at conferences, and in specialized journals; the press was filled with debates on a variety of subjects and with suggestions for reform, even political reform. Under Mao, except for the Hundred Flowers of 1956 and the first half of 1957, criticism was permitted only in veiled form and with subtle inferences; under Deng, in contrast, open, lively public debates by professionals, intellectuals, and officials were allowed until June 4, 1989. Periodically, basic policies were discussed and challenged in public forums, and different newspapers and journals openly took sides on public issues. The official party newspaper, *People's Daily,* tended to express more reformist views; the official theoretical journal, *Red Flag,* more conservative views. Until they were closed down in June 1989, semi-independent papers such as the *World Economic Herald* in Shanghai and *Economic Weekly* in Beijing advocated radical political and economic change.

With the tacit support of the reform political leaders Hu Yaobang and Zhao Ziyang, intellectuals welcomed the opportunity to participate in policymaking. They were fulfilling the traditional role of the literati as advisers to the rulers. Yet considerable as these improvements were, they did not occur steadily nor were they secure, as proved by the ease with which the post-Tiananmen regime of Jiang Zemin and Li Peng was able to roll them back. Toleration of criticism and dissent was not institutionalized. With the purge of the reform leaders Hu Yaobang in January 1987 and Zhao Ziyang in June 1989, politically oriented intellectuals lost their protectors and ability to speak out publicly.

Similarities and Differences in the Treatment of Intellectuals Between the Mao and Deng Eras

Although the reform era from 1978 until mid-1989 allowed for some autonomy, especially in private life and on academic matters, the control of intellectuals the party had established in the Mao period remained. True, in sharp contrast to Mao's hostility toward the intellectuals after mid-1957, Deng Xiaoping and other reform leaders encouraged the intellectuals to participate in policymaking. They sought to change the relatively uneducated political elite into an intellectual-technocratic elite (just 4 percent of the party had a college education, and more than half were illiterate or had only a primary school education). But the more conservative leaders, the party's revolutionary elders and former Long Marchers—Peng Zhen, Chen Yun, Bo Yibo, Li Xiannian, Wang Zhen, Yang Shangkun, and their associates—sought to prevent any diminution of the party's authority in the intellectual as well as the political realm. Because of Deng's desire to maintain consensus within the top leadership, he periodically gave in to their demands.

On the local level, officials were reluctant to give intellectuals responsibilities and appropriate positions and, in some cases, refused to make restitution for past abuses. Working under untutored, jealous cadres, many intellectuals endured poor working conditions, inadequate housing, relatively low salaries, and continuing discrimination. Even the reform leaders did not fully trust the intellectuals, as evidenced in the continuation of political campaigns against them. They were subjected to the cycles of relative repression and relative relaxation that characterized the Mao era, though the cycles of relaxation had become much longer and more frequent and periods of repression were shorter and less intense. The repression also lacked the mass participation, ideological fanaticism, and potential violence and condemnation of one's whole work, family, and profession that had marked Mao's campaigns. Nevertheless, the Deng regime continued Mao's contradictory approach toward the intellectuals: On the one hand, it wanted them to be productive and creative in their professions in order to modernize China; on the other, it set limits on their ideas and indoctrinated them in the party line, whatever it was at any given time.

As under Mao, the shifts in policy toward intellectuals also had a dynamic of their own. The party tightened its controls until the intellectuals appeared reluctant to produce; it then loosened its grip until its political authority appeared threatened. In the intervals of relative relaxation, the party fostered or at least permitted intellectual debates, Western influence, and criticism of the bureaucracy in order to root out abuses and make the economy run more efficiently. It initiated and established the framework within which intellectuals were to express themselves, at least in the beginning of a cycle of relaxation. But although the party limited the scope and fixed the terms in which the discourse was to be carried on, it could not fully control the response. Some intellectuals demanded individual self-expression in their own work; others demanded a voice on broader political issues. When discussion went beyond criticism of individual bureaucrats to criticism of the system and suggestions of alternatives, the regime invariably cracked down with varying degrees of intensity.

The oscillations in policy toward the intellectuals under each regime were also determined by political factors, particularly factional maneuvering and power struggles in the top leadership. Once the remaining Maoists were pushed out of top levels of power in 1981, divisions reflected policy as well as power differences. In post-Mao China, the conservative and reform leaders alike advocated economic modernization, but the conservatives viewed party hegemony, ideological unity, and social stability as prerequisites for economic development, and they opposed fundamental systemic change. Fearing the disruption and chaos of the Cultural Revolution—of which they had been the chief victims—China's conservative leaders objected to mass movements and spontaneous demonstrations. When they talked of legal reform, they did not mean legal checks on the abuse of power but the regularization of party procedures and supervision over society. They wanted contact with the

West in order to import Western science, technology, and capital, but they did not want to import Western values, culture, and political ideas. They drew their support from the bureaucracy and military, who were fearful that change would reduce their prerogatives, and from the general public, which was afraid that change could lead to open conflict and another Cultural Revolution.

The reform leaders were more willing to experiment with economic practices such as the stock market and political procedures such as allowing more democratic practices on the local level. Most important, they formed a tacit alliance with the intellectuals not only to gain their cooperation and support in economic reforms but also in opposition to the remnant Maoists and conservatives in the leadership. Hu Yaobang, as the head of the Organization Department from December 1977 to December 1978, director of the Propaganda Department from 1978 until 1981, and the party's general secretary from 1981 until January 1987, gathered around him a group of politically oriented intellectuals first to get rid of the remaining Maoists in the leadership and to revoke Maoist policies and then to oppose the obstructions of the revolutionary elders to political reforms. Despite increasing attacks upon them, these intellectuals continued to speak out for a more open, democratic society until they were themselves purged in the June 4, 1989, crackdown. Hu Yaobang also oversaw the rehabilitation of thousands of intellectuals who were victims of the Cultural Revolution and also of the antirightist campaign of 1957–1959. He gained the reputation as the official patron of the intellectuals. Along with Zhao, he was willing to tolerate intellectual diversity, even reinterpretations of Marxism-Leninism. He and Zhao may not have wanted genuine democratic reforms, but they were willing to tolerate discussion of them and permit a more pluralistic intellectual environment.

Deng at times sided with these reform leaders but even then would contemplate only administrative, not systemic, changes. He was much less tolerant of demands for democratic reforms. He allowed the activists of the democratic movement of late 1978 to early 1979 to criticize Mao and the Maoists in the top leadership, but once he purged the Maoists, he suppressed the movement and jailed its leaders. By March 1979 he asserted that all discussion had to take place within the limits of the Four Cardinal Principles: adherence to socialism, people's democratic dictatorship, the party, and Marxism-Leninism-Maoism. Although he wanted more scope for technical and managerial talent, he, like his fellow revolutionary elders, insisted on the party hegemony for which they had given their lives. Although Deng was the head of the reform leadership, at certain times (such as mid-1981, late 1983, early 1987, and mid-1989) he joined with the conservatives not only because of the need to compromise with them in order to undercut their opposition and ensure implementation of economic reforms but also because he agreed with their view on the party's monopoly of power. Thus policy and ideological conflicts were intertwined with power interests.

The conservatives—and sometimes Deng—revived the strategy of the late nineteenth-century Qing officials—the self-strengtheners—who sought to combine the *ti,* Chinese principle, and the *yong,* Western function. They attempted to blend traditional political culture with Western technology. Whereas the reform leaders at least tolerated debate and the intellectuals even suggested revisions of the *ti,* the conservatives, like their nineteenth-century predecessors, distrusted, resisted, and even sabotaged efforts to change the *ti,* which in the twentieth century is Marxism-Leninism rather than Confucianism. They realized that even a partial revision of the *ti* might loosen their monopoly on the exercise of power. Therefore, they staunchly opposed any introduction of the Western *ti*—specifically, democratic practices and intellectual freedom, which they denounced as spiritual pollution and bourgeois liberalization. By contrast, the reform leaders were not against introducing and most intellectuals wished to import some Western *ti* with the Western *yong* and modify certain aspects of Marxism-Leninism in order to adapt it to the changing economy. Moreover, the reform political leaders were more in the tradition of the Hundred Days reformers of 1898, who radically reinterpreted the orthodox ideology of Confucianism; in contrast, some of their intellectual associates were more in the tradition of their May Fourth predecessors, who sought to replace the orthodoxy with Western political ideas and institutions. Thus there was even a tension between the reformers and some of their intellectual allies, as well as between the reformers and the conservatives.

As under Mao, political factions used and manipulated the intellectuals for their own political purposes. They attempted to seize the initiative by directing intellectuals to write articles, conduct debates, and hold conferences in order to influence elite public opinion. Because the reform leaders had an implicit alliance with the intellectuals, they had an advantage in this propaganda struggle, but the conservatives had advocates among a number of older intellectuals who had allied with them in the revolutionary Yanan period and in the 1950s. In what Carol Hamrin[1] has characterized as reform "surges," the intellectuals who sided with the reform leaders provided positive reinforcement for the leaders' proposals but, as in the Mao years, invariably went much further and asked for greater change than even their reform patrons desired, thereby weakening their patrons and provoking conservative "backlashes." At such times, the intellectuals allied with the conservatives retaliated against their more liberal counterparts. Until the June 1989 crackdown, there were more genuinely intellectual discussions on specific academic issues than at any other time in the PRC, but debates reflecting conflicts between the top leaders over power as well as issues still dominated the intellectual scene. For example, Wang Ruoshui, the philosopher and deputy editor of the party's official newspaper (*People's Daily*), tried to point out that the concepts of humanism and alienation existed in Marxism, intending to undermine ideological orthodoxy and the revolutionary elders who upheld it. Similarly, the head of the Institute of Literature of the Chinese Academy of Social Sciences, Liu Zaifu, called for a more subjective, more experimental literature, his demands meant to diminish the use of socialist realist and politicized literature that simply spouted the doctrines of the revolutionary elders. These elders retorted to such "intellectual" offenses with a vigorous defense of orthodoxy and charges of bourgeois liberalization and spiritual pollution against the exponents of such heterodoxies.

Because of the regime's commitment to economic and technological modernization, however, even the conservatives until June 1989 did not pressure intellectuals to conform to the point of producing an atmosphere that would altogether stifle their productivity and initiative. Without Mao's charismatic leadership and animosity toward intellectuals—and especially after the trauma of the Cultural Revolution—even if the regime wished to launch mass movements, incite fanaticism, and direct violence against the intellectuals as in the past, it would have been very difficult. Equally important, most intellectuals were no longer willing to obey the party's efforts to mobilize them against their colleagues. The Deng era was more moderate not only for fear of reviving the Cultural Revolution's repressive practices and disrupting economic modernization but also because the party no longer had the unquestioning allegiance of the population, particularly the intellectuals. The party still had the power to isolate, discredit, and coerce any intellectual, but until the 1989 Tiananmen crackdown, it was more selective in its discrimination than it had been under Mao. Moreover, the victims did not become nonpersons. After a time, they returned to positions somewhat related to their skills and spoke out again publicly, sometimes even more provocatively.

Scientists and Engineers in the Deng Era

That similar demands for far-reaching departures were also being heard in the Soviet Union and Eastern Europe in the 1980s suggests that Chinese intellectuals' and reform officials' calls for radical change were more than a reaction to the Cultural Revolution and demolished faith in the party. They, like their Communist counterparts elsewhere, were also responding to the technological backwardness of their countries vis-à-vis the West and Japan. Thus the updating of science and technology became crucial to the reform process. Until at least June 1989, China's opening to the outside world under Deng had been more extensive and lasted longer than at any other time in the PRC. The influx of Western ideas and methodologies and the direct exposure of China's intellectuals to the West through travel and personal contacts engendered skepticism not only about Marxism-Leninism and the one-party state but also about the party leadership and political system that had allowed China to fall so far behind scientifically and economically, especially in comparison to its East Asian neighbors, who until modern times had followed China's lead.

Since the party's takeover in 1949, one of its major goals was to modernize Chinese science and technology. Like China's nineteenth-century self-strengtheners and their Soviet mentors, party leaders regarded the development of science and technology as the means to achieving wealth, power, and status in the international arena. Despite the twists and turns of policies, this goal has remained quite consistent. The one exception was the decade of the Cultural Revolution, after which China's leaders and intellectuals alike became increasingly aware of China's backwardness. This consciousness generated a sense of urgency to make up for the lost time. To become an advanced scientific and technological society by the twenty-first century became an obsession.

Deng's China, however, was constrained by previous Chinese emulation of the Soviet model during the 1950s.[2] Along with considerable Soviet assistance in technological expertise, equipment, and training of Chinese students in the Soviet Union, China had also received the Soviet system of scientific and technological organization. It was characterized by a deemphasis on research in universities and centralization of research in institutes under an academy of science, giving high priority to research related to military and heavy-industrial needs. As in the Soviet Union, the scientific advances in the Chinese research institutes did not flow into industry and the economy; research activities became isolated from production activities. Furthermore, achieving production quotas rather than quality goods was the measure of success. Power over activities related to science and technology and within the research institutes was determined by a handful of political leaders who had little understanding of the matter.

Periodically, Mao shook up the encrusted Soviet model, as in the Great Leap Forward and the Cultural Revolution, in which he imposed his own rather than the Soviet criteria onto technological and economic activities. He stressed mass participation, egalitarianism, self-reliance, and indigenous scientific and technological development. At such times, Maoist activists took over scientific and technological tasks from professionals who were sent to the countryside and factories to learn from peasants and workers. Political mobilization and ideological exhortation rather than scientific research and laboratory experiments were to achieve technological breakthroughs. Central planning of science and technology was disrupted, and power devolved to ministries and local areas, with even less interaction than before. More damaging were the political campaigns that demoralized and decimated several generations of scientists, particularly in the Cultural Revolution, when most academic, professional, and scientific activities were stopped as scientists, along with writers and social scientists, were persecuted, reeducated, and sent away for labor reform merely for possessing expertise.

The Deng regime attempted not only to rectify the mindlessness of Mao's policies but, more important, to do away with the Soviet system, which it regarded as obstructing China's entrance into the age of high technology. It decentralized resources and authority to lower levels in order to reduce stifling effects of the Soviet-style centralized control, but at the same time it concentrated overall direction in the State Council Leading Group for Science and Technology. It also encouraged universities to engage in scientific research as they had before 1949.

Research centers and universities were encouraged to participate in the market, compete for projects, and contract their services to economic enterprises. Supposedly, as these practices took hold, institutes would become increasingly self-supporting, and the central government would gradually decrease its direct funding of research except in high-priority areas, such as defense. As the role of the party diminished in scientific and technological matters, scientific research became more and more independent of political control. Some research institutes even formed joint ventures with economic enterprises and gradually merged with them. "Research development production alliances" were created in industrial cities such as Harbin, Shanghai, and Dalian. To facilitate diffusion of ideas, methodologies, and more rational distribution of skilled personnel, some vertical mobility was allowed in the form of contracts, private consulting, and moonlighting. Revision in ideology also buttressed use of the market in science and technology.[3] In Deng's China, science and technology were no longer treated as free goods but as commodities that could be bought and sold. This revision was institutionalized in a patent system established in April 1985, which legally provided material incentives for scientific and technological innovation. For those engaged in both basic and applied research, a Chinese Science Foundation was established in February 1986 to allocate funds through peer review and competition rather than by administrative decree and party favors.

Another reform that helped insulate science and technology from political interference was the election of directors of institutes by their colleagues. In 1981 Lu Jiaxi was elected by his peers to the presidency of the Academy of Sciences; when he was forced to resign in 1987, however, at the time of the purge of the astrophysicist Fang Lizhi (who was blamed for inciting the student demonstrations of December 1986), Lu's replacement was appointed by the party. Still, the new president, Zhou Guangzhao, was a highly respected physicist, trained in the Soviet Union, who became directly involved in advising the political leadership on scientific matters. Until Zhao Ziyang's purge in June 1989, such scientists and economists in the Economic Institute of the Academy of Social Sciences, along with think tanks established by Zhao in the State Council and Central Committee, advised on policy matters.

These reforms—decentralization of research, introduction of a scientific market, private consulting, increased mobility, and peer evaluation—have the potential for fundamental structural change because they undermine the party's monopoly of control over science and technology. Like the reforms in other areas, such as agriculture, they obviated the party's entrenched bureaucracy and lessened its authority to intervene in such critical activities as the selection of research projects, promotion of particular scientists, and distribution of financial resources. Equally important in undermining the party's control over the scientific and technological realm was the reestablishment of ties with the international scientific community that had been severed in 1949.

Precisely because such reforms and international contacts were a threat to the bureaucracy's vested interests, party officials in science and technology obstructed and in some cases even resisted their full implementation. Furthermore, their antagonism was exacerbated by the scientists' opportunities to earn additional income and study abroad, opportunities not readily available to bureaucrats. Ideological factors also stiffened the bureaucracy's resistance. The scientific bureaucrats were not against scientific and technological development per se, but some shared the concern Mao tried to redress in the Great Leap Forward and the Cultural Revolution—a concern that faces all modernizing societies: As science and technology modernize, they become the preserve of a core of apolitical experts engaged in specialized activities that exclude the masses and inevitably increase inequalities. Perhaps it is impossible to create a modern science without a degree of exclusiveness. Nevertheless, despite the destructiveness of Cultural Revolution policies toward science and technology, Mao was facing an important issue in a nation's development—can it truly be modernized scientifically if the masses of people are excluded from the process? As it was, the reforms in science and technology were only beginnings, most of which still remained more in the realm of intent than reality. As in other areas, there was a difference between enunciation of policies and their effective implementation, which was thwarted by the very bureaucrats and cadres who were to carry them out.

The resistance of the entrenched bureaucracy was reinforced by the Deng regime's continuing use of political campaigns against the intellectuals. The campaigns were not directed against scientists; in fact, scientists were explicitly exempt from them. With the important exception of Fang Lizhi and his associates, most of the targets were nonscientific intellectuals, but the way in which the regime treated the nonscientists affected the scientists. If the nonscientific intellectuals were inhibited from adopting ideas from abroad and were subjected to arbitrary, repressive treatment, it intimidated scientists as well, especially those who from 1966 to 1976 had been subjected to violence and humiliation because of their Western orientation and expertise. Scientists need sustained effort and extensive, ongoing interaction with the international community to be productive. Periodic restrictions on the flow of experts, information, and initiative disrupt the continuity and contacts that transcend disciplines, institutions, and borders and that are necessary for modernizing science and technology.

True, even with the much longer and more drastic political interruptions under Mao, China was able to imitate and even modify some Western science and technology. Relying on the Soviet model and using a centralized system of direction, it developed rocket and space technology and made synthetic insulin, synthetic ribonucleic acid, germanium crystal, and state-of-the-art advances in superconductivity at relatively low temperatures. Certain pockets of excellence may be created through a combination of trained personnel, local initiatives, and central government priorities. But China's aspirations are much higher—an advanced science and technology that requires experimentation, uncertainty, questioning, and alternative views. Even in the sciences, so prized by the Deng regime, the effort to break away from the Soviet and Maoist models ran not only into bureaucratic resistance but also the still overall restraining Marxist-Leninist ideology that inhibits inquiry and schools of thought outside the established orthodoxy.

The sudden opening to the outside world, even the exaltation of Western science and technology as the panacea for all China's problems, may be as superficial and short-lived as in the May Fourth era (1919), when after a brief interlude the new orthodoxy of Marxism-Leninism soon replaced the traditional orthodoxy of Confucianism. There is no question that China has the potential for a modern science and technology. Even with the beginnings of structural reform in science and technology, the research improved and the professional quality rose quickly. The real problem is not the talent or even the age of the equipment in the laboratories; it remains the overriding weight of a political system whose controls, while lessened somewhat by the reforms, still do not allow this talent to express itself fully. Modern science requires the establishment of a relatively independent research community with its own norms and objectives. Its criteria for achievement, based on ability and scholarly attainment, conflict with the party's criteria based on seniority and political orthodoxy.

The ideological orthodoxy of a Leninist party-state, even one that gives its scientists a degree of autonomy, stifles the ethos of wide-ranging scientific inquiry, tolerance of error, testing of new ideas, open communication, and free exchange with the outside world on a continuing basis that is required for scientific advancement. Scientific methods inherently challenge dogma. For these reasons, China's scientists in the Deng era joined with their nonscientific colleagues for the first time in the PRC to demand the establishment of political institutions and laws that will encourage and protect this ethos—which ultimately challenges the party's authority based on Marxism-Leninism.

In their book *Intellectuals on the Road to Class Power,* the Hungarian writers George Konrad and Ivan Szelenyi argued that as Communist regimes in post-Stalinist Eastern Europe abandoned their revolutionary goals and made concessions to technocrats in order to modernize, an alliance gradually formed between the political leadership and technocrats. This alliance opened the way for increasing wealth, status, and political clout for scientists and engineers, who desire expensive equipment, foreign travel, and membership on important advisory councils. The interests of scientists and technocrats increasingly became identified with those of the political leaders than with those of their fellow intellectuals. Thus this alliance has not benefited and has even hurt intellectuals in the humanities and social sciences.

The experiences of scientists in China, as well as in other Communist regimes in the late 1980s, however, have disproved this assumption. It is difficult to isolate the fate of the scientists from the fate of other intellectuals. A number of talented Chinese scientists suffered in the antirightist campaign. In the Cultural Revolution, Mao tried to protect scientists from the violence of the Red Guards, but the dynamics of the campaign inevitably swept up virtually all the intellectuals. Even in the Deng period, when China's scientists and technocrats have readier access to training, responsibility, study abroad, and influence on policies in their areas of expertise than intellectuals in the humanities and creative arts, the split that Konrad and Szelenyi described as supposedly happening in Eastern Europe did not occur in China. In fact, among the leaders of the 1989 student demonstrations, nearly half came from scientific disciplines. In addition, members of the Academy of Sciences as well as the Academy of Social Sciences demonstrated in support of the students' demands for political reform.

Moreover, allowing scientists access to the outside world inevitably affects other intellectuals as well. Once the door is open, as China discovered in the late nineteenth century, it is impossible to control what comes in and who is influenced by it. Western political and philosophical concepts flow in along with scientific ideas and technological gadgets. Li Honglin, a member of Hu Yaobang's intellectual network, has pointed out that the nonscientific realm cannot be excluded from foreign influence without hurting the scientific realm. He acknowledges that "decadent and degenerate ideology and culture will enter our culture along with Western science and technology and contaminate the air. But even if the door were closed somewhat, such 'dirty things' would enter anyway from outside through the cracks in the walls."[4] Despite the party's continuing domination of the media, even more than Qing officials in the nineteenth century, it would be impossible to regulate the flow of ideas into and within China today.

Even if the regime should play off scientists against nonscientists, neither group appears willing to take part in the game. Not only would nonscientists like Li Honglin protest, but, more important, the periodic threat of repression and closing off contact with the outside world, though primarily directed against nonscientists, frightens scientists. They may be less directly affected, but they also are buffeted by shifts in the political winds. Furthermore, with scientists more involved politically in post-Mao China, they, too, are bound to become scapegoats, as happened to Fang Lizhi in the campaign against "bourgeois liberalization" in 1987 and in the June 1989 crackdown. Perhaps most important, scientists still remember their persecution in the Cultural Revolution, when their attackers made little distinction between writer and scientist. The threat of another Cultural Revolution unites all intellectuals as they had never been united before to resist an attack against any group among them. The scientists share with nonscientific intellectuals an interest in building institutions and establishing laws to protect themselves. Finally, as the scientific elite is expanded by students and scholars who have studied abroad, this elite exposed to greater intellectual freedom and professional autonomy will greatly strengthen the constituency for their right to engage more freely in their professional work, unencumbered by political demands. Unfortunately, these processes had not gone far enough by June 1989 to protect intellectuals. Once again, the regime made no distinction in charging that those calling for democracy and freedom, whether scientists or nonscientists, were infected with "bourgeois liberalization."

The Nonscientific Intellectuals

At least until June 4, the reform of the social sciences also had the potential for challenging the party's political monopoly. As in the Maoist period, scholarship still was subordinated to the political line, ideology, and factions, but there was greater diversity in the subject matter studied and the techniques used. For the first time since 1949, Western approaches in the social sciences and humanities were considered objectively. More attention was given to factual accuracy and periodically more tolerance was given to wide-ranging debates on doctrinal issues. The disciplines of anthropology, sociology, and political science were revived after twenty years of virtual suppression. As at the turn of the century, when thousands of Chinese students went abroad in search of political and economic theories to strengthen Chinese society, so in the Deng era thousands flocked to Japan and the West in search of ways to reform Chinese society. Like their predecessors, they shared a commitment to making China wealthy and powerful.

The modern social sciences, introduced into China around the turn of the century through translations of Western books, were meant from the onset to serve the political purpose of reforming China and facilitating its national survival. In addition to medicine, science, and engineering, new Western-style universities also taught history, literature, political economy, and political philosophy. Although they were turning away from their heritage, they were actually building on the traditional subjects of study and shared the traditional concern with political issues. Although most of the social scientists were educated in the West, their work was politically oriented, especially toward strengthening China.

With the reorganization of higher education along Soviet lines after 1949, the teaching of the humanities and the social sciences was done primarily in the universities and research primarily in the Institute of Philosophy and Social Sciences in the Academy of Sciences. When a separate Academy of Social Sciences was established in May 1977, the social sciences were given importance in their own right and were at least theoretically assured the same degree of autonomy as were the sciences. In the slogans of the day, they were to "emancipate minds" and "seek truth from facts." Controversies were no longer to be initiated or resolved by political leaders and ideological doctrine but with reference to empirical data and rigorous debate. All of these activities, however, are ultimately political in that they are to contribute to China's modernization.

By August 1984, the Academy of Social Sciences had thirty-two research institutes, a postgraduate school, and a publishing house. It employed more than 5,000 researchers and 3,000 staff members.[5] Its specific role was to advise the reform leaders on policy. Its economic institutes studied Western economic institutions, foreign investment, technology transfer, and theories of modernization. In addition to the think tanks under the State Council and the Central Committee, they were among a number of different sources contributing to policy formulation. The humanists were in charge of developing a modern culture and revising ideology in line with the changes in the economy. They were to inculcate social and political values deemed necessary for modernization.

Sociologists, political scientists, and anthropologists experimented with Western techniques such as quantitative analysis, survey research, and opinion polls to ascertain the views of the population. These methods were to provide objective sources of information with which the leadership could devise policies more responsive to the people's will than those based on the leaders' ideology, political interests, or personal whims. They could even provide a "truer" version of the people's wishes than the ones the literary intellectuals perceived and presented in their writings. After the Tiananmen massacre, however, it is unlikely that the social sciences will be allowed to develop as an independent profession and carry on their inquiries, unimpeded by political considerations, at least until the revolutionary elders pass from the scene. Even if the social scientists are totally committed to their methodologies and have no desire to make political statements, if their work presents information that contradicts the party's view of society or the party's interests, it is unlikely that it will be listened to and can easily be suppressed.

As much as the differing content, differing methodologies also challenged the party and Marxism-Leninism. In 1985 a major controversy arose over economic methodology. Ma Ting, a young scholar at Nanjing University, suggested that Western economic theories, such as econometrics and quantitative techniques, might be more helpful in developing the economy than the Marxist political-economy approach. It is not surprising that the conservatives were enraged at these recommendations because, as they rightly charged, Ma Ting was implicitly rejecting the party's ideology and thereby its leadership. Without institutional protections, the capacity of the social scientists to present alternative views remains problematic.

In the Deng era as in traditional times and under Mao, literature remains a principal means for expressing criticism of the regime. This criticism began with "wound" literature: stories, plays and poems on the officially approved topic of persecution by the Gang of Four in the Cultural Revolution. But by the early 1980s, writings on the Cultural Revolution were gradually restricted because, as Deng pointed out, to criticize Mao's policies also meant to criticize party leaders (like Deng) who had supported Mao's policies. In addition, the genre of "wound" literature became outmoded as the mood of the nation turned more to the present. It was replaced by the genre of "exposure" literature, which reveals the corruption and abuses of officials in the present as well as in the past. This genre was not new in China; it existed in traditional times, the May Fourth era, and even under Mao, especially during the Hundred Flowers, when the writers Liu Binyan and Wang Meng exposed incompetent officials who were undermining the system. A new trend to emerge in the Deng era involved literary works concerned less with overt political issues and more with the emotions, frustrations, and relationships of everyday life. In this innovative genre, Wang Meng (who was to become minister of culture in 1985) and a number of younger writers experimented with a variety of styles—intricate language, folktales, imagery, symbolism, and stream of consciousness—to evoke memories, inner feelings, and random associations. These new techniques were regarded as more appropriate to their subject matter.

Even though the Deng regime initially encouraged greater leeway in style and content in an effort to win the support of the creative intellectuals, to be artistically apolitical in a society in which politics hitherto permeated every aspect of life expressed a rejection of political interference in one's creative work. It was a direct challenge to the party's politicization of culture. In addition, writers such as Wang Meng believe that using literature for didactic purposes stifles the writer's ability to express genuine emotions and create artistic works. This apolitical trend was most noticeable among writers in their thirties and early forties, who were in their formative years during the Cultural Revolution. Utterly disillusioned by that experience, they were skeptical of all politics. For the first time in the PRC, serious writers explicitly departed from the moral-political orientation of their traditional and May Fourth predecessors and senior colleagues by shunning political commentary for self-expression. Although the Deng regime periodically criticized what it called "obscure" poetry, unintelligible to ordinary people, it treated apolitical writers less harshly than the politically oriented intellectuals. Academic discussions of modernism, for example, were regarded as less of a threat than academic discussions of political reform and modern capitalism. There was greater tolerance of experimentation with style than with content because it challenged the regime less directly.

Although political control of high literary culture continued, the Deng regime showed greater restraint than Mao in coercing the whole literary profession. Individual writers were singled out as negative examples, but not the whole profession, as in the Great Leap Forward and the Cultural Revolution. Equally important, instead of insisting that literature serve politics and the political line, Deng asked it to serve the more general cause of socialism and especially modernization. Supposedly writers could write in any style they pleased and on any subject they wished as long as they assisted the cause of modernization. Furthermore, until June 4, 1989, literature no longer had to cater only to workers, peasants, and soldiers but to all social groups. None of these injunctions provided autonomy, yet they made it possible to write less politicized literature. More important, breaking away from the realistic and socialist-realist legacy and experimenting with styles led to experimentation with content as well. They explored new, previously "forbidden" topics such as extramarital love and sexual dysfunction. In reaction to the collectivist, heroic emphasis of the Cultural Revolution, some fiction in the Deng era dwelled on the individual and the outsider.

The Critical Intellectuals

Whereas the scientists, engineers, professionals, and relatively apolitical writers challenged the party's monopoly of power indirectly and potentially, the critical intellectuals challenged it directly and immediately until they were silenced in June 1989. As in the past, a tiny minority of intellectuals, the critical intellectuals, exposed repression, bureaucratic privilege, arbitrary rule, corruption, and irrational practices and made political demands. Most of them were Marxists, such as the writer Liu Binyan, the philosopher Wang Ruoshui, the ideological theorist Su Shaozhi, and the political scientist Yan Jiaqi. Even under the Deng regime, with which they were initially allied, they pointed out the difference between Marxist ideals and the realities of life. Most sought change not by destroying the prevailing political order but by reforming it.

In the initial period after Deng's accession to power in late 1978, they saw themselves as they had in the early Mao years, as the conduit through which the "people's" views reached the political leaders and through which the leaders learned of the effects of their policies. They were the intermediaries who interpreted the murmurings of the people to the government. If the leaders would listen and respond to the voices of the people as interpreted by these self-appointed spokespersons, then the relationship between the leaders and the led would be strengthened and their interests harmonized. They presented the government as inherently good and wanted to ensure that it lived up to its benevolent image. This elitist view, which looks on "the people" as an undifferentiated mass, is in the traditional image of the literati's paternalistic responsibility for the common people. It gives the critical intellectuals, like the literati, a special status and implicitly accepts an autocratic polity.

By the second half of the 1980s, however, the critical intellectuals were no longer willing merely to accept concessions from the political leadership. In addition to their experience in the antirightist campaign and the Cultural Revolution, the continuing attacks by the Deng regime (specifically, the campaigns against spiritual pollution in 1983–1984 and against bourgeois liberalization in early 1987) made them realize that even when rights were given to them by an enlightened leadership, they could be taken away. Moreover, official patrons like Hu Yaobang might be purged or Deng Xiaoping withdraw support. Thus they began to demand institutional and legal guarantees of civil rights and freedom of expression and the establishment of some form of representative government in order to check abuses of the political leadership. They sought protection from the retribution they endured in the Deng era as well as the Mao period for expressing critical views. They were no longer willing to rely on the good services of party patrons, even when those leaders seemed to be in sympathy with their views.

Consequently, they pointed out the gap between state and society that began with the alienation of the peasants in the Great Leap Forward and widened still further in the Cultural Revolution when virtually the whole population suffered from its violence and anarchy. As the famous writer Ba Jin declared, "Never before in the history of man nor in any other country have people had such a fearful and ridiculous, weird and tragic experience as in the Cultural Revolution."[6] One legacy was the readiness of some leaders, such as Hu Yaobang and Zhao Ziyang, as well as intellectuals to question the political and economic system that had allowed such a tragedy to occur. Another legacy was that for the first time the critical intellectuals questioned the elitist assumption they had inherited from their literati predecessors, that they spoke on behalf of, or at least for the benefit of, the people. They also questioned their previous assumption that leaders, when properly informed of the people's will, would respond accordingly. An important departure in the Deng era was the critical intellectuals' realization that these assumptions may have contributed to the repressive system itself and that perhaps the democratic practices of representative government accountable to the people and freedom of speech guaranteed by law might more effectively close the gap between the leaders and the led.

Although certain leaders acknowledged the need for political reform, then, the intellectuals associated with them believed that the Cultural Revolution did not come about merely because of the abuses of a single leader, however tyrannical he may have been, but because of the very nature of the system in which he operated. Consequently, they called for more far-reaching departures from prevailing practices across all areas of life—economy, society, and culture in addition to the political system. Not only did the nature of their demands differ from those made in the Mao era, their methods also differed. Because the Deng regime was less intimidating and oppressive, they spoke out much more directly and publicly and resorted less to the traditional use of oblique, subtle criticism. Moreover, whereas under Mao most critical intellectuals were literary intellectuals, under Deng their ranks were expanded with scientists, social scientists, ideological theorists, and economists who also actively engaged in public debate. Most importantly, in the second half of 1986 and again in the first half of 1989, they called for fundamental changes in the political system.

The leaders of the critical intellectuals were mainly in their fifties and early sixties. Many of them had been "rightists" in the late 1950s; they had "lost" not only the ten years of the Cultural Revolution but more than twenty years that followed. Their protests were against the people—such as Deng Xiaoping and Peng Zhen—and the system that had allowed repressions like the antirightist campaign, the Cultural Revolution, and the post-Mao campaigns to occur.

Most of the critical intellectuals justified their actions in Marxist terms, but their interpretations of Marxism drew on their Confucian heritage, the Western democratic concepts introduced into China in the early decades of the twentieth century, and Western Marxism. Their ideas and practices also resembled those of their Soviet and East European counterparts, with whom they had continuing contact and shared structural similarities in their critical roles vis-à-vis the ruling Communist parties. Although some of their ideas overlapped with those of the ex–Red Guard democratic activists of the late 1970s and the student demonstrators of the 1980s, the way in which the critical intellectuals protested until the 1989 Tiananmen incident was closer to the style of their literati predecessors than to the more Westernized tactics of the democratic activists and students, who expressed themselves through unofficial channels—self-printed pamphlets, wall posters, demonstrations, and talks with Western journalists. Like their literati predecessors, the critical intellectuals were well connected and, under Deng, linked directly and indirectly to Zhao Ziyang and particularly to Hu Yaobang, for whom several of them had worked in the 1950s, when Hu was the head of the Communist Youth League. They published in the most prestigious newspapers and journals and held positions high up in the intellectual hierarchy.

In return for these positions, the reform leaders expected the critical intellectuals to perform the practical function of lobbying for reform and attacking those opposed to reform. Like a number of enlightened emperors of the imperial era, Mao in the Hundred Flowers, and even Gorbachev during the 1980s and 1990s in the Soviet Union, the Deng leadership not only encouraged criticism of abusive officials in order to make the system run more efficiently, they also encouraged attacks on their political opponents who obstructed the reforms. Similarly, as under Mao, the critical intellectuals used their access to the party's newspapers and journals to insert their own ideas. What was different in the Deng period was that the memory of the Cultural Revolution and desire for acceptance in the international community limited the party's repression of the critical intellectuals at the same time that it impelled the critical intellectuals to speak out more persistently and more daringly than they had before the Cultural Revolution.

Under Mao's rule as well as in the Confucian system, there was no clear distinction between the state and society. Most intellectuals, even the Western-trained ones, had accepted this undifferentiated view because at the time of the 1949 revolution, they believed the Communist party was the only political organization that could unite and save the nation. Because of this unreflective patriotism, in 1955 most of them went along with the party's persecution of the nonconformist writer Hu Feng and his coterie as "traitors." In 1957–1959 many acquiesced and even participated in condemning as "rightists" close to 1 million of China's brightest and best intellectuals who, at Mao's behest in the Hundred Flowers, had criticized bureaucratic abuses. Even those designated as "rightist" initially believed that their criticism of the party bureaucracy had disunited the nation. In addition to feeling a sense of patriotism, which justified closing ranks against officially designated scapegoats, intellectuals feared that if they did not acquiesce, they, too, would be labeled "traitors" or "rightists," which could result in public disgrace, isolation, labor reform, and even imprisonment for themselves, their families, and their friends.

However, as the regime increasingly equated loyalty to the nation with loyalty to the party—and in the Cultural Revolution to Mao himself—the intellectuals became more and more alienated. With the persecution of virtually all intellectuals in the Cultural Revolution, the tension between loyalty to their nation and people and loyalty to the party and its political leaders burst out into the open in the post-Mao period. The critical intellectuals, in particular, began to redefine the traditional and Maoist identification of government with society. If leaders ignore the people's cries and draw apart from the people as they did in the Cultural Revolution, a number of critical intellectuals urged, then the intellectuals' articulation of the grievances of the masses must take precedence over the expression of the will of the leaders and the party. They no longer equated their support for their country and society or even their view of Marxism with support for the party or for a particular political faction with which they may have been allied. The party and the leaders they had served had turned against some of them in the antirightist campaign, against the peasants in the Great Leap Forward, and against virtually the whole population in the Cultural Revolution. Those experiences plus their continuing persecution in the Deng era made them realize that what the party or any leader decreed was not necessarily good for the nation and society.

These views were spelled out by the preeminent critical intellectual, the writer-journalist Liu Binyan, when he returned after twenty-two years in exile as an alleged rightist. In his first major address (appropriately entitled "The Call of the Times") at the Fourth Congress of the All-China Federation of Literary and Art Circles in fall 1979, he recalled that only when he was sent to the countryside for labor reform did he discover that the lives of the peasants were "exactly the opposite of what the higher levels were saying and what the newspapers were publishing." No matter how much he wanted to believe what the party told him, "I saw the peasants wanted one thing, the leadership and newspapers something else." When the demands of the people and the demands of the party contradict each other, Liu insisted, "We should listen to the people; we owe allegiance to the welfare and needs of the people" because, as Liu observed, "The party is not infallible." Consequently, "When this sort of double truth . . . appears in our lives, writers should obey their feeling of great responsibility to the people."[7] Liu called on his fellow writers to be independent spokespersons who, when confronted with a conflict between what the party decreed and what the people wanted, sided with the people.

He dealt with this conflict in a kind of investigative reporting carried to an art form, reportage (*baogao wenxue*), a genre he had learned from the Soviet-thaw writers of the mid-1950s. The conflict between party decrees and popular desires was most directly expressed in "In the Second Kind of Loyalty," published in spring 1985. Liu talked of various kinds of loyalties: The most common is the safe one personified by Lei Feng and promoted by the party because Lei Feng was a model soldier who followed the party's orders, whatever they were. The second kind of loyalty, the one Liu most admired, is personified by two protagonists—Chen Shizhong, a mechanical engineer, and Ni Yuxian, a former soldier enrolled in the Shanghai Naval Transport College—whose loyalty to their country and society is much more valuable than Lei Feng's slavish loyalty to the political line. In the Maoist period, they risked death to expose abuses of power or to defend others against injustice. Even in the Deng period, where at least in the early stage there was a closer relationship between the government and the people, they continued to point out unpleasant facts of party corruption, privilege, and deceit. Their loyalty was to the led, not to the leaders.[8]

In the post-Mao period, Liu expressed a less elitist view than in his earlier work during the Hundred Flowers, when his heroes were educated party youth who fought against bureaucratic officiousness and incompetence. His later protagonists, though somewhat educated and skilled, are figures on the fringes of society whose moral courage leads them to condemn the Great Leap Forward, the Cultural Revolution, and even certain aspects of the Deng period. They are isolated individuals, loners with little power, surrounded by the overwhelming majority who commit and acquiesce in abuses. Their cries are no match for the evil around them: Liu's view is pessimistic, like that of Lu Xun in his early stories. His only solution for the conflict between the leaders and the led is moral outrage—voiced through letters, petitions, and visits—by individuals like himself who investigate the incidents brought to his attention. His reportage functions as remonstrations to the leadership, a traditional approach to redressing grievances.[9] Nevertheless, his distinction between the country and society on the one hand and the government and leaders on the other is revolutionary in the Chinese context.

Disillusionment with the party extended to its orthodox ideology—Marxism-Leninism-Maoism. Actually, the reform leaders themselves, most prominently Hu Yaobang, acknowledged this disillusionment in calls to revise the ideology in line with changes in China, as well as in the rest of the world. A controversial December 7, 1984, *People's Daily* editorial, supposedly based on notes of Hu Yaobang, stated, "We cannot expect the writings of Marx and Lenin of that time to provide solutions to our current problems." The next day, "all" was added to "our current problems," reflecting a disagreement over the editorial. Yet even with the revision, the conclusion was that the orthodox ideology was largely irrelevant. In 1979 the Institute of Marxism-Leninism and Mao Zedong Thought had been established to update and revise the ideology. Su Shaozhi, who became its head in 1982, admitted in an October 21, 1985, article in *People's Daily,* written with his student Deng Xueliang, that "the Cultural Revolution seriously set back Marxism . . . because of all the vicious things done in the period under the guise of Marxism." Therefore, it is necessary "to adopt a creative attitude and developmental view toward Marxism so as to maintain its vitality." Equally subversive to the orthodox ideology was Su's assertion that the intellectuals, not the workers, will lead the way to an advanced industrial society: "Information has replaced material resources as well as man's labor to become the dominant resource for the growth of social wealth." Moreover, "the productive forces of knowledge have become the key factors in productivity, competitiveness, and economic success." He did not blame Marxism itself as the cause of irrelevance but praised its emphasis on the role of technology in transforming society. Rather, he blamed "some of our comrades, ignorant of the latest trends of science and technology." This ignorance, he insisted, is a consequence not only of the traditional legacy but also "a rigidity in thinking resulting from years of autocracy and 'leftist' influence."[10] Implicit in his argument is criticism of the ideology and system that allowed these negative forces to gain ascendancy. Although his views and those of his colleagues were influenced by the West European Marxists' reinterpretations, their analyses stem primarily from their awareness of China's backwardness in the aftermath of the Cultural Revolution.

In the late 1970s, as part of the outpouring of works that explored the tragic dimensions of the Cultural Revolution, Wang Ruoshui (deputy editor of the *People's Daily* until he was dismissed in fall 1983) began writing on alienation existing under socialism. He argued that the system had produced so much suffering and so much violence that it had given rise to the opposite of what was intended. Instead of enhancing man's worth, it had diminished it. Specifically, this alienation was caused by (1) the cult of personality during Mao's leadership, (2) irrational economic policies such as the Great Leap Forward and emphasis on heavy industry, and (3) the doings of the party cadres, supposedly "the servants of the people, [who had transformed] themselves into the masters of the people." Merely to overthrow the Gang of Four and to be on guard against another Cultural Revolution were not enough to end the alienation. It was necessary to limit the power of "the high and mighty officials" who were "indifferent to the interests of the people."[11] Although Wang mentioned the need to restrict official power by means of genuine democracy and a legal system, his emphasis, like that of his literati predecessors, was still on ideological rather than institutional change. To counter the oppressive, dehumanizing society that he described, he called for a revival of humanism, whose principles he said could be found in Marxism.

Up until the mid-1980s, most critical intellectuals were more concerned with ideological rather than institutional means to achieve their goals.

But as the Deng era evolved, a number of critical intellectuals began to shift this emphasis, calling for new institutions as well as humaneness in order to check abusive political power. Despite their courage and willingness to challenge injustice, their emphasis on the traditional moral suasion certainly had not saved them under Mao, had not protected them from attacks under Deng, and in fact had provoked counterattacks. Thus the political scientist Yan Jiaqi called for limited terms of office for leaders, strengthening the National People's Congress in the fashion of Gorbachev's strengthening of the Supreme Soviet, and establishing a system of checks and balances. Fang Lizhi demanded basic human rights, which he declared were not bestowed as gifts by the party but were inalienable. These views were voiced in the student demonstrations of December 1986 and again in the spring 1989 demonstrations.

The increasing attention that the critical intellectuals gave to institutional political change, legal protections, and human rights as the Deng regime proceeded was not only because China had become more exposed to Western ideas and the reforms under way in Eastern Europe but also because Chinese society was no longer passive. Once Mao himself had desanctified the party and incited various groups to rebel against authority in the Cultural Revolution, it was no longer possible to impose a "single truth" or dictate to a "unified society." Moreover, the retreat from Mao's utopian visions in the Deng period engendered distrust of social engineering not only among the educated but also among the peasants and workers, who no longer could be treated as mere objects of official policy. Despite the reform leaders' greater willingness to recognize a more diverse society and govern in a more conciliatory, flexible way, they still expressed the traditional and Leninist view that only a small elite can govern and be entrusted with the ideological truth that they periodically attempted to impose. Thus the critical intellectuals' shift in the mid-1980s—from emphasizing moral persuasion to stressing political and legal checks on power—could not be attributed to outside influences alone; it came about in part as a result of their own treatment and the actions of the Deng regime, their supposed political patrons.

Implications for the Future

If history has taught anything, it is that nothing is inevitable; certainly reform is not inexorable nor is a continuing loosening of controls over China's intellectuals. In the aftermath of the Tiananmen crackdown, China faces another period of tightening control and emphasis on orthodox ideology. The revolutionary elders may not have a program, but they can obstruct and even reverse reforms. Nevertheless, the reforms of the previous ten years had some residual effects. The atmosphere after June 4, 1989, was less stifling than under Mao, but for a time the forces for change, the students and critical intellectuals, were silenced and withdrew to their private lives or overseas. Virtually all the members of Hu Yaobang's network of intellectuals who had opposed the remaining Maoists and conservatives in the leadership and demanded democratic reforms for nearly ten years (despite periodic repression) were suppressed. They either were imprisoned for at least a year (like Li Honglin), escaped abroad (like Yan Jiaqi and Su Shaozhi), or are no longer able to speak out publicly (like Wang Ruoshui).

Because of the Cultural Revolution, it was thought that China's leaders would never again repress intellectuals. But after initially facing up to the horrors of the Cultural Revolution, the efforts of intellectuals to bear witness in their writings and even the writer Ba Jin's attempts to establish a museum of the Cultural Revolution were frustrated. The denunciation of Mao has not been as thorough as the Soviet condemnation of Stalin. Consequently, the memory of the Cultural Revolution was not sufficient to prevent the June 1989 crackdown.

As of 1991 it appeared that even if economic reforms would resume, political change would be illusory. Nevertheless, that the students failed in their demands for democracy in the spring 1989 demonstrations has more to do with the Leninist political system, the internal dynamics of the power struggle, and the revolutionary elders' continuing control over the military than with any inherent obstacles to political reform. If the elders had already left the scene, Zhao Ziyang might have prevailed and the students and intellectuals might at least have been given a hearing. The social and intellectual forces for change and the desire to restrain political power remain—and are perhaps even greater today. Just because China reverted to totalitarian practices does not mean that the desire for political reform is lacking. Ostensibly, the population appears to have fallen into line. In addition to ubiquitous military and police presence, the party still controls assignment of jobs, housing, ration tickets, medical treatment, and education of most of the population. The difference this time, however, is that there has been a popular uprising not just by students and intellectuals but by people from all walks of urban life in defiance of the party for the first time since 1949.

Equally important, as in other Communist societies today, even China needs the tacit consent of the people in order to govern. Because of the Tiananmen crackdown, Deng has lost the mandate he was given when he promised to end the traumas of the Mao era. Historically, once intellectuals feel a regime's mandate has been lost, it is almost impossible to retrieve. But in traditional China when new leaders gained the mandate, they were able to govern effectively within the existing system; at present that appears increasingly difficult. Since the fall of the last dynasty in 1911, China has not been able to find the political system appropriate for its needs. The seventieth anniversary of the May Fourth movement, the first student protest demanding democracy, was celebrated by the 1989 demonstrators, who made the very same demand. Will those honoring the seventieth anniversary of the 1989 Tiananmen demonstration still be making the same demand? Until democracy is realized in some way, China will continue to endure cycles of autocratic rule interspersed with periods of reformist benevolence.

Jiang Zemin, the party general secretary who replaced Zhao Ziyang, has a record of tough treatment of the critical intellectuals, but, like Deng, he is within the self-strengthening tradition that wants Western science, technology, and business yet rejects the Western ideas that accompany them. But as Li Honglin observed, there is no way to keep Western notions from coming in "through the cracks." As the self-strengtheners were unable to stop Western ideas from undermining Confucian orthodoxy in the late nineteenth century, so, too, will China's present-day self-strengtheners be unable to prevent Western thought from subverting their Marxist-Leninist orthodoxy and power in the late twentieth century.

So long as the party's goal remains economic modernization, the critical intellectuals will resume their demand for fundamental political changes some time in the future. Even though Hu Yaobang's intellectual network has been crushed, other critical intellectuals will emerge as they have throughout Chinese history. The party cannot repress them altogether without also alienating the scientists and engineers needed for scientific and economic modernization and jeopardizing its relations with the outside world. Yet until new political institutions are established that change the party-dominated state and separate the state from society, the age-old tradition of small numbers of intellectuals' pointing out the government's misdeeds and demanding reforms will continue. What makes the critical intellectuals of the Deng period different from those of the traditional and Mao periods is that what they propose—democratic institutions—renders their traditional role as spokespersons for the people obsolete. But if and when new political institutions emerge, it may be because of the efforts of the critical intellectuals as well as the underlying forces of modernization.

Notes

1. Carol Hamrin, "New Trends Under Deng Xiaoping and His Successors," in *China's Intellectuals and the State,* edited by Merle Goldman, with Timothy

Cheek and Carol Hamrin (Cambridge: Harvard University Press, Council on East Asian Studies, 1987), 275–304.

2. Robert Suttmeier, "New Directions in Chinese Science and Technology," in *China Briefing, 1985,* edited by John Major (Boulder: Westview Press, 1986), 91–102.

3. Robert Suttmeier, "Impact of Modernization of Science and Technology on the Political System," in *China's New Technological Revolution,* edited by Denis Simon and Merle Goldman (Cambridge: Harvard University Press, 1989), 375–396.

4. Li Honglin, "Socialism and Opening to the Outside World," *Renmin ribao* (People's daily), October 15, 1984, 5.

5. For a full discussion of the social sciences, see *New Directions in the Social Sciences and Humanities in China,* edited by Michael B. Yahuda (New York: St. Martin's Press, 1987), particularly 114–130.

6. Ba Jin, *Random Thoughts,* trans. Geremie Barmé (Hong Kong, 1984), 16.

7. Liu Binyan, "The Call of the Times," in *Chinese Literature for the 1980s,* edited by Howard Goldblatt (Armonk, N.Y.: M. E. Sharpe, 1982), 104.

8. Liu Binyan, "Dierzhong Zhongcheng" (The second kind of loyalty), *Kaituo* (Exploration), No. 1, 1985, 4–23.

9. An excellent discussion of the traditional aspects of Liu Binyan is provided by Leo Oufan Lee, "The Tragic Vision of Liu Binyan" (unpublished manuscript).

10. Su Shaozhi and Deng Xueliang, "China and the Coming Post-Industrial Society," *Renmin ribao,* October 21, 1985, 5.

11. Wang Ruoshui, "On Estrangement," originally in *The Journalist Front,* No. 8, 1980; reprinted in *Selected Works on Studies of Marxism* (Beijing), Nos. 1–20, 1981.

Selected Bibliography

Balazs, Etienne. *Chinese Civilization and Bureaucracy: Variation on a Theme.* Trans. H. M. Wright. New Haven: Yale University Press, 1964.

Barmé, Geremie. *New Ghosts, Old Dreams: Chinese Rebel Voices.* New York: Random House, 1991.

Barmé, Geremie, and John Minford, eds. *Seeds of Fire: Chinese Voices of Conscience.* New York: Hill and Wang, 1988.

Barnett, A. Doak. *Cadres, Bureaucracy, and Political Power in Communist China.* New York: Columbia University Press, 1967.

Baum, Richard, ed. *Reform and Reaction in Post-Mao China: The Road to Tiananmen.* London: Routledge, Chapman, and Hall, 1991.

Bergère, Marie-Claire. *The Golden Age of the Chinese Bourgeoisie.* New York: Cambridge University Press, 1989.

Binyan, Liu. *China's Crisis, China's Hope.* Cambridge: Harvard University Press, 1990.

_____. "People or Monsters?" In Perry Link, ed., *China After Mao.* Bloomington: Indiana University Press, 1983.

Brugger, Bill, and David Kelly. *Chinese Marxism in the Post-Mao Era.* Stanford: Stanford University Press, 1990.

Chance, Norman A. *China's Urban Villagers: Changing Life in a Beijing Suburb.* 2d ed. Troy, Mo.: Holt, Rinehart & Winston, 1991.

Chang, Parris H. *Power and Policy in China.* 2d enl. ed. University Park: Pennsylvania State University Press, 1978.

Cheng, Chu-Yuan. *Behind the Tiananmen Massacre: Social, Political, and Economic Ferment in China.* Boulder: Westview Press, 1990.

Cheng, Joseph Y., ed. *China: Modernization in the 1980s.* New York: St. Martin's Press, 1990.

Christiansen, Flemming. "Private Land in China? Some Aspects of the Development of Socialist Land Ownership in Post-Mao China." *Journal of Communist Studies* 3, 1 (March 1987): 55–70.

Davis, Deborah. "Chinese Social Welfare: Policies and Outcomes." *China Quarterly* (Spring 1989): 577–597.

_____. "Unequal Chances, Unequal Outcomes: Pension Reform and Urban Inequality." *China Quarterly* (1988): 223–242.

Davis, Deborah, and Ezra F. Vogel, eds. *Chinese Society on the Eve of Tiananmen: The Impact of Reform.* Cambridge: Council on East Asian Studies, Harvard University, 1990.

Dittmer, Lowell. *Liu Shao-ch'i and the Chinese Cultural Revolution.* Berkeley: University of California Press, 1974.

Esherick, Joseph W. "Xi'an Spring." *Australian Journal of Chinese Affairs* 24 (June 1990): 209–235.

Fewsmith, Joseph. "Agricultural Crisis in China." *Problems of Communism* 37 (November-December 1988): 78–93.

Gold, Thomas B. "China's Private Entrepreneurs." *China Business Review* (November-December 1985): 46–50.

———. "Guerrilla Interviewing Among the Getihu." In Perry Link, Richard Madsen, and Paul G. Pickowicz, eds., *Unofficial China: Popular Culture and Thought in the People's Republic,* 175–193. Boulder: Westview Press, 1989.

———. "The Resurgence of Civil Society in China." *Journal of Democracy* 1, 1 (Winter 1990): 18–31.

———. *State and Society in the Taiwan Miracle.* Armonk, N.Y.: M. E. Sharpe, 1986.

———. "Urban Private Business in China." *Studies in Comparative Communism* 22, 2-3 (Summer-Autumn 1989): 187–201.

Goldman, Merle. *China's Intellectuals: Advise and Dissent.* Cambridge: Harvard University Press, 1981.

Gu, Zhibin. *China Beyond Deng: Reform in the PRC.* Jefferson, N.C.: McFarland, 1991.

Hamrin, Carol Lee. *China's Intellectuals and the State: In Search of a New Relationship.* Cambridge: Council on East Asian Studies, Harvard University, distributed by Harvard University Press, 1987.

Hamrin, Carol Lee, and Timothy Cheek, eds. *China's Establishment Intellectuals.* Armonk, N.Y.: M. E. Sharpe, 1986.

Harding, Harry. *Organizing China: The Problem of Bureaucracy, 1949–1976.* Stanford: Stanford University Press, 1981.

Hayhoe, Ruth, ed. *Education in China's Modernization: Historical and Contemporary Perspectives.* London: Pergamon Press, 1991.

Hershkovitz, Linda. "The Fruits of Ambivalence: China's Urban Individual Economy." *Pacific Affairs* 58, 3 (Fall 1985): 427–450.

Hicks, George, ed. *The Broken Mirror: China After Tiananmen.* Chicago: St. James Press, 1990.

Honig, Emily, and Gail Hershatter. *Personal Voices: Chinese Women in the 1980s.* Stanford: Stanford University Press, 1988.

Hooper, Beverly. *Youth in China.* New York: Penguin Books, 1985.

Kane, Anthony J., ed. *China Briefing, 1989.* Boulder: Westview Press, 1989.

Kraus, Willy. "Private Enterprise in the People's Republic of China: Official Statement, Implementations and Future Prospects." In Joseph C. H. Chai and Chi-Keung Leung, eds., *China's Economic Reforms.* Hong Kong: University of Hong Kong, Centre of Asian Studies, 1987.

Lampton, David M., with Yeung Saicheung. *Paths to Power: Elite Mobility in Contemporary China.* Ann Arbor: Center for Chinese Studies, University of Michigan, 1989.

Lee, Chiu-chuan, ed. *Voices of China: The Interplay of Politics and Journalism.* New York: Guilford Publications, 1990.

Lee, Hong Yung. *From Revolutionary Cadres to Party Technocrats in Socialist China.* Berkeley: University of California Press, 1991.
Lewis, John Wilson. *Leadership in Communist China.* Ithaca, N.Y.: Cornell University Press, 1963.
Li, Lulu, et al. "The Structure of Social Stratification and the Modernization Process in Contemporary China." *International Sociology* 6 (March 1991): 25–36.
Lieberthal, Kenneth, and Michel Oksenberg. *Policy Making in China: Leaders, Structures, and Processes.* Princeton: Princeton University Press, 1988.
Link, Perry, ed. *Stubborn Weeds: Popular and Controversial Chinese Literature After the Cultural Revolution.* Bloomington: Indiana University Press, 1983.
Link, Perry, Richard Madsen, and Paul G. Pickowicz, eds. *Unofficial China: Popular Culture and Thought in the People's Republic.* Boulder: Westview Press, 1989.
Lizhi, Fang. *Farewell to an Era.* New York: Alfred A. Knopf, 1991.
Lockett, Martin. "Small Business and Socialism in Urban China." *Development and Change* 17, 1 (1986): 35–67.
Lu, Feng. "Dan wei—A Special Form of Social Organization." *Social Sciences in China* 10 (Spring 1989): 100–122.
Lu, Li. *Moving the Mountain: My Life in China.* London: Macmillan, 1990.
Ma, Jisen. "A General Survey of the Resurgence of the Private Sector of China's Economy." *Social Sciences in China* 9, 3 (September 1988): 78–92.
McCormick, Barrett L. *Political Reform in Post-Mao China: Democracy and Bureaucracy in a Leninist State.* Berkeley: University of California Press, 1990.
MacFarquhar, Roderick. *Origins of the Cultural Revolution.* Vol. 1, *Contradictions Among the People.* New York: Oxford University Press, 1974. Vol. 2, *The Great Leap Forward.* New York: Columbia University Press, 1983.
Meaney, Connie Squires. "Market Reform in a Leninist System: Some Trends in the Distribution of Power Strategy and Money in Urban China." *Studies in Comparative Communism* 22, 2-3 (Summer-Autumn 1989): 203–220.
Minzhu, Han, ed. *Cries for Democracy: Writings and Speeches from the 1989 Chinese Democracy Movement.* Princeton: Princeton University Press, 1990.
Myers, Ramon H., ed. *Two Societies in Opposition: The Republic of China and the People's Republic of China After Forty Years.* Stanford: Hoover Institution Press, 1991.
Nathan, Andrew J. *China's Crisis: Dilemmas of Reform and Prospects for Democracy.* New York: Columbia University Press, 1990.
O'Brien, Kevin J. *Reform Without Liberalization: China's National People's Congress and the Politics of Institutional Change.* New York: Cambridge University Press, 1990.
Orleans, Leo A. *Chinese Students in America: Policies, Issues and Numbers.* Washington, D.C.: National Academy Press, 1988.
Pepper, Suzanne. *China's Education Reform in the 1980s: Policies, Issues, and Historical Perspectives.* Berkeley: Institute of East Asian Studies, University of California, 1990.

Rosen, Stanley. "The Chinese Communist Party and Chinese Society: Popular Attitudes Toward Party Membership and the Party's Image." *Australian Journal of Chinese Affairs* 24 (July 1990): 51–92.

______. "Political Education and Student Response: Some Background Factors Behind the 1989 Beijing Demonstrations." *Issues and Studies* 25, 10 (October 1989): 12–39.

______. "The Private Economy." *Chinese Economic Studies* 21, 1 (Fall 1987): 3–9.

______. "Youth and Students in China Before and After Tiananmen." In Winston L. Y. Yang and Marsha L. Wagner, eds., *Tiananmen: China's Struggle for Democracy,* 203–227. Baltimore: University of Maryland School of Law, 1990.

Saich, Tony. "The Rise and Fall of the Beijing People's Movement." *Australian Journal of Chinese Affairs* 24 (July 1990): 181–208.

______, ed. *The Chinese People's Movement: Perspectives on Spring 1989.* Armonk, N.Y.: M. E. Sharpe, 1990.

Schram, Stuart. *The Thought of Mao Tse-tung.* New York: Cambridge University Press, 1989.

Solinger, Dorothy J. *Chinese Business Under Socialism: The Politics of Domestic Commerce, 1949–1980.* Berkeley: University of California Press, 1984.

______. "The Petty Private Sector and the Three Lines in the Early 1980s." In Dorothy J. Solinger, ed., *Three Visions of Chinese Socialism,* 73–111. Boulder: Westview Press, 1984.

Teiwes, Frederick C. *Leadership, Legitimacy and Conflict in China.* Armonk, N.Y.: M. E. Sharpe, 1984.

Tong, Shen, and Marianne Yen. *Almost a Revolution.* Boston: Houghton Mifflin, 1990.

Vogel, Ezra F. *One Step Ahead in China: Guangdong Under Reform.* Cambridge: Harvard University Press, 1989.

Walder, Andrew G. *Communist Neo-Traditionalism: Work and Authority in Chinese Industry.* Berkeley: University of California Press, 1986.

______. "Communist Social Structure and Workers' Politics in China." In Victor C. Falkenheim, ed., *Citizens and Groups in Contemporary China,* 45–89. Ann Arbor: Center for Chinese Studies, University of Michigan, 1987.

______. "The Political Sociology of the Beijing Upheaval of 1980." *Problems of Communism* 38, 5 (September-October 1989): 30–40.

______. "Workers, Managers, and the State: The Reform Era and the Political Crisis of 1989." *China Quarterly* 127 (September 1991): 467–492.

Warner, Shelley. "Shanghai's Response to the Deluge." *Australian Journal of Chinese Affairs* 24 (January 1990): 121–132.

Watson, Andrew. "The Family Farm, Land Use and Accumulation in Agriculture." *Australian Journal of Chinese Affairs* 17 (January 1987): 1–27.

Whyte, Martin K., and William L. Parish. *Urban Life in Contemporary China.* Chicago: University of Chicago Press, 1984.

Womack, Brantly, ed. *Contemporary Chinese Politics in Historical Perspective.* New York: Cambridge University Press, 1991.

Xiaoping Deng. *Selected Writings*. Beijing: Foreign Languages Press, 1984.

Yudkin, Marcia. *Making Good: Private Business in Socialist China*. Beijing: Foreign Languages Press, 1986.

Zhang, Shou, ed. *Zhongguo Nongcun Sishi Nian* (Forty years of Chinese agriculture). Henan: Zhongyuan Nongmin Chubanshe, 1989.

Zhou, Yueli. "Lun nongcun de jingji lienhe" (On amalgamation in the rural economy). *Honggi* 11 (1986): 11–15.

Zhufeng, Luo, ed. *Religion Under Socialism in China.* Armonk, N.Y.: M. E. Sharpe, 1991.

Zweig, David. "Content and Context in Policy Implementation: Household Contracts in China, 1977–1983." In David Lampton, ed., *Policy Implementation in the Post-Mao Era,* 253–283. Berkeley: University of California Press, 1987.

About the Book and Editor

Thirteen years of reform initiated by Deng Xiaoping have dramatically shifted the balance between state and society in the People's Republic of China. Despite the growing strength of the people, the domination of the hegemonic party-state remains intact. In this book, leading scholars trace long-term trends, considering whether current developments favor the emergence of a pluralistic civil society or the preservation of a state-controlled society, either in its Marxist-Leninist guise or in a modernizing authoritarian reincarnation.

The book begins by portraying the subtle, irreversible changes in China and revealing the leadership's major failure to create a set of rational, workable political institutions. The contributors then consider the changing role of social classes and their relationship to the state. All implicitly question whether the existing changes imply the eventual transformation of China's political-social order. Advancing new research and research-based speculation, the contributors move beyond the immediate images and emotions of Tiananmen. What emerges is a balanced, critical evaluation that will be valuable for undergraduate and graduate courses on Chinese politics and comparative communism.

Arthur Lewis Rosenbaum is the China program coordinator at the Keck Center, Claremont McKenna College, where he is also associate professor of East Asian history. He received a Ph.D. in Chinese history from Yale University. In 1990–1991 Rosenbaum served as a Fulbright lecturer at Beijing Foreign Studies University. His writings include *The China Missionaries Oral History Project* and numerous articles on modern Chinese history.

About the Contributors

Thomas P. Bernstein is professor of political science at Columbia University and a member of its East Asian Institute. He received his Ph.D. in political science from Columbia and has taught at Indiana and Yale universities. A specialist on Chinese politics, he has written on a variety of topics, including youth and peasants. He has published numerous articles on Chinese domestic and foreign politics as well as a book on Chinese youth; his most recent study is on the politics of rural reform.

Lowell Dittmer received his Ph.D. from the University of Chicago and taught at SUNY, Buffalo, and the University of Michigan before joining the Department of Political Science at the University of California, Berkeley, in 1978. His principal works include *Liu Shao-ch'i and the Chinese Cultural Revolution* (1975), *China's Continuous Revolution* (1986), and *Sino-Soviet Normalization and Its International Implications* (1991). He is now engaged in a study of the Chinese reforms.

Merle Goldman is professor of Chinese history at Boston University and research associate at the Fairbank Center for East Asian Research at Harvard. She is the author of *Literary Dissent in Communist China* (1977) and *China's Intellectuals: Advise and Dissent* (1981). She is completing a book on China's democratic movement.

Hong Yung Lee is professor of political science and chair of the Center for Korean Studies at the University of California, Berkeley. He is also affiliated with the International Relations Program of the East-West Center in Honolulu as adjunct research associate. Among his publications are *The Politics of the Cultural Revolution* (1978), *From Revolutionary Cadres to Party Technocrats in Socialist China* (1991), and *Research Guide to Red Guard Publications* (1991).

Stanley Rosen is associate professor of political science at the University of Southern California. He specializes in political and social change in China. His current research includes the Chinese debates over neoauthoritarianism, the television series "River Elegy," and the status of Chinese women.

Dorothy J. Solinger is professor in the Department of Politics and Society at the University of California, Irvine. She received a Ph.D. in political science from Stanford University. She is the author of *Chinese Business Under Socialism* (1984), *From Lathes to Looms: Chinese Industrial Policy in Comparative Perspective* (1991), and *China's State-shaped Transition to Markets: Socialist Legacies and Economic Reforms* (forthcoming).

Andrew G. Walder is professor of sociology at Harvard University, where he is also an associate of the Fairbank Center for East Asian Research. The author of *Communist Neo-Traditionalism: Work and Authority in Chinese Industry* (1986), he has also published on the subjects of social stratification and political conflict in contemporary urban China.

Martin K. Whyte is professor of sociology at the University of Michigan. He received a Ph.D. in sociology from Harvard University. His writings include *Village and Family in Contemporary China* (1980) and *Urban Life in Contemporary China* (1984) (both coauthored with William L. Parish) and numerous articles on contemporary Chinese social life.

Index